Ashley George

W9-CZN-945

# HaYesod™

## THE FOUNDATION

### THE LAND, THE PEOPLE,
### AND THE SCRIPTURES OF ISRAEL

First Fruits of Zion is a 501(c)(3) registered nonprofit educational organization.

**First Edition 1998**
**Second Edition 2010**
**Printed in the United States of America**

Unless otherwise noted, Scripture quotations taken from the New American Standard Bible®, Copyright © 1960, 1962, 1963, 1968, 1971, 1972, 1973, 1975, 1977, 1995 by The Lockman Foundation. Used by permission. (www.Lockman.org)

ISBN: 978–1–892124–39–5

Cover Design: Joel Powell, First Fruits of Zion
Photography: ©iStockphoto/Horst Puschmann

Illustrations: Illustrations throughout the HaYesod manuals were created by Phil Rose and are under the copyright of First Fruits of Zion. They may not be duplicated. Phil Rose can be contacted at Phil@philrosestudios.com.

## First Fruits of Zion

PO Box 649, Marshfield, Missouri 65706–0649 USA
Phone (417) 468–2741, www.ffoz.org

Comments and questions: www.ffoz.org/contact

HaYesod: www.hayesod.org

## HaYesod Production Team

President and Founder: Boaz Michael
Creative Director: Avner Wolff
Educational Director: D.T. Lancaster
Administrative Director: Michael Cundiff
Audio/Video Director: Joel Powell

Director of Israel segments: David Vermeesch
Director of Beit Midrash segments: Joel Powell
Assistant Director: Jeremy Schoenwald
Post Production and Film Editor: Jeremy Schoenwald
Associate Designer and Print Production: Anne Mandell
Lesson Development: D.T. Lancaster, Toby Janicki, Boaz Michael
HaYesod Project Manager: Toby Janicki
Editing/Proofing: Robert Morris, Steven Lancaster, Jeff and Sarah Croswell, Bill Beyer, Mia Powell, Amber Michael
HaYesod Administrative Director: Michael Badgley
HaYesod Branding and Identity: Joel Powell
Transcription: Mia Powell
Music performed and arranged by: Gary L. Moore, with Christine Adkins

General: Asaf ben-Ami, Shannon Janicki, Sean Deakyne, Brian Nicholas

Special thanks to all of the financial supporters and contributors to this project—may the Father richly bless you. To you my brothers and sisters the words of James are most appropriate: "Whoever brings back a sinner from his wandering will save his soul from death and will cover a multitude of sins" (James 5:19–20).

# HaYesod™

## THE FOUNDATION

THE LAND, THE PEOPLE,
AND THE SCRIPTURES OF ISRAEL

Shalom from First Fruits of Zion,

Thank you for dedicating the time to study God's Word with us in the HaYesod program. *HaYesod* is a Hebrew word that means "the foundation." Before trying to build a house, it is important to make sure the foundation is secure. The ten lessons of this program are all about the foundations of our faith in the Land, the People, and the Scriptures of Israel.

HaYesod is a Messianic Jewish Bible study, but students need not be Messianic, Jewish, or from any one particular sect of Christianity. That's because HaYesod is meant for everyone, not just Messianic Jews. Other students in your group might be Jewish, Messianic, Catholic, Orthodox, Lutheran, Baptist, Episcopalian, Evangelical, Adventist, or any flavor of Christianity, because the HaYesod teachings are non-denominational. They are not affiliated with any particular church; instead, they are about something that every church has in common: the same origin and the same foundation—the Jewish Roots of Christianity.

First Fruits of Zion originally created HaYesod in 1998 to address the growing interest in the Jewish origins of the Christian faith. Over the last ten years, thousands of Christians and Jewish believers have reconnected with the Land, the People, and the Scriptures of Israel through the HaYesod program. If you studied with us in the original program and enjoyed those lessons, you will be blessed with the new program. Our ministry has learned a lot in ten years, and the second edition of the program (2010) takes students further into the foundations of our Jewish roots with fresh material, new insights, and trips to Israel.

Jesus says, "Ask, and it will be given to you; seek, and you will find; knock, and it will be opened to you" (Matthew 7:7). Have you been asking for answers, seeking for truth, and knocking on doors closed to understanding? I pray that through these ten lessons of HaYesod our Father in Heaven will give you answers, help you find truth, and open up the Scriptures to you. Like the old hymn says, "How firm a foundation … is laid for your faith in His excellent word."

Shalom in Messiah,

Boaz Michael
Founder and Director
First Fruits of Zion
Boaz.m@hayesod.org

# HOW FIRM A FOUNDATION

How firm a foundation ye saints of the Lord,
Is laid for your faith in His excellent word.
What more can He say, than to you He hath said;
To you, who for refuge to Jesus have fled?

Fear not, I am with thee, oh be not dismayed
For I am thy God, and will still give thee aid.
I strengthen thee, help thee, and cause thee
    to stand,
Upheld by my righteous, omnipotent hand.

When through fiery trials thy pathway shall lie,
My grace all-sufficient shall be thy supply.
The flame shall not hurt thee, I only design
Thy dross to consume, and thy gold to refine.

The soul that on Jesus hath leaned for repose,
I will not, I will not desert to His foes.
That soul, though all hell should endeavor
    to shake
I'll never, no never, no never forsake.

– by John Keith, 1787

# HaYesod Group Information

## HaYesod Group Leader(s)

Leader name(s) _____

Church or congregation _____

Website _____

Address _____

City _____ State/Prov. _____ Zip Code _____

Home _____ Cell _____

E-mail _____

## Group Host(s)

Leader name(s) _____

Church or congregation _____

Address _____

City _____ State/Prov. _____ Zip Code _____

Home _____ Cell _____

E-mail _____

## HaYesod Meeting Calendar

| Meeting Date and Time | Meeting Date and Time |
|---|---|
| **Lesson One:** | **Lesson Six:** |
| **Lesson Two:** | **Lesson Seven:** |
| **Lesson Three:** | **Lesson Eight:** |
| **Lesson Four:** | **Lesson Nine:** |
| **Lesson Five:** | **Lesson Ten:** |

*Please do your best to attend each HaYesod lesson. The lessons depend upon one another, progressively building upon the concepts and teachings of the previous classes. If you miss a lesson, you can get a summary of its contents in the booklet,* HaYesod: Exploring The Jewish Foundation of Christianity. *Or, you can arrange a time to meet with your HaYesod Group Leader to make up the class.*

**The HaYesod Program DVDs cannot be loaned out to individual students.**

# CONTENTS

To Our Parents:

Some of our most vivid childhood memories are of our homes being filled with people learning, discussing, and fellowshipping over the Scriptures. This Bible study program is yet another fruit of the example you set for us on all of those late nights, Sunday afternoons, and Wednesday evenings. Thank you for the love, encouragement, and sacrifice that you have invested into the lives of your children. We are blessed to have been raised in godly homes of love and passion for the things of the Lord.

Our hope is that we honor you with the work of our hands and continue to build on the firm foundation of faith and devotion that you established for us.

Boaz, Daniel, Toby, Jeremy, and Joel

TEVET 5770
JANUARY 2010

# THE PURPOSE OF HAYESOD

What is a Christian's connection to Israel? A Gentile Christian living in the Greek city of Corinth 1,900 years ago would have replied, "I am a part of the greater people of Israel; I worship with God's people; the Jewish Messiah is my Messiah; the God of Israel is my God."

In those days, being a Christian meant affinity with Israel. Today, Christianity accepts the God of Israel and proclaims the Jewish Messiah as Savior of the world, but does not necessarily understand or foster its connection to the Land, the People, and the Scriptures of Israel.

The HaYesod discipleship program attempts to educate believers on their relationship with the Promised Land, the historic people of God, and the Scriptures of the Jewish people. Knowing the Jewish foundation of Christianity deepens the faith of the believer, clarifies the meaning of the Bible, and reveals God's purpose for all of His people.

Each of HaYesod's ten lessons develops the believer's relationship to the Land, the People, and the Scriptures of Israel. It is our goal to bring clarity, understanding, and unity through these teachings to the body of Messiah as she recognizes her place and role within the greater community of Israel.

## Land of Israel

The land of Israel is the physical stage on which the drama of the Bible was played out. Christians unfamiliar with the Promised Land find the Scriptures difficult to understand. God Himself sanctified the land of Israel; that is why it is called the Holy Land. His glory resided in the Temple in Jerusalem, and He sent His Son to be born and to minister in the land. The land of Israel is at the center of biblical prophecies, including the return of the people of Israel, the return of the Messiah, the final wars of the Messianic Era, and the allotment of the land to God's people.

## People of Israel

The people of Israel—the Jewish people—are the chosen people of God. The children of Israel are God's special portion, His prized possession, and the apple of His eye. Not all Jewish people acknowledge the Messiah; nevertheless, "as regards election, they are beloved for the sake of their forefathers" (Romans 11:28). In every generation, a faithful spiritual remnant has existed among our people—the Jewish people.

Jesus, the apostles, and all the first followers of Jesus were Jewish. In every generation since the gospel was first proclaimed, there have been Jewish people who confessed Jesus of Nazareth as the Messiah. All believers in Jesus should find a spiritual connection with this core remnant within Israel. Gentile believers in Jesus have not replaced the Jewish people; instead they are grafted into Israel and made fellow citizens with Israel. For too long Christianity has been disconnected from Israel. It is time to renounce the theological anti-Semitism of the past and rediscover our connection with the people of Israel.

## Scriptures of Israel

By "Scriptures of Israel," we mean the Bible. The Bible is a definitive collection of the Scriptures of Israel. Just about the entire Bible was written by Jewish people. The people of Israel received the Scriptures under the inspiration of the Holy Spirit, and since then, the Jewish people have been the faithful custodians of the Old Testament while the Christian Church has preserved the New Testament. Nevertheless, both the Old and New Testaments are Jewish writings. It is no exaggeration to call the Bible the "Scriptures of Israel."

Even though the Bible can be called the "Scriptures of Israel," those Scriptures have a universal message for all mankind. The Bible is for everyone. But when the Bible is read outside of a connection to the land and the people of Israel, its words are inevitably misunderstood. Historic Christianity has often strayed from the straight and narrow path of biblical revelation simply because we have failed to recognize the Bible as the Scriptures of Israel.

## Message of Restoration

For almost two thousand years, Christianity has been disconnected from the Land, the People, and the Scriptures of Israel. Today, all of that is changing. An explosion of new scholarship about the origins of Christianity coupled with the return of the Jewish people to the land of Israel has started a restoration and reformation of "biblical proportions."

After almost two thousand years, Jewish people are beginning to reconsider Jesus, and many are declaring Him to be the Messiah. Christians are rediscovering their relationship to Israel and the Jewish people. New insights into the Bible are yielding rich results. God is on the move, and the wheels of biblical prophecy have begun to turn. This is one of the most exciting times in history to be alive, and HaYesod is your introduction to the excitement.

# INTRODUCTION

## So Far as it Depends on You

Shalom from First Fruits of Zion. We are blessed to have the opportunity to partner with you and your HaYesod Group Leader in studying the Land, the People, and the Scriptures of Israel. The HaYesod classes are an opportunity for serious study, thrilling discovery, and precious fellowship. May the LORD bless you as you immerse yourself in His Word!

Help create a peaceful and godly learning environment at your HaYesod class by committing to the governing principle of love. "Love one another with brotherly affection. Outdo one another in showing honor" (Romans 12:10, ESV). Refrain from "foolish controversies … and strife and disputes about the Law, for they are unprofitable and worthless" (Titus 3:9). Set aside any critical spirit, and commit to seeing the good. "If possible, so far as it depends on you, be at peace with all men" (Romans 12:18).

Resolve now to finish the whole program. HaYesod is a long program, packed with information. It's not like some of the devotional-style Bible studies common in church groups today. Don't be discouraged by the amount of material covered in the lessons or the duration of the program. Serious Bible study takes serious work. Think of this as something like a college class. A committed student is "not lagging behind in diligence, [but] fervent in spirit, serving the Lord" (Romans 12:11).

## About First Fruits of Zion

First Fruits of Zion (FFOZ) is a Messianic Jewish educational ministry dedicated to "Proclaiming the Torah and its way of life, fully centered on Messiah, to today's People of God." A non-profit (501(c)(3)) organization with offices in North America and Israel, FFOZ has both Jewish and Gentile staff and contributors. We are on a mission to restore the original faith and practice of the apostles and first followers of Jesus of Nazareth. We rejoice in our rootedness in Judaism as well as our relationship with Christianity.

For more information on the ministry and message of First Fruits of Zion please visit our website at www.ffoz.org.

## Resource and Participation Policies

The *FFOZ Friends* have strengthened our hand to create these resources through their prayers and financial support. Our intention is to see the integrity of the program preserved as a tool that can serve the greater body of Messiah for years to come. We ask that:

1. *HaYesod Student Workbook, HaYesod Program DVDs,* and any related material are not to be duplicated.
2. Each student that participates in the program should purchase a *HaYesod Student Workbook.* Student workbooks cannot be shared. Workbooks cannot be re-used or recycled by others who are not the original purchasers. Every participant must be properly registered and have a *HaYesod Student Workbook* to be allowed to be a part of the HaYesod program.

3. HaYesod Leadership resources and *HaYesod Program DVDs* are not to be loaned out to others. For more additional information on the role and regulations for HaYesod Group Leaders, please see page xxix or the HaYesod web site for more information.

## Corners of the Field

First Fruits of Zion is a non-profit ministry. In keeping with Torah's commandment to leave the corner of the field for the poor, First Fruits of Zion makes a portion of all materials available to those in legitimate need at a discount or without charge. Requests for materials need to be submitted in written form to feedback@ffoz.org or by writing us at: PO Box 649, Marshfield, Missouri 65706. To learn more about our Corners of the Field policies, see www.ffoz.org.

# MEET YOUR TEACHERS

Toby Janicki, Boaz Michael, and Daniel Lancaster

Your teachers on the ten DVD lessons of HaYesod are from the First Fruits of Zion teaching team. They will be guiding you through each lesson, opening the Scriptures with you, and speaking to you from the First Fruits of Zion study hall (*beit midrash*) and from the land of Israel.

**Toby Janicki** is a disciple of Jesus of Nazareth and a teaching team member, Staff Writer, and Project Manager for First Fruits of Zion. He and his wife Shannon have four children: Aharon, Channah, Isaac, and Abigail, and reside in Marshfield, Missouri. Toby is a second-generation Messianic Gentile believer. See Toby's testimony at the end of Lesson Seven.

**Daniel Thomas Lancaster** is a disciple of Jesus of Nazareth and a teaching team member, Staff Writer, and Educational Eirector for First Fruits of Zion. He and his wife Maria have four children: Isaac, Gabriel, Simon, and Miriam, and reside in Saint Paul, Minnesota. Daniel is a Messianic Gentile believer and congregational leader of Beth Immanuel Sabbath Fellowship in Hudson, Wisconsin. See Daniel's testimony at the end of Lesson Six.

**Boaz Michael** is a disciple of Jesus of Nazareth, a teaching team member, and the Founder and Director of First Fruits of Zion. He and his wife Amber (Tikvah) have four children: Jeremiah, Shayna, Rebekah, and Noach, and reside in Marshfield, Missouri. Boaz is a second-generation Messianic Jewish believer. See Boaz's testimony at the end of Lesson Five.

# HOW TO GET THE MOST OUT OF HAYESOD

Brace yourself for a challenging study. HaYesod is an in-depth study program. Each lesson is packed with information.

Throughout the program we will be presenting many concepts and dealing with a host of wide-ranging biblical topics and themes. You may find that you disagree with some things that we will present. It is important that you do not allow differences in minor interpretations to get in the way of the larger message.

Be sure to protect your time and make a commitment to each lesson. Make attendance at each HaYesod lesson one of your priorities each week. If you miss one lesson, you miss a lot! Each of the ten comprehensive lessons systematically builds on the previous one, enabling you to make connections and form logical conclusions from lesson to lesson.

Each DVD lesson runs approximately ninety minutes and may include additional, optional segments with more information. As you watch the DVD presentations you will need to have your *HaYesod Student Workbook* open and follow along, filling in blanks, answering questions, and completing the exercises.

Each lesson in your workbook closes with a review and study questions. Optional, additional studies and extra credit homework are found at the end of each lesson, or on the HaYesod website.

After watching each DVD lesson you will be invited to ask questions, engage in discussions with your group, and then utilize the website for the additional studies, extra credit material, and participation in the HaYesod student forums.

# HaYesod Program Resources

## HaYesod Student Workbook

The beautifully illustrated *HaYesod Student Workbook* presents the entire lesson outline and material in detail and runs parallel to the video teachings. Students fill in the blanks in the workbooks while watching the DVDs. The workbook is full of additional helps such as a glossary of terms, pertinent Scripture quotations, additional sources, references, and citations.

## HaYesod Leadership Manual

The *HaYesod Leadership Manual* is a copy of the *HaYesod Student Workbook* with many critical additions. It is a complete answer key to the student workbook and has additional leadership notes and helps. It is linked to the DVD tracks for lesson planning and review. HaYesod facilitators will be confident and equipped to lead a successful study in the foundations of our faith from a Hebraic perspective with the leadership manual.

## HaYesod Leadership Guide

Years of successful Torah teaching tips are at the registered group leader's fingertips in the *HaYesod Leadership Guide*. This invaluable tool is the group leader's guide to starting, hosting, and facilitating a successful HaYesod study.

## HaYesod Program DVDs

The video lessons combine teachings on location in Israel with lectures from a messianic *beit midrash* to give you a careful and articulate presentation of the Jewish roots of our faith. The package contains: *HaYesod Program DVDs* and ten additional video segments covering topics ranging from evangelism and doctrine to personal testimonies and group Bible studies.

## HaYesod Leadership Training & Program Promotion DVDs

This resource is an overview of the program discussing the responsibilities and approaches for leaders within the HaYesod program. The *HaYesod Leadership Training DVD* develops the ideas presented in the *HaYesod Leadership Guide*. The promotional material includes the "Menorah of Israel" presentation, which is used in conjunction with the HaYesod Israel Night.

## HaYesod Book & AudioBook

You may desire to review the material presented in the program outside of the group setting. The *HaYesod* book provides a print version of the lectures presented in the video course and in some cases expands upon them. This book is a perfect supplement for the student going through the full program, and a good choice for individuals unable to participate with a group. The majority of the text in the book is taken directly from the lecture notes of the HaYesod teachers. This resource is scheduled for release in late 2010.

## HaYesod: Exploring the Jewish Foundation of Christianity

To assist you in sharing what you are learning in the HaYesod program with others, and to help solidify each lesson, we have created a short summary that captures the heart of the matter of every lesson. The *HaYesod: Exploring the Jewish Foundation of Christianity* booklet is also available as an audiobook.

## HaYesod Website

The HaYesod website is a place of learning, discussion, and accessing additional materials that supplement your HaYesod materials. A monitored discussion forum is available for you to discuss your thoughts, ask questions, or to help you work through the concepts introduced in the HaYesod program.

**www.hayesod.org**

# HaYesod Workbook Key

**❶ Lesson title page**

The name of that week's lesson.

**❷ Theme verse**

A selected Scripture passage which summarizes the main concept of the lesson.

**❸ Lesson overview**

Review this section each week to see how this fits into the overall lesson structure of the HaYesod program. The overview gives you a bird's-eye view of the lesson and helps you understand how it builds upon previous lessons.

**❹ Lesson purpose**

Here you will find the intended purpose of the weekly lesson. Major concepts you should know or understand by the time the lesson is completed are listed as bullet points.

**❺ Field trips to Israel**

Each HaYesod lesson contains four teachings from the land of Israel. Use this list to find out where you are going in the Land before the lesson begins.

**❻ Lesson teaching outline**

This outline is a summary of the lesson's contents. This is a helpful tool to determine the overall flow and content of the lesson and a good way to review the material.

**❼ Lesson worksheets**

The lesson worksheets are designed to track with the DVD lesson. While watching the DVDs, it will be important for you to keep one eye on the lesson worksheets.

Fill-in-the-blank sections feature citations, quotations, and Scripture passages quoted by the teacher in the DVD lessons. Main points are summarized here, and occasionally you will find charts that need to be completed during the lesson. The fill-in-the-blank icon will cue you to be ready to write. If you miss a blank, don't panic—your Group Leader has an answer key and can help you after the lesson.

**Refer to Resource**

FFOZ Video:
*Hey! That's Not In the Bible*

Most of the discussions raised in the HaYesod course are treated quickly and summarily. First Fruits of Zion has many additional resources if you would like to delve deeper into the topics. The "Refer to Resource" box will direct you to those resources and remind you that HaYesod is only the beginning of your studies in the Jewish Roots of Christianity.

## ❽ Lesson endnotes

## ❾ Lesson summary

The lesson summary is casually formatted to serve as a simple review of the lesson. It is important at the close of every lesson to summarize what you have studied that evening.

## ❿ Lesson discussion and review questions

Eight questions about the material taught in that lesson facilitate review for personal study or group interaction. Answers are available from the Group Leader.

## ⓫ Extra Credit

Each lesson concludes with optional "Extra Credit" work in the form of Bible exercises, investigations, and further studies to be done at home.

## ⓬ Digging Deeper

Excerpts from First Fruits of Zion resources augment concepts from the lesson and provide further reading. The "Extra Credit" and "Digging Deeper" sections are not repetitions of the lesson material. Instead these are supplemental materials associated with the theme of the lesson you just completed. Relax! The homework will not be collected or graded. However, it goes without saying that if you do the homework, you will learn much more.

---

# 🔍 Video Icons Key

SCRIPTURE: *Indicates a passage or reference from the Bible.*

VOCABULARY: *Visual Hebrew or Greek word reminders and definitions.*

QUOTE: *Notes a passage from an extra-biblical text or Bible commentary.*

LEADERSHIP: *Represents topics specifically relating to a HaYesod Group Leader.*

WORKBOOK: *Denotes a fill-in-the-blank section from the HaYesod Student Workbook.*

VIDEO: *Denotes "field trip to Israel" DVD segments.*

HAVE A LOOK: *Distinguishes additional points of interest to HaYesod students.*

# Workbook Key

1 Lesson title page
2 Theme verse
3 Lesson overview
4 Lesson purpose
5 Field trips to Israel
6 Lesson teaching outline
7 Lesson worksheets

    7a Interactive fill-in-the-blank and note sections
    7b Refer to reference box: Pointing to resources for further study
    7c Charts and reference materials

7d Sidebars with key verses covered, key words used (with definitions), and key concepts presented
7e Israel location picture and information
7f Points of emphasis
7g Visual illustrations

8 Lesson endnotes
9 Lesson summary
10 Lesson discussion and review questions
11 Extra Credit
12 Digging Deeper

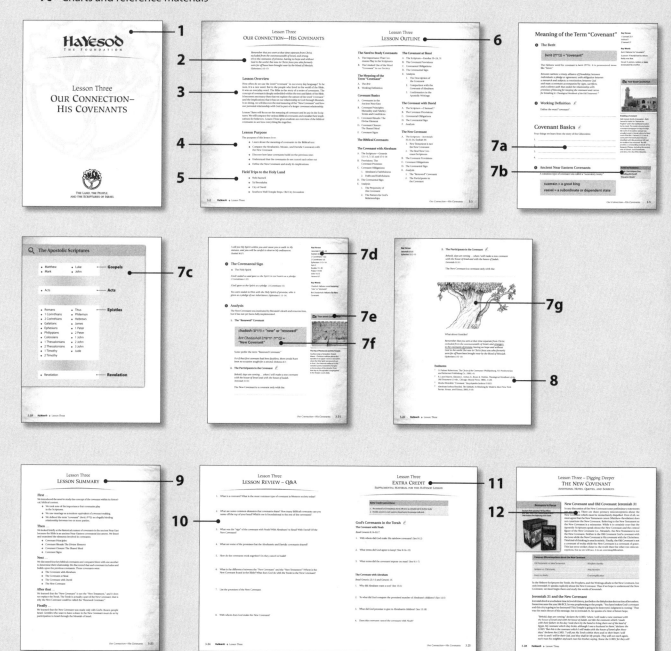

# HaYesod Lesson Summary

The HaYesod program is composed of ten compelling lessons that explore the foundational truths of the entire Word of God from a Hebraic perspective. Lessons are taught from locations throughout the land of Israel and from the studio setting of the First Fruits of Zion study hall (*beit midrash*). Students will enjoy a unique, messianic, yeshiva-style learning experience and will fall in love with the land of Israel through several visual tour clips.

### Lesson One:
## Our Foundation—His Torah

An introduction to the concept of Torah, the five books of Moses. Lesson One teaches students that Torah means "instruction." It is God's loving instruction for His people—the wedding vows of the sacred marriage between God and His people.

### Lesson Two:
## Our Birthright—His Salvation

When we become believers in Jesus we receive a new identity. We receive the righteousness of Messiah through His salvation. Now we have a responsibility to live it out. Lesson Two explores the practical implications of being a new creation in Messiah.

### Lesson Three:
## Our Connection—His Covenants

The Bible is the story of a series of covenants. New covenants do not cancel previous covenants; they build on top of one another. Lesson Three gives students an overview of the biblical covenants to see how everything fits together.

### Lesson Four:
## Our Rabbi—His Teachings

It is one thing to know Jesus as savior; it is something else to know Him as teacher. Lesson Four introduces students to the Torah teacher, Rabbi Yeshua of Nazareth, in His first-century Jewish context. Discover the Jewish background to the Gospels and the Torah teachings of Jesus.

### Lesson Five:
## Our Call—His Yoke

What does it mean to be a disciple? Lesson Five brings students back to a first-century Jewish understanding of discipleship. Students find out why Torah and discipleship to Jesus are inseparable.

## Lesson Six:
## Our Identity—His Apostle

What about the Apostle Paul? Did he convert to Christianity and forsake Torah? Did Paul teach against keeping Torah? Lesson Six introduces students to Paul, the misunderstood man, and the major issues that defined his mission.

## Lesson Seven:
## Our Mail—His Letters

The letters of Paul can be hard to understand. On the surface some passages sound like they are anti-Torah or anti-Jewish. Lesson Seven clarifies several key passages in Paul's epistles by placing them back into their original context.

## Lesson Eight:
## Our Calendar—His Appointments

The Torah spells out appointed times for meeting with God: times of prayer, holy days, and sacred festivals. Are these relevant for believers? Lesson Eight gives students a quick overview of the biblical calendar.

## Lesson Nine:
## Our Boundaries—His Commandments

The commandments of Torah are not burdensome or beyond our reach. Lesson Nine demonstrates the simple wisdom of living according to God's instructions by highlighting a few sample commandments.

## Lesson Ten:
## Our Walk—His Path

Are you ready to take hold of your rich biblical inheritance? Torah is for all of God's people. Lesson Ten explores the relationship of Christianity and Judaism, discusses Jewish and Gentile relationships to Torah, and reveals the place of the believer in Jesus amidst the people of Israel.

# HaYesod Group Leaders

## Sharing the Mission

HaYesod Group Leaders are individuals and congregations that feel led to host and facilitate a HaYesod program. While First Fruits of Zion does not formally approve or endorse HaYesod Group Leaders, we support their efforts to share this message. They are individuals that have expressed a shared calling in our mission to educate the people of God in their relationship to the Land, the People, and the Scriptures of Israel.

Not knowing all of the leaders personally we place a great deal of faith in their personal standards of integrity. The HaYesod Commitment of Integrity statement pertains to HaYesod Group Leaders. The association between a HaYesod Group Leader and FFOZ is grounded in trust and shared mission. All HaYesod Group Leaders have agreed to the following:

## Commitment of Integrity

❖ **Trustworthy leaders** do not officially represent FFOZ; however, they do indirectly represent FFOZ through their leadership in the HaYesod program. All HaYesod leaders do directly represent the Messiah. This should fundamentally guard and govern every action.

❖ **Upright leaders** will avoid using the HaYesod program outside of its intended use. For example, a leader should not allow viewing of the program DVDs unless all viewers have properly registered, paid the appropriate registration fees, and have their own copy of the *HaYesod Student Workbook*. The leader should facilitate the course in its entirety and present all of the lessons in their established order. To avoid confusion and discord, the leader should not insert personal commentary or doctrinal views during the lessons. Leaders will be able to share their views at established times of discussion.

❖ **Respectful leaders** will guard their students' time commitment by avoiding the use of the platform of HaYesod to promote non-related teachings or materials. Additionally, a respectful HaYesod leader will not present himself to his group in an ostentatious manner, wearing ritual garb, or using unnecessary Hebrew terminology.

❖ **Accountable leaders** recognize that they have a responsibility to honor and respect others. They respect established congregational leadership, pastors, and other teachers, etc. They will not speak ill of others or other institutions and will not solicit students to leave their communities of worship. While it is not necessary for a HaYesod class to be conducted under the consent and covering of established congregations or churches, we feel that this is the healthiest scenario under which to present the program.

❖ **Leaders who exercise good-faith leadership** will protect the integrity of the HaYesod program. Such a leader recognizes the expense and effort that went into the creation of this program and:

1. Will not copy, modify, or duplicate any of the materials or allow others to do so;

2. Will not allow non-registered members to participate in the program or view the DVDs;

3. Will remember that HaYesod leadership materials (Guide, Workbook, DVDs) remain the property of FFOZ and will not transfer these in any form to any other individual;

4. Will return those leadership materials (Guide, Workbook, DVDs) upon the request of FFOZ.

## The Leadership Responsibilities

Group leaders are responsible for leading group discussions, communicating with the students, answering administrative questions about the program, and serving your HaYesod group to ensure an environment and opportunity for you to learn and grow in the Word of God. Please contact First Fruits of Zion with any concerns or comments.

To review all of the leadership forms and agreements or for more information on HaYesod leadership please visit www.hayesod.org.

Lesson One

# OUR FOUNDATION– HIS TORAH

THE LAND, THE PEOPLE,
AND THE SCRIPTURES OF ISRAEL

# Lesson One
# OUR FOUNDATION—HIS TORAH

*You, however, continue in the things you have learned and become convinced of, knowing from whom you have learned them, and that from childhood you have known the sacred writings which are able to give you the wisdom that leads to salvation through faith which is in Christ Jesus. All Scripture is inspired by God and profitable for teaching, for reproof, for correction, for training in righteousness; so that the man of God may be adequate, equipped for every good work.* (2 Timothy 3:14–17)

## Lesson Overview

*HaYesod* means "the foundation." HaYesod is a study series that explores the believer's relationship to the Land, the People, and the Scriptures of Israel. The primary source for learning about Israel is the Bible, and the foundation of the Bible is the Torah: Genesis, Exodus, Leviticus, Numbers, and Deuteronomy. Torah is the foundation because it is God's first revelation to humanity. Torah means "teaching and instruction." It is God's loving instruction for His people. The Torah serves a role for both believers and unbelievers. It is relevant to believers today. Moreover, the discovery of what it means to be related to the people of Israel is laid out in the Torah.

All of our studies in HaYesod will be built upon the foundation of Torah that we will examine in this first lesson.

## Lesson Purpose

Here are the main points that you can expect to learn in this lesson:

- ❖ The revelation, inspiration, infallibility, inerrancy, and authority of the Bible.
- ❖ The definition(s) of the word "Torah."
- ❖ The function of Torah for both believers and unbelievers.
- ❖ Why some laws of Torah do not apply today.
- ❖ The purpose which the Torah was designed to accomplish.

## Field Trips to the Holy Land

- ❖ Jaffa Gate, Old City Jerusalem
- ❖ Qumran, Dead Sea Region
- ❖ Road to Emmaus, Mevaseret Zion
- ❖ Southern Steps, Jerusalem Temple Mount

# Lesson One
# LESSON OUTLINE

## The Nature of the Scriptures

A.  Revelation
    1.  Creation
    2.  Jesus
    3.  Scripture
B.  Inspiration
C.  Inerrant and Infallible
D.  Authority

## Defining the Word Torah

A.  Torah and Law
B.  What is Torah (תורה)?
    1.  The Root Word Yarah (ירה)
    2.  Torah (תורה) means Teaching
    3.  Torah (תורה) vs. Chata (חטא)
C.  Uses of the Word Torah
    1.  Rabbinic Teachings
    2.  Written Torah
    3.  Oral Torah
        a.  Mishnah (משנה)
        b.  Talmud (תלמוד)
    4.  TaNaK (תנ״ך)
    5.  Chumash (חמש)

## TaNaK: Torah, Nevi'im, Ketuvim

A.  "T" is for Torah (תורה)
B.  "N" is for Nevi'im (נביאים)
C.  "K" is for Ketuvim (כתובים)

## The Biblical Function of Torah for Unbelievers

A.  The Torah is a Witnessing Tool
B.  The Torah Reveals Sin
C.  The Torah Brings Wrath
D.  The Torah is a Pedagogue
E.  The Torah Points to Yeshua

## The Biblical Function of Torah for the Redeemed

A.  Trains in Righteousness
    1.  Torah is Good for Teaching
    2.  Torah is Good for Rebuking
    3.  Torah is Good for Correcting
    4.  Torah is Good for Training in Righteousness
B.  Teaches the Lifestyle of Godliness
C.  A Source of Blessing
D.  Points to Yeshua

## Parts That Don't Apply Today

A.  Death Penalty and Court-Imposed Punishments
B.  Animal Sacrifices and Levitical Laws

## The Designs of Torah

A.  History Book
B.  Training Manual
C.  Covenant/Constitution
D.  Ketubah (כתבה)
    1.  A Marriage Contract
    2.  God's Marriage Contract with His Bride Israel

**Key Verses**

Psalm 19:1–2

John 1:14

John 14:9

1 Thessalonians 2:13

**Key Words**

*HaYesod:* Hebrew word meaning "the foundation."

# The Nature of the Scriptures

The Bible is God's book, it's our foundation (our *yesod*) of faith and practice.

**A** **Revelation**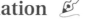

The three primary ways God reveals Himself to us:

Mount Sinai

1. Creation

*The heavens are telling of the glory of God; and their expanse is declaring the work of His hands. Day to day pours forth speech, and night to night reveals knowledge.* (Psalm 19:1–2)

2. Jesus

*And the Word became flesh, and dwelt among us, and we saw His glory, glory as of the only begotten from the Father, full of grace and truth.* (John 1:14)

*He who has seen Me has seen the Father.* (John 14:9)

**Refer to Resource**

*Boundary Stones*

"The New Testament Cannot Overturn the Old"

Pages 65–66

3. Scripture

*When you received the word of God which you heard from us, you accepted it not as the word of men, but for what it really is, the word of God.* (1 Thessalonians 2:13)

## B Inspiration

Inspiration

> **inspired = "God-breathed"**

*All Scripture is inspired by God.* (2 Timothy 3:16)

*No prophecy was ever made by an act of human will, but men moved by the Holy Spirit spoke from God.* (2 Peter 1:21)

## C Inerrant and Infallible

Inerrant and infallible

> **inerrant = "without error"**
>
> **infallible = "unbreakable, reliable"**

*The law of the LORD is perfect … the testimony of the LORD is sure … The precepts of the LORD are right … the judgments of the LORD are true; they are righteous altogether.* (Psalm 19:7–9)

## Ⓓ Authority

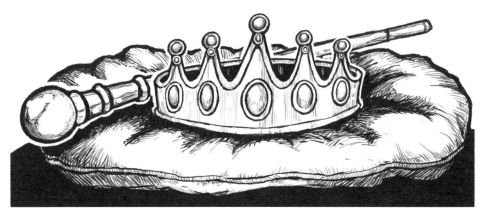

Authority

The Bible alone is our standard and text for all faith and practice.

## 🔍 Foundational Points to Discuss and Remember

**Revelation**
The material

**Inspiration**
The source of the material

**Inerrant, Infallible**
The character and recording
of the material

**Authority**
The power and command of
the material

# Defining the Word Torah

Torah is the Hebrew word translated as "law" in our English Bibles.

**Key Verses**

Deuteronomy 6:4–9
Deuteronomy 11:13–21
Deuteronomy 30:11–14
Luke 1:16
Psalm 119:1–7

## A  Torah and Law

Torah  ≠  Law

Torah does not mean "law"

**Key Words**

*Yarah*: Hebrew word meaning "to throw" or "to cast."

*Torah*: Hebrew word meaning "teaching" or "instruction;" the five books of Moses.

**📹 Your Israel Connection**

**Torah, Torah, Torah**

*Jaffa Gate, Old City Jerusalem* – Jaffa Gate is one of the main entrances to Old City Jerusalem. The Jewish people of Jerusalem have affixed mezuzahs to the gates—small scroll cases containing parchments with the words of Deuteronomy 6:4–9 and 11:13–21 in fulfillment of the commandment, "You shall write them on the doorposts of your house and on your gates" (Deuteronomy 6:9).

## B  What is Torah (תורה)?

The Hebrew word *Torah* (תורה) is derived from the root word *yarah* (ירה).

### 1.  The Root Word Yarah (ירה)

*The basic idea of the root yara is "to throw" or "to cast" with the strong sense of control by the subject … The three most frequent uses of this root deal with shooting arrows, sending rain, and teaching.* (*Theological Wordbook of the Old Testament*)[1]

### 2.  Torah (תורה) Means Teaching

*The word tôrâ means basically "teaching" whether it is the wise man instructing his son or God instructing Israel. The wise give insight into all aspects of life so that the young may know how to conduct themselves and to live a long blessed life. So too God, motivated by love, reveals to man basic insight into how to live with each other and how to approach God. Through the law God shows his interest in all aspects of man's life which is to be lived under his direction and care.* (*Theological Wordbook of the Old Testament*)[2]

Torah is  God's instruction about how to live with each other & how to approach God

**Refer to Resource**

*HaYesod Student Workbook*
"What is the Torah?"
Pages 1.21–1.23

**Key Words**

*Chata:* Hebrew word meaning "to miss a mark or a way."

*Mishnah:* Hebrew for "repetition." A collection of rulings, applications, and legal disputes that were passed along orally until being written down in the third century CE. Also called the Oral Torah.

*CE:* "Common Era." This abbreviation replaces the previously used AD. (*anno Domini,* Latin for "in the year of the Lord"). The Common Era covers the time from Christ's birth to the present day.

3. **Torah (תורה) vs. Chata (חטא)**

*The basic meaning of the root [chata] is to miss a mark or a way. (Theological Wordbook of the Old Testament)*[3]

Chata means <u>to fall short or miss the target</u>

*The root occurs about 580 times in the Old Testament and is thus its principal word for sin. (Theological Wordbook of the Old Testament)*[4]

Sin means <u>Missing the mark</u>.

*For all have sinned and fall short of the glory of God.* (Romans 3:23)

Torah hits the mark

**C** **Uses of the Word Torah**

The word has come to be used in several different ways in traditional Jewish thinking.

1. **Rabbinic Teachings**

*Torah* means "teaching." In Judaism, all the authoritative teachings of the rabbis are considered to be Torah.

2. **Written Torah**

The written Torah is the books of Moses and the rest of the Old Testament.

3. **Oral Torah**

a. *Mishnah* (משנה)

The Hebrew word *Mishnah* means "repetition." The *Mishnah* is a third-century CE written version of the oral traditions of the rabbinic community.

**Refer to Resource**

FFOZ Video:
*Hey! That's Not In the Bible*

b. *Talmud* (תלמוד)

The Hebrew word *Talmud* means "study." The *Talmud* is a multi-volume discussion of the *Mishnah* completed in the fifth and sixth centuries CE.

4. **TaNaK** (תנ״ך)

The term *TaNaK* is often used as a synonym for the whole of what Christians call the Old Testament.

5. **Chumash** (חמש)

*Chumash* means "five" and is used as a synonym for the Torah. The "Torah" most specifically refers to just the five books of Moses: Genesis, Exodus, Leviticus, Numbers, and Deuteronomy.

# TaNaK: Torah, Nevi'im, Ketuvim

In Judaism the Hebrew Bible is called the *TaNaK* (תנ״ך), an acronym for Torah, Prophets, and Writings.

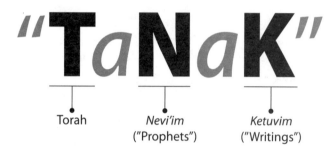

"TaNaK"

Torah | Nevi'im ("Prophets") | Ketuvim ("Writings")

Ⓐ **"T" is for Torah** (תורה)

5 books of Moses

Ⓑ **"N" is for Nevi'im** (נביאים)

Prophets

Ⓒ **"K" is for Ketuvim** (כתובים)

Writings

**Key Verses**

2 Timothy 3:14–17

**Key Words**

*Talmud:* Hebrew word meaning "study." A voluminous record of rabbinic discussions about the Oral Law.

*TaNaK:* Acronym from the Hebrew words for "Torah," "Prophets," and "Writings."

*Chumash:* Hebrew word meaning "five." A bound volume containing the five books of Moses and selections from the Prophets, arranged according to the reading schedule.

*Nevi'im:* Hebrew word meaning "prophets," used to refer to the prophetic sections of the Hebrew Scriptures.

*Ketuvim:* Hebrew word meaning "writings," used to refer to the narrative/historical sections of the Hebrew Scriptures.

**Your Israel Connection**

**TaNaK: Torah, Nevi'im, Ketuvim**

*Qumran, Dead Sea Region* – The ruins at Qumran are widely believed to have been the home of an ascetic Jewish sect called the Essenes. Many scholars believe that the Dead Sea Scrolls, which were found in caves around Qumran, were created by Essene scribes.

# Compare the Christian and Jewish Bibles

## The Old Testament

### Pentateuch

Genesis
Exodus
Leviticus
Numbers
Deuteronomy

### Historical Books

Joshua
Judges
Ruth
1 & 2 Samuel
1 & 2 Kings
1& 2 Chronicles
Ezra
Nehemiah
Esther

### Poetry Books

Job
Psalms
Proverbs
Ecclesiastes
Song of Solomon

### Prophetic Books

**Major Prophets**

Isaiah
Jeremiah
Lamentations
Ezekiel
Daniel

**Minor Prophets**

Hosea
Joel
Amos
Obadiah
Jonah
Micah
Nahum
Habakkuk
Zephaniah
Haggai
Zechariah
Malachi

---

In Christianity, the Hebrew Bible is referred to as the "Old Testament" because it contains covenants which later Christianity deemed obsolete.

In Judaism, the Hebrew Bible is referred to by the acronym *TaNaK*: **T** for Torah; **N** for *Nevi'im* ("Prophets"); and **K** for *Ketuvim* ("Writings").

Books like Joshua, Judges, 1 and 2 Samuel, and 1 and 2 Kings are called prophetic books because they were originally authored by the prophetic schools. These historical works are collectively referred to as the "former prophets," whereas books of prophecy proper are referred to as "latter prophets."

Judaism refers to the twelve minor prophets as the *Trei Asar*, that is, "The Twelve."

According to tradition, Jeremiah wrote the book of Lamentations, so Christian-published Bibles place it immediately after his book.

The Christian ordering of the prophets follows that of the Jewish Bible, but the arrangement is not chronological.

In a Jewish-published Bible, the book of Daniel is not ranked with the other books of the prophets.

---

## The Hebrew Bible

### Torah (Pentateuch)

Genesis
Exodus
Leviticus
Numbers
Deuteronomy

### Prophets (*Nevi'im*)

**Former Prophets**

Joshua
Judges
1 & 2 Samuel
1 & 2 Kings

**Latter Prophets/ Major Prophets**

Isaiah
Jeremiah
Ezekiel

**Twelve Minor Prophets**

Hosea
Joel
Amos
Obadiah
Jonah
Micah
Nahum
Habakkuk
Zephaniah
Haggai
Zechariah
Malachi

### Writings (*Ketuvim*)

Psalms
Proverbs
Job

**Five Megillot**

Song of Songs
Ruth
Lamentations
Esther
Ecclesiastes

Daniel
Ezra and Nehemiah
1 & 2 Chronicles

# The Biblical Function of Torah for Unbelievers

**Key Verses**

Deuteronomy 4:6–8
Romans 7:7
Exodus 20:17
1 John 3:4
Romans 4:15

The Torah serves several foundational functions, even for unbelievers.

## Ⓐ The Torah is a Witnessing Tool

When the nations see the People of Israel living the Torah, they will desire to have a relationship with God too. Torah-life is to be a light to the nations.

*Keep and do them, for that is your wisdom and your understanding in the sight of the peoples who will hear all these statutes and say, "Surely this great nation is a wise and understanding people." For what great nation is there that has a god so near to it as is the LORD our God whenever we call on Him? Or what great nation is there that has statutes and judgments as righteous as this whole law which I am setting before you today?* (Deuteronomy 4:6–8)

## Ⓑ The Torah Reveals Sin

The meaning of Torah for unbelievers is that it reveals what sin is. Remember that Torah basically means instruction that "hits the mark," while sin means "missing the mark."

*I would not have come to know sin except through the [Torah]; for I would not have known about coveting if the [Torah] had not said, "You shall not covet."* (Romans 7:7; quoting Exodus 20:17)

*Everyone who practices sin also practices lawlessness; and sin is lawlessness.* (1 John 3:4)

## Ⓒ The Torah Brings Wrath

Since the Torah defines sin, it brings God's wrath in the form of punishment for sin.

*For the [Torah] brings about wrath, but where there is no [Torah], there also is no violation.* (Romans 4:15)

**Key Words**

*Pedagogue:* Teacher of young children; a schoolmaster, like a bodyguard to help ensure that the student got to the teacher; from the Greek word *paidagogos*.

## Ⓓ The Torah is a Pedagogue

The Torah is a custodian that leads us to Messiah.

*Why the [Torah] then? It was added because of transgressions, having been ordained through angels by the agency of a mediator, until the seed would come to whom the promise had been made. Now a mediator is not for one party only; whereas God is only one. Is the [Torah] then contrary to the promises of God? May it never be! For if a [Torah] had been given which was able to impart life, then righteousness would indeed have been based on [Torah]. But the Scripture has shut up everyone under sin, so that the promise by faith in Jesus Christ might be given to those who believe. But before faith came, we were kept in custody under the [Torah], being shut up to the faith which was later to be revealed. Therefore the [Torah] has become our tutor to lead us to Christ, so that we may be justified by faith. But now that faith has come, we are no longer under a tutor. For you are all sons of God through faith in Christ Jesus.* (Galatians 3:19–26)

The word "tutor" in Galatians 3:24 comes from the Greek *paidagogos* (παιδαγωγος), a type of caretaker entrusted with supervising and directing a child's conduct and moral behavior; used figuratively of the Torah in the book of Galatians.

### pedagogue = literally "child-conductor"

Galatians 3:23–24 retranslated: "But before faith came, we were kept _Protected_ under the Torah, being _kept inside for_ the faith which was later to be revealed. Therefore the Torah has become our _caretaker_ to lead us to Christ, so that we may be justified by faith."

## Ⓔ The Torah Points to Yeshua

Everything in the Torah, from the forefathers to the Passover redemption, to the prophet Moses, to the giving of the Torah at Sinai, to the Tabernacle, to the priesthood, to the sacrifices, teaches about and points to Messiah.

**Your Israel Connection**

**The Road to Emmaus**

*Road to Emmaus, Mevaseret Zion* – The way to the village that many scholars believe to have been the Emmaus of Luke 24 runs past modern Mevaseret Zion, a modern Israeli city. Somewhere on this road, the risen Christ appeared to two of His disciples and taught them about Messiah in the Torah.

**Refer to Resource**

*HaYesod Student Workbook*
"A Closer Look at Galatians 3:23–25"
Pages 1.24–1.25

# The Biblical Function of Torah for the Redeemed

The Torah has important functions for believers.

**Key Verses**

2 Timothy 3:16–17

**Key Words**

*Didaskalia*: Greek word meaning "sound, doctrinal teaching."

*Elegmos*: Greek word meaning "conviction of sin."

*Epanorthosis*: Greek word meaning "restoring, setting straight, untwisting."

*Paideia*: Greek word meaning "raising God's children in righteousness."

All Scripture is inspired by God

## A  Trains in Righteousness

*All Scripture is inspired by God and profitable for teaching, for reproof, for correction, for training in righteousness; so that the man of God may be adequate, equipped for every good work:* (2 Timothy 3:16–17)

### What's the Torah Good For Anyway?

| | Key Word | Meaning | Definition |
|---|---|---|---|
| 1. | *Didaskalia* διδασκαλια | Teaching | sound, Doctrinal teaching |
| 2. | *Elegmos* ελεγμος | Rebuking | Conviction of sin |
| 3. | *Epanorthosis* επανορθωσις | Correcting | Restoring, Setting straight, untwisting |
| 4. | *Paideia* παιδεια | Training | Raising Gods children in righteosness |

**Key Verses**

Malachi 4:4

Leviticus 26

Deuteronomy 28

Psalm 1:1–2

Luke 24:44–45

Exodus 21:23–25

John 8:1–11

Deuteronomy 16:18–20

Deuteronomy 17:2, 8–13

### Ⓑ Teaches the Lifestyle of Godliness

The Torah is intended for those already redeemed by God. The Torah contains teaching and instruction that covers every conceivable part of a person's life.

*Remember the Torah of Moses My servant, even the statutes and ordinances which I commanded him in Horeb for all Israel.* (Malachi 4:4)

### Ⓒ A Source of Blessing

The Torah promises blessings for obedience, but it also warns of curses for disobedience. Sin has bad consequences in our lives; godly living has good consequences.

Leviticus 26, Deuteronomy 28

*How blessed is the man who does not walk in the counsel of the wicked, nor stand in the path of sinners, nor sit in the seat of scoffers! But his delight is in the law of the LORD, and in His [Torah] he meditates day and night.* (Psalm 1:1–2)

**⌕◄ Your Israel Connection**

**The Difficult Commands of Torah**

*Southern Steps, Jerusalem Temple Mount* – In the days of the apostles (70 AD/CE), the Temple of God in Jerusalem was destroyed by the Romans. Not one stone of the Temple remains upon another, but below the southern wall of the Temple Mount archaeologists discovered the remains of a monumental stairway pilgrims used to ascend on their way up to worship the God of Israel. The feet of Jesus and the apostles once climbed those stone stairs.

### Ⓓ Points to Yeshua

The Torah is filled with shadows of Messiah: prophecies, foretellings, and types of Christ.

*All things which are written about Me in the Law of Moses and the Prophets and the Psalms must be fulfilled. Then He opened their minds to understand the Scriptures.* (Luke 24:44–45)

# Parts That Don't Apply Today

The Torah is not done away with or cancelled, but some parts of it do not apply to us today.

**Refer to Resource**

*Torah Club Volume One: Unrolling the Scroll*

"Behukotai: In My Statutes"

### Ⓐ Death Penalty and Court-Imposed Punishments ✍

Death penalty does not apply __out side land or with out sanhedrin__.

(Deuteronomy 16:18–20, 17:2, 8–13)

## B  Animal Sacrifices and Levitical Laws

**Key Verses**
Leviticus 17:1–9
Deuteronomy 12:5–14
Deuteronomy 16:5–6

Altar sacrifices and Levitical laws do not apply _Outside the temple in jerusalem_ .
(Leviticus 17:1–9; Deuteronomy 12:5–14, 16:5–6)

# The Designs of Torah

The Torah is written in several genres.

## A  History Book

The Torah is a history book because it contains the history of the creation of the world, the origin of sin, the story of the great flood, and the history of Israel's origins.

## B  Training Manual

The Torah is a "user's manual" for human life.

## C  Covenant/Constitution

The Torah is Israel's national covenant with God, the national constitution of the People of God.

1.  Torah defines what it means to be _Part_ of Israel.

2.  It describes what a member of Israel _looks like_ .

3.  It delineates the parameters of Israel's _government_ .

4.  It defines the geographical _Borders_ of the nation.

5.  It documents the _Land titles_ of the nation and
    the nation's right to _Exist_ .

## D  Ketubah (כתבה)

The Torah is like a marriage contract between God and Israel.

**Key Verses**

Exodus 19:5–6
Jeremiah 31:32
Hosea 1–3
Hosea 4:6

**Key Words**

*Ketubah:* A legal document which spells out the terms and conditions of a marriage and establishes the roles and responsibilities of both husband and wife.

The marriage canopy (*chuppah*)

### 1. A Marriage Contract

*ketubah* (כתבה) = a marriage contract

A *ketubah* spells out the terms and conditions of a marriage and establishes the roles and responsibilities of both husband and wife.

### 2. God's Marriage Contract with His Bride Israel

God is compared to a husband and His people are referred to as the bride.

*Now then, if you will indeed obey My voice and keep My covenant, then you shall be My own possession among all the peoples, for all the earth is Mine; and you shall be to Me a kingdom of priests and a holy nation.* (Exodus 19:5–6)

*"Not like the covenant which I made with their fathers in the day I took them by the hand to bring them out of the land of Egypt, My covenant which they broke, although I was a husband to them," declares the LORD.* (Jeremiah 31:32)

Hosea 1–3

*My people are destroyed for lack of knowledge … Since you have forgotten the Torah of your God, I also will forget your children.* (Hosea 4:6)

### Endnotes

1   R. Laird Harris, Gleason L. Archer, Jr., and Bruce K. Waltke, *Theological Wordbook of the Old Testament* (2 vols.; Chicago: Moody Press, 1980), 1:403.

2   Ibid., 1:404.

3   Ibid., 1:277.

4   Ibid.

# Lesson One
# LESSON SUMMARY

## First …

We introduced the Bible as the foundation of our faith.

- ❖ We saw that the Bible is God's infallible revelation to mankind.
- ❖ We learned that the Bible is "God-breathed."
- ❖ We agreed that the Bible should be the authority over our lives.

## Then …

We explored the definition, function, and design of the document known as the "Torah." We saw that:

- ❖ Torah is "teaching and instruction that hits the mark."
- ❖ Torah is "God's instruction about how to live with each other and how to approach God."
- ❖ In Judaism, Torah can refer to rabbinical teachings and traditional Oral Law as well as the Hebrew Scriptures.
- ❖ In its narrowest definition, Torah refers to the first five books of the Bible: Genesis, Exodus, Leviticus, Numbers, and Deuteronomy.

## After that …

We learned that in Judaism the Hebrew Scriptures are not called the "Old Testament." They are called the *TaNaK*, which is an acronym for Torah, *Nevi'im* ("Prophets"), and *Ketuvim* ("Writings").

## Next …

We learned that Torah has functions for both unbelievers and believers:

- ❖ The Torah functions for unbelievers as a witnessing tool, a revealer of sin, a bringer of wrath, a "pedagogue" that leads to Messiah.
- ❖ For believers, the Torah trains in righteousness, teaching, rebuking, and correcting us in the lifestyle of righteousness, and it is a source of blessing that points us to Messiah.

## After that …

We learned that not all parts of the Torah apply in today's circumstances.

## Finally …

We looked at the overall design of the Torah as a:

- ❖ History of the redemption of God's people
- ❖ User's manual for human life
- ❖ A national covenant-constitution for Israel
- ❖ A wedding contract (*ketubah*) between God and Israel

# Lesson One
# LESSON REVIEW – Q&A

1. What does "HaYesod" mean? What is the foundation of faith and practice?

2. What is the best definition of the word "Torah"? Why is this better than defining it as "law"?

3. What are the three parts of the *TaNaK*?

4. What are some of the functions that the Torah serves for those who are not believers in Messiah?

5. What functions does the Torah serve for believers in Yeshua?

6. Why are there no stonings or animal sacrifices carried out by Jews or Christians today?

7. Why is the Torah likened to a history book, a user's manual, a national constitution, and a *ketubah*?

8. Did you have any preconceptions about the Torah which have been challenged by this first lesson of HaYesod?

# Lesson One
# EXTRA CREDIT
### SUPPLEMENTAL MATERIAL FOR THIS HAYESOD LESSON

> **Extra Credit Instructions:**
>
> 1. This material is not mandatory, but it will serve as a helpful tool for further study.
> 2. Fill in the missing words for each of the verses indicated.

## Psalm 119: The Song of the Torah

David loved the Torah. Psalm 119, the longest continuous poem in the Bible, contains 176 verses of David's adoration of God's law. It is structured as an acrostic on the Hebrew alphabet, 22 stanzas corresponding to the 22 letters of the alphabet. Each stanza consists of a number of lines which begin with that particular letter. Therefore the Hebrew of the first eight verses of the Psalm all begin with letter *alef*—the first letter of the alphabet. The second stanza of eight verses begins with the letter *beit*—the second letter of the alphabet—and so on. In this way, David intentionally celebrates the letters of the Hebrew alphabet because they are the letters which comprise the Torah. They are the letters and shapes which are joined in various combinations to spell out the Word of God. They are the building blocks of the Torah.

King David, the poet-warrior of ancient Israel, sang under the inspiration of the Holy Spirit. The words of his psalms were authored by the Holy Spirit.[1] While his harp sang in his hands, the Spirit of God sang through his words. In his psalms, he sang the praises of the LORD, he sang prophecies of the Messiah, and he sang the merit of the Torah. Psalm 119 is David's ode to the Torah.

The following lines are excerpts from Psalm 119, one line from each *alef-beit* section. Use your Bible (NASB) to look up the passage and fill in the missing word.

א How blessed are those whose way is _____, who walk in the Torah of the LORD. (119:1)

ב How can a young man keep his way pure? By keeping it according to Your word … do not let me wander from Your _____. (9–10)

ג Open my eyes, that I may behold _____ from Your Torah. (18)

ד Remove the false way from me, and _____ me Your Torah. (29)

ה Make me walk in the path of Your commandments, for I _____ in it. (35)

ו I shall delight in Your commandments, _____. (47)

ז Your statutes are my _____ in the house of my pilgrimage. (54)

ח At midnight I shall rise to give thanks to you because of your _____. (62)

ט  The law of Your mouth is better to me than _____

_____ . (72)

י  May my heart be blameless in Your _____ , so that I will not be ashamed. (80)

כ  Though I have become like a _____ , I do not forget Your statutes. (83)

ל  I will never forget Your precepts, for by them You have _____ . (93)

מ  I have more insight than all _____ , for Your testimonies are my meditation. (99)

נ  I have inherited Your testimonies forever, for they are the _____ . (111)

ס  Uphold me that I may be safe, that I may have regard for _____ continually. (117)

ע  Therefore I love Your _____ above gold, yes, above fine gold. (127)

פ  My eyes shed streams of water, because they do not _____ . (136)

צ  Your righteousness is an everlasting righteousness, and Your _____ . (142)

ק  My eyes anticipate the night watches, that I may _____ on Your word. (148)

ר  The sum of Your word is truth, and every one of Your righteous ordinances is

_____ . (160)

שׁ  Those who love Your Torah have _____ , and nothing causes them to stumble. (165)

ת  I long for Your salvation, O LORD, and _____ is my delight. (174)

## Endnotes

1  The long standing rabbinic explanation of the book of Psalms is that they are the songs of King David dictated by the Holy Spirit. Yeshua and the apostles follow the same interpretation; e.g., Mark 12:36, Acts 1:16, Acts 4:25.

# Lesson One – Digging Deeper
# WHAT IS THE TORAH?
## ADDITIONAL NOTES, QUOTES, AND SOURCES

The Torah is the Law of Moses. Specifically, it is the books of Genesis, Exodus, Leviticus, Numbers, and Deuteronomy. This is the "law" that Paul often spoke of in his epistles. Paul used the Greek word *nomos* to translate the Hebrew word *torah*. The word *nomos* means "law," but the Torah is more than just law. It is more than just a legal code.

Paul wrote in Greek, but the concepts he was communicating were Hebrew. They were concepts taken from the Hebrew Scriptures and the Hebrew religion. Although the Greek word *nomos* means "law," its Hebrew equivalent, *torah*, is considerably broader.

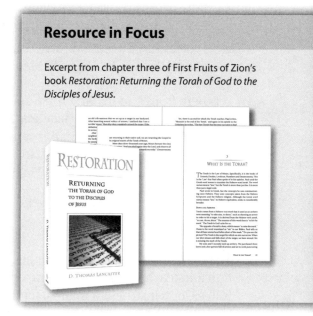

**Resource in Focus**

Excerpt from chapter three of First Fruits of Zion's book *Restoration: Returning the Torah of God to the Disciples of Jesus.*

## Bows and Arrows

*Torah* comes from a Hebrew root word that is used as an archery term meaning "to take aim, to shoot," such as shooting an arrow in order to hit a target. It is derived from the Hebrew verb *yarah*, "to cast, throw, shoot." The essence of this word then is "to hit the mark." The Torah is God's aim for us.

The opposite of *Torah* is *chata*, which means "to miss the mark." *Chata* is the most common word translated as "sin" in our Bibles. Paul tells us that all have sinned and fallen short of the mark.[1] Do you see the picture? The Torah is the target at which we aim our arrow. When our shot misses and falls short of the target, we have sinned. Sin is missing the mark of the Torah.

My sons and I recently took up archery. We purchased three bows and a few quivers full of arrows and set to work puncturing an old crib mattress that we set up as a target in our backyard. After launching several volleys of arrows, I realized that I am a terrible "sinner." Shot after shot completely missed the target. If the definition of sin is to be understood as "missing the mark," then, in terms of archery, I am hopelessly sinful indeed!

After I buried several arrows into the planks of our next-door neighbor's wooden fence, my wife forbade me from shooting in the backyard. Like Paul in his epistle to Timothy, I can claim to be among the worst of sinners, in regard to archery and in regard to Torah. In archery I can't even hit the target, much less a bull's-eye. In regard to Torah I have a heart prone toward sin. I am a mark-misser.

Torah is the mark for which we are to aim. It is God's standard of righteousness. Sin is our failure to hit that mark. And we all do fail to hit the mark. "The law [Torah] of the LORD is perfect" (Psalm 19:7), but we are not. "All have sinned and fall short of the glory of God" (Romans 3:23). The Apostle John described it in no uncertain terms: "Everyone who practices sin also practices lawlessness [Torahlessness]; and sin is lawlessness" (1 John 3:4). Sin, properly defined, is transgression of Torah. We all miss the target. We all sin.

# The End of the Torah

There is a point at which the Torah aims. The bull's-eye of Torah, the careful aim of Torah, is the perfect Messiah. This is why Paul wrote in his epistle to the Romans: "Messiah is the end of the law [Torah]" (Romans 10:4).

Unfortunately, Christians have traditionally misunderstood Paul's words to mean that Messiah is the cancellation of the Torah. The Greek of Romans 10:4 is best understood to mean that Messiah is the "goal" of the Torah. The Greek word *telos*, which is translated as "end," is the same word we use in English words like telephone, television and telescope. *Telos* implies arrival at a goal. The sound of one's voice on the telephone arrives at the goal of the telephone on the other end. That reading fits the context of Romans 10:4 as well: Messiah is the destination at which the journey of Torah arrives.

Yet there is an end for which the Torah reaches. Paul writes, "Messiah is the end of the Torah," and again in his epistle to the Galatians he writes, "The law [Torah] has become our tutor *to lead us* to Messiah" (Galatians 3:24). In this sense, Messiah is the goal of the Torah. Is Messiah to be understood as the ending of the Torah then? No. He is the end, but not the ending. He is the goal of the Torah, but not the termination of it. In fact, He Himself said, "Do not think that I came to abolish the law [Torah]" (Matthew 5:17).

# The Instructions

The Hebrew archery term *yarah* is also used to mean "teaching." Torah in many contexts means instruction and teaching. Torah is the impartation of God's direction, instruction, teaching, and guidance. It is like God's instruction manual for life.

Several years ago I purchased a VCR with a built-in digital clock and timer. I plugged in the VCR and started to use it, but I never knew how to program it. I could not use it to its fullest potential because I did not know how to set the clock or program the timer. Instead I left the clock endlessly blinking. "12:00 … 12:00 … 12:00 … 12:00." One day I finally dug out the instructions that came with the VCR and learned how to program it.

A short time later we bought a DVD player to replace the VCR. According to the DVD player, the time is still 12:00.

When God made human beings, He made an instruction manual to accompany them. It is called the "Torah." We do not function to our fullest potential without the instructions. The Ten Commandments, for example, are one part of the instruction manual for human life.

# All Scripture Is Torah

When we speak of the Law (or Torah), we immediately think in terms of Genesis, Exodus, Leviticus, Numbers, and Deuteronomy. Those are the books of Moses. But Torah is not limited to the five books of Moses. As we learned above, Torah does not just mean "law;" it also means "teaching." Genesis, Exodus, Leviticus, Numbers, and Deuteronomy are the teaching of Moses, the Torah of Moses. But in a broader sense, all of Scripture is God-breathed. Therefore, when the rabbis spoke of the Torah, they generally included all of the Scriptures in the term. The Psalms and the Prophets, and even the little scrolls of Esther and the book of Ruth, are all considered parts of the Torah of Israel. That is why Paul sometimes said, "It is written in the Law," and then quoted from Isaiah.[2] The Master Himself did the same thing.[3] In one sense, the entire Old Testament is Torah.

For believers in Yeshua, the Torah is broader yet. The Gospels, Acts and the Epistles, and the Revelation of John, are also Torah. The entire Bible is God's teaching built upon the Torah of Moses.

In classical Judaism, even the rabbis' extended teachings came to be termed "Torah." The oral traditions, customs, and law, including the *Talmud* and other later writings, are regarded as additional members of the extended family of Torah.[4] They all teach, in one form or another, and they are all based upon the five books of Moses.

For the purposes of this book, when I speak of the Torah, I am speaking of the formal Torah in its narrowest sense—the five books of Moses: Genesis, Exodus, Leviticus, Numbers, and Deuteronomy.

## The Wedding Vows

Covenants are not something we generally encounter in the modern world. One form of covenant that is still with us today, however, is the marriage covenant. The Torah is like a marriage covenant between God and Israel.

Their romance actually began while Israel was still in Egypt. There the Lord declared to Israel, "I will take you for My people, and I will be your God" (Exodus 6:7). This expression is close to an ancient legal formulation from the sphere of marriage. In ancient Near-East marriages, the groom declared, "You will be my wife and I will be your husband."[5] In a sense, it is as if God had declared His intention to marry the people of Israel.

The people of Israel are the object of God's affection. At Mount Sinai, He was like the suitor asking for her hand in marriage. He was to be their God; they were to be His people.

The giving of the law at Mount Sinai is described in Jewish literature as a betrothal and a wedding. In Jewish tradition, one's wedding vows are written out in a formal legal document called a *ketubah*. It is a contract containing all the terms and conditions incumbent upon the bride and groom. The responsibilities of both parties are spelled out clearly. It is a covenant document. Typically, the married couple displays this wedding contract prominently in their home as a piece of artwork celebrating their union. Even in modern Western weddings, the repeating of vows retains vestiges of these nuptial contracts.

The rabbis compared the Torah to a *ketubah*.[6] Whereas God is likened unto the groom and Israel is likened unto the bride, the Torah is likened unto the *ketubah* that spells out the terms and conditions of their marriage. The Ten Commandments form the summary of their marital statement. Treasured like the *ketubah* in the married couple's home, the tablets of the Ten Commandments were kept inside the Ark at the center of the Tabernacle.

# Lesson One – Digging Deeper
# A CLOSER LOOK AT GALATIANS
### FURTHER STUDY FROM THIS WEEK'S HAYESOD LESSON

## A Closer Look at Galatians 3:23–25

In Galatians 3:23–25, Paul was drawing upon a familiar illustration from the ancient Greco-Roman world of which he was a part. Well-to-do families often hired someone or assigned a household slave to serve as a warden for their children. This warden was called a *paidagogos* (παιδαγωγος). The English word "pedagogue" (which means tutor) is derived from *paidagogos*, but the terms are not synonymous. The word *paidagogos* is actually a compound consisting of two Greek words. It could most literally be translated as "child-conductor," or "someone responsible for the conduct of a child."

The *paidagogos* was a type of caretaker entrusted with supervising and directing a child's conduct and moral behavior. He was responsible for overseeing the child's activities, particularly as the child became a teen and young adult. He was to ensure that the child was safe, stayed out of trouble, attended to his responsibilities, and did not fall in with the wrong crowd. The pedagogue taught the child social skills and manners. Moreover, the warden was responsible for coordinating and overseeing the child's education by arranging tutors, lesson schedules, and courses of study. Thus the warden's job was "to conduct the boy or youth to and from school and to superintend his conduct … he was not a "teacher."[7] In that regard, he was a type of bodyguard responsible to ensure the student's safety and good behavior on the way to school and back.

This understanding of the function of the *paidagogos* clears up Galatians 3:23 where Paul says, "But before faith came, we were kept in custody under the law, being shut up to the faith which was later to be revealed" (Galatians 3:23). Being "kept in custody" sounds like a prison sentence. It seems that the apostle Paul is casting the Torah as a cruel prison guard. "Being shut up to the faith" sounds like the Torah was keeping us away from faith. These are very unfortunate translations. The translators have depicted the Torah as something that holds people captive like prisoners and bars them from faith.

When we understand that the *paidagogos* was responsible for protecting, supervising, and directing a child, then we have a better understanding of how the Greek of Galatians 3:23 should be rendered into English. The Greek word *phroureo* which the NASB translates as "kept in custody" has a different connotation. It can also be rendered as "protected," "kept safe," or "guarded." The word should be understood as speaking about how a pedagogue kept a child safe and out of trouble. Similarly, the Greek word *sugkleio* which the NASB translates as "shut up to the faith" can be rendered as "kept in," or "enclosed" in a positive sense. Seen in this light, the word should be understood as speaking about how a pedagogue kept a child inside for his school lessons. He did not allow the child to run off and follow his friends into trouble. He kept him shut up inside for the purpose of education.

That explains why we have asked you to retranslate Galatians 3:23–24 as follows:

> But before faith came, we were kept ~~in custody~~ PROTECTED under the Torah, being ~~shut up to~~ KEPT INSIDE FOR the faith which was later to be revealed. Therefore the Torah has become our ~~tutor~~ CARETAKER to lead us to Christ, so that we may be justified by faith.

This re-translation of Galatians 3:23–24 makes much better sense in the context of what Paul was writing. In Paul's metaphor, the Torah is the warden appointed to watch over and protect the people of Israel and to arrange for their education by taking them to the teacher: the Messiah. The Torah did this by creating moral boundaries which kept Israel inside the parameters of ethical monotheism until the fullness of faith in Christ was revealed. The revelation of Torah was the only place from which the people of Israel could draw hope for salvation, relationship with God, and the expectation of eternal life. For that reason, prior to the coming of Messiah, some people believed that converting to Judaism and keeping the Torah was the way to earn salvation.

Paul goes on to explain: "But now that faith has come, we are no longer under a tutor" (Galatians 3:25). Just as the pedagogue brought the student to the teacher, the Torah brings us to Christ. But the pedagogue is not the teacher. Neither is the Torah a way to earn salvation. When Paul says, "We are no longer under a tutor," he does not mean that the Torah is done away with or cancelled. He means that we should not look to obedience to Torah or legal conversion to Judaism as a means of earning salvation. We now know that salvation is (and always was) through the grace of God in Jesus Christ for Jews and Gentiles both.

## Endnotes

1   Romans 3:23.

2   1 Corinthians 14:21.

3   John 10:34, 15:25.

4   For more information about the oral traditions, Oral Law, and the *Talmud*, see *Restoration* chapter 14.

5   Moshe Weinfeld, "Covenant," *Encyclopedia Judaica* (1st Edition) 5:1011–1022.

6   For example, *Exodus Rabbah* 46:1.

7   William Arndt and J. Wilbur Gingrich, *A Greek-English Lexicon of the New Testament and Other Early Christian Literature* (Chicago: University of Chicago Press, 1979), 603.

# Notes:

# Lesson Two
# OUR BIRTHRIGHT–HIS SALVATION

THE LAND, THE PEOPLE,
AND THE SCRIPTURES OF ISRAEL

# Lesson Two
# OUR BIRTHRIGHT—HIS SALVATION

*For if we have become united with Him in the likeness of His death, certainly we shall also be in the likeness of His resurrection, knowing this, that our old self was crucified with Him, in order that our body of sin might be done away with, so that we would no longer be slaves to sin. Therefore if anyone is in Christ, he is a new creature; the old things passed away; behold, new things have come.* (Romans 6:5–6; 2 Corinthians 5:17)

## Lesson Overview

Christianity sometimes teaches that grace and Torah are opposites. This false dichotomy arises from a misunderstanding of salvation. To really understand how the believer relates to the Land, the People, and the Scriptures of Israel, it is important to understand the biblical meaning of grace, redemption, and salvation. The Torah illustrates salvation with the story of the exodus from Egypt and it lays a pattern of "Progressive Revelation," slowly and deliberately revealing Messiah and the way of salvation. As we lay hold of the powerful truths of our new identity in Messiah, we will realize that we are no longer just "sinners saved by grace," but we have been transformed into the righteousness of Messiah.

## Lesson Purpose

Here are the main points that you can expect to learn in this lesson:

- ❖ Grace and law are not opposites. Grace and legalism are opposites.
- ❖ The sinful state of humanity and our need for grace.
- ❖ The function of "Progressive Revelation."
- ❖ The means of salvation in the Old Testament.
- ❖ Our new identity in Messiah.

## Field Trips to the Holy Land

- ❖ Beit Shean, Upper Jordan Valley
- ❖ Mount of Olives, Outside Jerusalem
- ❖ Tel Beersheva, Negev Region

# Lesson Two
# LESSON OUTLINE

## The Passover Seder

A. A Remembrance

B. Telling the Story of Salvation

## Grace vs. Law

A. Moses vs. Messiah

B. Grace vs. Legalism

C. Defining Legalism

D. All Have Sinned

E. Paying the Wages

F. Amazing Grace

## The Servants of God

A. Slaves in Egypt

B. Slaves to Righteousness
   1. From Pharaoh's Slaves to God's Slaves
   2. From "Slaves to Sin" to "Slaves to Righteousness"
   3. Anomia = Torahlessness

C. Redemption
   1. Redemption in Messiah
   2. Free from the Law?

## Progressive Revelation

A. Progressive Revelation Defined

B. What Progressive Revelation Is Not

C. God Does Not Change

D. Messianic Prophecy in Torah
   1. Genesis 3:15
   2. Genesis 12:1–3
   3. Genesis 22
   4. Joseph Stories
   5. Moses Stories
   6. Tabernacle and Priesthood
   7. Prophecies in the Torah

E. Messianic Prophecy in the Prophets

## The Centrality of the Cross

A. "Saved" before Christ

B. Did Animal Sacrifices Save Them?

C. Saved by Faith

## Our Transformation

A. Bad Analogies
   1. The Filter: Christ-Goggles
   2. The New Clothes

B. The New-Creation Man
   1. Lay Aside the Old Self
   2. Justification and Sanctification
   3. No Longer "Just Sinners"
   4. Our New Family

## The Birthright

A. Importance of a Proper Understanding of Salvation

B. Importance of Proper Understanding of Family

C. New-Creation Theology

D. The Soul Mirror

**Key Verses**

Exodus 6:6–7
Exodus 12:14
Exodus 13:14

**Key Words**

*Seder* (pl. *Sedarim*): lit. "order," with specific reference to the Passover meal.

# The Passover Seder

A Passover Seder is a ritual meal commemorating the exodus from Egypt. The Last Supper in the Synoptic Gospels was a Passover Seder.

> *Seder* (סדר) = "set order"

The set order of the Passover Seder meal includes eating unleavened bread and bitter herbs, drinking four cups of wine, eating a ritual substitute for the Passover lamb, and a retelling of the story of the exodus.

*Say, therefore, to the sons of Israel, "I am the LORD, and I will bring you out from under the burdens of the Egyptians, and I will deliver you from their bondage. I will also redeem you with an outstretched arm and with great judgments. Then I will take you for My people, and I will be your God; and you shall know that I am the LORD your God, who brought you out from under the burdens of the Egyptians." (Exodus 6:6–7)*

Moses parting the Red Sea

### Ⓐ Remembrance

Passover is a "memorial" of the story of the exodus.

*Now this day will be a memorial to you, and you shall celebrate it as a feast to the LORD; throughout your generations you are to celebrate it as a permanent ordinance. (Exodus 12:14)*

### Ⓑ Telling the Story of Salvation

*And it shall be when your son asks you in time to come, saying, "What is this?" then you shall say to him, "With a powerful hand the LORD brought us out of Egypt, from the house of slavery."* (Exodus 13:14)

Passover is an opportunity to tell the story of salvation to the next generation.

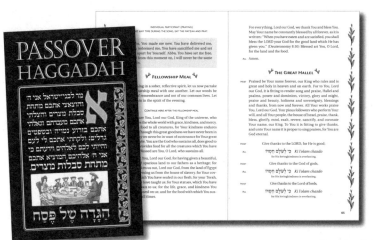

Sample of a Haggadah

**Key Verses**

John 1:17

**Key Words**

*Haggadah* (pl. *Haggadot*): lit. "telling." A book used during a Passover Seder as a guide to each of its steps.

**Key Concepts**

*Legalism:* Trying to earn God's salvation by doing good works.

> *Haggadah* (הגדה) = "telling"

# Grace vs. Law

"Grace vs. Law" is the idea that grace and the Torah are opposed to one another.

## Ⓐ Moses vs. Messiah

*The [Torah] was given by Moses, <u>but</u> grace and truth came through Jesus Christ.* (John 1:17, NKJV)

An italicized word in the New King James Version means that it was supplied by the translator for clarity and not part of the original Greek manuscripts.

There is no ___but___ in John 1:17. ___torah___ and ___grace___ are not opposites.

*As a principle, therefore, grace is set in contrast with law, under which God demands righteousness from men, as, under grace, He gives righteousness to men. Law is connected with Moses and works; grace, with Christ and faith. Under law, blessings accompany obedience; grace bestows blessings as a free gift.* (*The Scofield Study Bible*)[1]

## Ⓑ Grace vs. Legalism

In Christianity, it is often taught that, before Jesus came, people earned eternal life by keeping the Torah.

Completely pointless

## C Defining Legalism

"Legalism" is the concept of earning salvation by being good enough.

"Good people go to heaven. Bad people go to hell."

"The way to get to heaven is by being a decent person."

"If you are a good enough person, you can be pretty sure you will go to heaven when you die."

"If you keep the commandments of the Torah, you will earn salvation."

Legalism is the attempt to _earn salvation through good works._

No one is good enough to earn salvation

## D All Have Sinned

Legalism doesn't work because no one is good enough.

*All have sinned and fall short of the glory of God.* (Romans 3:23)

*For the wages of sin is death.* (Romans 6:23)

> **all have sinned = condemnation = eternal death**

All have sinned

### E Paying the Wages

*For the wages of sin is death, but the free gift of God is eternal life in Christ Jesus our Lord.* (Romans 6:23)

*He made Him who knew no sin to be sin on our behalf, so that we might become the righteousness of God in Him.* (2 Corinthians 5:21)

### F Amazing Grace

Salvation is God's free gift to us. You can't earn or deserve a free gift.

*For by grace you have been saved through faith; and that not of yourselves, it is the gift of God; not as a result of works, so that no one may boast.* (Ephesians 2:8–9)

**Saved by Grace**

| Key Word | Definition |
|---|---|
| 1. **Grace** <br> *Charis / Chen* <br> χαρις / חן | Gods unmarited favor |
| 2. **Faith** <br> *Pistis / Emunah* <br> πιστις / אמונה | belief & faithfulness |
| 3. **Works** <br> *Erga / Ma'asim* <br> εργα / מעשים | Good deeds, observances of the torah |

# The Servants of God

The exodus from Egypt was not the end of the journey; it was the beginning of Israel's walk with God. In the same way, our salvation is not the end of our spiritual journey, it is a new beginning.

### A Slaves in Egypt

*The mind set on the flesh is hostile toward God; for it does not subject itself to the law of God, for it is not even able to do so, and those who are in the flesh cannot please God.* (Romans 8:7–8)

> slaves to <u>Pharaoh</u> = slaves to <u>sin</u>

**Key Verses**

Romans 6:23
2 Corinthians 5:21
Ephesians 2:8–9
Romans 6:16
Romans 8:7–8

**Key Concepts**

*Charis/Chen:* Greek/Hebrew words meaning grace; unmerited favor, the free gift of salvation.

*Pistis/Emunah:* Greek/Hebrew words meaning belief and faithfulness.

*Erga/Ma'asim:* Greek/Hebrew words meaning good deeds, observances of Torah.

**Your Israel Connection**

**Let My People Go**

*Beit Shean, Upper Jordan Valley* – Beit Shean is actually one of the cities in the Galilee that Joshua and the Israelites did not manage to conquer. When David became king, he conquered the city and brought it under Israelite control. In the days of Moses and Joshua, Beit Shean was an Egyptian outpost. Archaeologists have discovered numerous Egyptian artifacts, including a nearly life-sized statue of Ramses III.

**Key Words**

*Eved*: "Servant" or "slave"

*Nomos*: lit. "law," this is the word used throughout the Bible to translate the Hebrew word "Torah."

*Anomia*: "Lawlessness" or, specifically, "Torahlessness."

**Ⓑ Slaves to Righteousness**

The children of Israel were set free from being slaves to Pharaoh in order to become God's "servants."

**1. From Pharaoh's Slaves to God's Slaves**

*For the sons of Israel are My servants; they are My servants whom I brought out [of] the land of Egypt.* (Leviticus 25:55)

*What have we been saved for?*

> *eved* (עבד) = "servant" or "slave"

The Hebrew term translated as "servant" (*eved*, עבד) in Leviticus 25:55 is actually the same word translated "slave" elsewhere in the Bible.

**2. From "Slaves to Sin" to "Slaves to Righteousness"**

> *Do you not know that when you present yourselves to someone as slaves for obedience, you are slaves of the one whom you obey, either of sin resulting in death, or of obedience resulting in righteousness? But thanks be to God that though you were slaves of sin, you became obedient from the heart to that form of teaching to which you were committed, and having been freed from sin, you became slaves of righteousness.* (Romans 6:16–18)

According to Romans 6:16–18:

1. We were slaves of _____Sin_____.

2. We have been freed from _____Sin_____.

3. We have become slaves of _____Rightcousness_____.

**3. Anomia = Torahlessness**

*For just as you presented your members as slaves to impurity and to lawlessness, resulting in further lawlessness [anomia, ανομια], so now present your members as slaves to righteousness, resulting in sanctification.* (Romans 6:19)

> *nomos* (νομος) = "law, Torah"
>
> *anomia* (ανομια) = "lawlessness, Torahlessness"

# Anomia     "Lawlessness"

$$\text{Anomia} = \text{Lawlessness}$$

*Equals*

**Key Verses**

Titus 2:13–14
Romans 8:2
Romans 6:18

**Key Concepts**

*Redemption:* Transferring ownership or buying back.

## C  Redemption

When the Bible says that God "redeemed" us, that means that He "bought us back," transferring our ownership to Himself.

> ### redemption = "buying back"

As our new owner, God has the sole authority over us.

1.  **Redemption in Messiah**

    *[Jesus Christ] gave Himself for us to redeem us from every lawless deed, and to purify for Himself a people for His own possession, zealous for good deeds.* (Titus 2:13–14)

    Messiah gave Himself to redeem us from ___every lawless deed___.

    Messiah gave Himself to redeem us as ___People for his own Possesion___.

    Messiah gave Himself to redeem us so that ___we would be zealous for good deeds___.

2.  **Free from the Law?**

    Was Israel saved from Egypt before or after God gave the Torah?

    ___Before___

    Did Israel have to earn salvation from Egypt by keeping the Torah?

    ___NO___

    Does God save us because of our righteous obedience to Torah?

    ___NO___

**Key Concepts**

*Progressive Revelation:* The idea that God disclosed His truths in a gradual and deliberate manner over time.

Should we keep God's commandments in order to be saved?

NO

Should we keep God's commandments because we are already saved?

yes

# Progressive Revelation

## Ⓐ Progressive Revelation Defined

> **Progressive Revelation = God's truths disclosed deliberately and gradually**

Progressive Revelation is the idea that God disclosed His truths in a gradual and deliberate manner over time. In other words, later books of the Bible build on the revelation revealed in earlier books of the Bible.

 **Your Israel Connection**

**Abraham saw the Day**

*Mount of Olives, Outside Jerusalem –* Pictured is the view of the Temple Mount from the Mount of Olives. The Temple Mount where the Muslim Dome of the Rock now sits marks the location of the first and second Temples. The Temple Mount, Dome of the Rock, and Church of the Resurrection make Jerusalem sacred to Judaism, Islam, and Christianity.

*Just as God provided a sacrificial lamb for abraham, Jesus will be the ultimate. sacrifice*

*Over time God will show himself more*

Progressive Revelation

## Ⓑ What Progressive Revelation is Not

Progressive Revelation does not mean that earlier books of the Bible are at all inferior to later books of the Bible. It does not mean that later revelations negate or cancel earlier revelations.

## C. God Does Not Change

**Key Verses**

1 Samuel 15:29
Psalm 55:19
Malachi 3:6
Genesis 3:15
Genesis 12:1–3
Genesis 22:18
Galatians 3:16

Progressive Revelation says that the truths of the New Testament were first revealed in rudimentary form in the Torah. They are not new truths, just further revealed truths.

*Also the Glory of Israel will not lie or change His mind; for He is not a man that He should change His mind.* (1 Samuel 15:29)

*Even the one who sits enthroned from of old—Selah. With whom there is no change.* (Psalm 55:19)

*For I, the LORD, do not change.* (Malachi 3:6)

## D. Messianic Prophecy in Torah    *stories that point to the messiah*

One easy way to see the pattern of Progressive Revelation in the Bible is through Messianic prophecy.

**1.   Genesis 3:15**

*And I will put enmity between you and the woman, and between your seed and her seed; He shall bruise you on the head, and you shall bruise him on the heel.* (Genesis 3:15)

> **seed of woman = Messiah**

**2.   Genesis 12:1–3**

*Now the LORD said to Abram, "Go forth from your country, And from your relatives And from your father's house, To the land which I will show you; And I will make you a great nation, And I will bless you, And make your name great; And so you shall be a blessing; And I will bless those who bless you, And the one who curses you I will curse. And in you all the families of the earth will be blessed."* (Genesis 12:1–3)

*In your seed all the nations of the earth shall be blessed.* (Genesis 22:18)

*Now the promises were spoken to Abraham and to his seed … that is, Christ.* (Galatians 3:16)

> **seed of Abraham = Messiah**

**Refer to Resource**

*Torah Club Volume Two: Shadows of the Messiah*
"B'reisheet: In the Beginning"
"Lech Lecha: Go Out"

3.  **Genesis 22**

*Abraham said, "God will provide for Himself the lamb for the burnt offering, my son." So the two of them walked on together.*
(Genesis 22:8)

The binding of Isaac foreshadows the crucifixion.

Abraham and Isaac

4.  **Joseph Stories**

Joseph foreshadows Messiah.

5.  **Moses Stories**

> **Moses = first redeemer**
> **Messiah = final redeemer**
>
> **Moses = prophet, priest, king**
> **Messiah = prophet, priest, king**

6.  **Tabernacle and Priesthood**

❖ Tabernacle foreshadows Messiah, the dwelling place of God on earth.

❖ Sacrifices foreshadow Messiah, the sacrifice for sin.

❖ Priesthood foreshadows Messiah, our high priest before the throne.

7. **Prophecies in the Torah**

For example: Genesis 49:8–12; Numbers 24:17; Deuteronomy 18:15.

**Ⓔ Messianic Prophecy in the Prophets**

For example: Micah 5:2; Daniel 9; Zechariah 14; Isaiah 53.

# The Centrality of the Cross

How were people "saved" before the death and resurrection of the Messiah?

**Ⓐ "Saved" before Christ**

None of the great men fully obeyed every written commandment, yet in some way, they must have been forgiven of their faults—even before Jesus' sacrifice.

*All these … gained approval through their faith.* (Hebrews 11:39)

**Ⓑ Did Animal Sacrifices Save Them?**

*It is impossible for the blood of bulls and goats to take away sins.* (Hebrews 10:4)

*Both gifts and sacrifices are offered which cannot make the worshiper perfect in conscience.* (Hebrews 9:9)

*For the Torah, since it has only a shadow of the good things to come and not the very form of things, can never, by the same sacrifices which they offer continually year by year, make perfect those who draw near.* (Hebrews 10:1)

*If righteousness comes through the Law, then Christ died needlessly.* (Galatians 2:21)

**Ⓒ Saved by Faith**

*Even so Abraham "believed God, and it was reckoned to him as righteousness."* (Galatians 3:6; quoting Genesis 15:6)

*I am the way, and the truth, and the life; no one comes to the Father but through Me.* (John 14:6)

**Key Verses**

Genesis 49:8–12
Numbers 24:17
Deuteronomy 18:15
Micah 5:2
Daniel 9
Zechariah 14
Isaiah 53
Hebrews 11:39
Hebrews 10:4
Hebrews 9:9
Hebrews 10:1
Galatians 2:21
Galatians 3:6
Genesis 15:6
John 14:6

*If this is how they were saved, Jesus dieing on the cross would be pointless* (handwritten note)

**Refer to Resource**

*HaYesod Student Workbook*
"What Were Animal Sacrifices For?"
Pages 2.27–2.29

Looking Back in Faith

Looking Forward in Faith

JEWISH AND GENTILE BELIEVERS

# THE SAME FAITH, HOPE, AND BELIEF

You are here ▶

◀ Abraham is here

*The Scripture, foreseeing that God would justify the Gentiles by faith, preached the gospel beforehand to Abraham, saying, "All the nations will be blessed in you."* (Galatians 3:8; quoting Genesis 12:3)

Messiah's sacrifice did not apply only to people who would sin in the future but in a timeless way, it was the means by which the LORD granted grace to those in the past.

*[handwritten: We look back they looked forward]*

# Our Transformation

Being "born again" is a lot more than just receiving the gift of eternal life. It is supposed to be a complete transformation.

*[handwritten: Hebrew = means one who has crossed over possibly making Abraham the first believer]*

## Ⓐ Bad Analogies

We often use bad analogies to illustrate our transformation in Messiah. For example:

### 1. The Filter: The Christ-Goggles

*[handwritten: Bad analogie ↓]*

The only thing that has changed is the way God sees me. Thanks to the Christ-goggles, He can't see my sin anymore, but I am the same old sinner I always was.

The Christ-goggles

**Key Verses**

Galatians 3:8
Genesis 12:3
Genesis 22:19
Genesis 12:1
Joshua 24:2–3
Genesis 10:21
1 Timothy 2:3–6

**📹 Your Israel Connection**

**Crossing Over**

*Tel Beersheva, Negev Region* – The archaeological remains at Tel Beersheva date from an Israelite city later than the age of Abraham. Abraham was a nomadic tent-dweller. "So Abraham returned to his young men, and they arose and went together to Beersheva; and Abraham lived at Beersheva" (Genesis 22:19).

**Refer to Resource**

***Boundary Stones***
"Salvation Is by Grace"
Pages 1–7

## Key Verses

Isaiah 64:6
2 Corinthians 5:17
Ephesians 4:22–24
John 3:3
1 Peter 1:15–16
Leviticus 19:2

## Key Concepts

*Justification:* Declaring free from the penalty of sin.

*Sanctification:* Setting apart or observing as holy.

### 2. The New Clothes

I am actually still the same old sinner, unchanged on the inside. I'm just dressed up in a costume of Messiah's righteousness.

*All our righteous deeds are like a filthy garment.* (Isaiah 64:6)

The new clothes

### B The New-Creation Man

*Therefore if anyone is in Christ, he is a new creature; the old things passed away; behold, new things have come.* (2 Corinthians 5:17)

#### 1. Lay Aside the Old Self

*You [should] lay aside the old self, which is being corrupted in accordance with the lusts of deceit, and that you be renewed in the spirit of your mind, and put on the new self, which in the likeness of God has been created in righteousness and holiness of the truth.* (Ephesians 4:22–24)

*Unless one is born again, he cannot see the kingdom of God.* (John 3:3)

Being "born again" is an <u>inward</u> and <u>spiritual</u> transformation.

**Refer to Resource**

*Boundary Stones*
"God's People Are His Servants"
Pages 21–24

#### 2. Justification and Sanctification

Justification: <u>becoming right with God</u>

Sanctification: <u>the act of setting something apart as holy</u>

*Like the Holy One who called you, be holy yourselves also in all your behavior; because it is written, "You shall be holy, for I am holy."* (1 Peter 1:15–16; quoting Leviticus 19:2)

*For we are His workmanship, created in Christ Jesus for good works, which God prepared beforehand so that we would walk in them.* (Ephesians 2:10)

**Key Verses**
Ephesians 2:8–10
1 John 3:5
1 John 3:6–7
Ephesians 2:11–13
Romans 4:16
Genesis 21:31

### 3. No Longer "Just Sinners"

*[Messiah] appeared in order to take away sins; and in Him there is no sin.* (1 John 3:5)

*No one who abides in Him sins; no one who sins has seen Him or knows Him. Little children, make sure no one deceives you; the one who practices righteousness is righteous, just as He is righteous.* (1 John 3:6–7)

This does not mean that believers are perfect, and will never sin; but it means that when we do sin, we are living inconsistently with our new and true identity in Messiah.

Living a life of obedience to the Bible's commandments is not _Adding_ to the work of Messiah, it is the _Result_ of the work of Messiah.

### 4. Our New Family

Believers have been brought into a new family: the family of Israel.

**Your Israel Connection**

**Sons of Abraham**

*Tel Beersheva, Negev Region* – Pictured is an ancient well outside the gates of Beersheva: "Therefore he called that place Beersheva" (Genesis 21:31). "Beersheva" means "Well of the Oath." Beersheva, the ancient home of Abraham later became an important Israelite city in the Negev.

Israel's flag

*Remember that formerly you, the Gentiles in the flesh … were at that time separate from Christ, excluded from the commonwealth of Israel, and strangers to the covenants of promise, having no hope and without God in the world. But now in Christ Jesus you who formerly were far off have been brought near by the blood of Christ.* (Ephesians 2:11–13)

*[Abraham] is the father of us all.* (Romans 4:16)

# The Birthright

When we have an improper understanding of biblical salvation, it affects the way we live out our spiritual lives.

## Ⓐ Importance of a Proper Understanding of Salvation

When we are told, over and over, that we are nothing but sinners whose righteous deeds are filthy rags, we will never aspire to be anything more than forgiven sinners. *When we reborn we aspire to fulfill our new identity*

## Ⓑ Importance of Proper Understanding of Family

When that same Gentile Christian realizes that, by faith, he has been brought near, into the commonwealth of Israel, and is a son of Abraham too—suddenly he realizes that the Land, the People, and the Scriptures of Israel are relevant to him.

## Ⓒ New-Creation Theology

Messiah resides within the believer.

*I have been crucified with Christ; and it is no longer I who live, but Christ lives in me.* (Galatians 2:20)

New-Creation Theology:

*The inner presence of the Messiah living through my outer person*

**Refer to Resource**

*HaYesod Student Workbook*
"New-Creation Theology"
Pages 2.25–2.26

## Ⓓ The Soul Mirror

James calls the Torah the "perfect Torah," and the "Torah of liberty." He compares it to a mirror that a person looks into to see himself.

*Prove yourselves doers of the word, and not merely hearers who delude themselves. For if anyone is a hearer of the word and not a doer, he is like a man who looks at his natural face in a mirror; for once he has looked at himself and gone away, he has immediately forgotten what kind of person he was. But one who looks intently at the perfect [Torah], the [Torah] of liberty, and abides by it, not having become a forgetful hearer but an effectual doer, this man will be blessed in what he does.* (James 1:22–25)

As believers, our truest and deepest identity is our new life in Messiah, a life of righteousness.

The "soul mirror"

### Endnotes

1   C.I. Scofield, *The Scofield Study Bible, New King James Version* (New York: Oxford University Press, 2002), 1451.

# Lesson Two
# LESSON SUMMARY

## First ...

We discussed the concept of "Grace vs. Law."

- ❖ We saw that grace is not opposed to Torah.
- ❖ We learned that "legalism" is the idea of earning salvation.
- ❖ We agreed that no one can earn their salvation by keeping Torah.
- ❖ We saw that all have sinned and are under condemnation.
- ❖ We learned that Messiah has paid the price for sin, and that faith in Him is the way to eternal life.

## Then ...

We compared our redemption in Messiah to the redemption of Israel from Egypt, and we learned that we used to be "slaves to sin" but now we are "slaves to righteousness."

## After that ...

We discussed the concept of "Progressive Revelation."

- ❖ God disclosed truth in a gradual, deliberate manner over time.
- ❖ Earlier books of the Bible are not inferior to later ones.
- ❖ Later revelations do not cancel earlier ones.
- ❖ God does not change.

## Therefore ...

We realized that Messiah and the way of salvation is revealed in the Torah and prophets, and the saints of the Old Testament were saved the same way we are—not by keeping the Torah or sacrificing animals.

## Next ...

We learned about what it means to be transformed in Messiah:

- ❖ Not viewed through the filter of "Christ-goggles"
- ❖ Not wearing a costume of righteousness
- ❖ Rather, a new creation, born again, justified, and sanctified
- ❖ No longer "just sinners" saved by grace
- ❖ Members of the family of Abraham

## Finally ...

We discussed the importance of a proper understanding of salvation. Messiah dwells within us, and the Torah is like a mirror that shows us who we really are.

# Lesson Two
# LESSON REVIEW – Q&A

*We don't follow the torah to be saved, we follow the Torah because, we have been saved*

1. What is the concept of "Grace vs. Law"?

   They aren't opposites

2. What is "legalism"? Does it work for attaining salvation?

   "earning your salvation," it doesn't work

3. From what does Messiah set us free? After we are set free, to what do we now become slaves?

   Sin, we become slaves of righteousness

4. What is Progressive Revelation?

   God showing himself bit by bit

5. How were the heroes of faith in the days of the *TaNaK* (Old Testament) saved?

   by faith

6. Did sacrifices take away sins?

   No

7. What are two problematic, theological analogies that contribute to a believer's misunderstanding of his identity in Messiah?

   "Christ goggles"   "New clothes"

8. What are some ways we can describe our new identity in Messiah?

   New creation
   Part of a New family

# Lesson Two
# EXTRA CREDIT
### SUPPLEMENTAL MATERIAL FOR THIS HAYESOD LESSON

**Extra Credit Instructions:**

1. This material is not mandatory, but it will serve as a helpful tool for further study.
2. Read Romans 5–6.
3. Provide answers to each question based upon the passages indicated.

## Our Identity: An Excursion into the Heart of the Epistle to the Romans

The epistle of Paul to the believers who were in Rome is often characterized as a treatise on justification and righteousness. In many ways it is. The Epistle to the Romans is deeply theological and is concerned with questions about Jewish and non-Jewish standing before God. Since God justified us through the blood of Messiah and not through our own personal merit, what difference does that make in our lives? As Paul explores the implications of salvation, he has a great deal to say about our identity in Messiah. The goal of this exercise is to help you see the ideal identity of the believer in Messiah from the Pauline perspective. Read Romans 5–6 and answer the following questions from the words in the text of the Scriptures.

1. How are we justified? (Romans 5:1) Note that Paul uses the Greek perfect tense, which indicates action that is completed in the past with results that continue into the present.

   By Faith

2. Every believer has three specific things as the result of being justified. What are they? (Romans 5:1–3)

   1. Peace   2. hope   3. Perseverance

3. Before becoming believers and followers of Messiah, we were _Sinners_ (5:8–10, 12), but now, in Messiah, we are made _Righteous_ (5:19).

4. What does it mean to be "baptized into Messiah"? (6:3–4)

   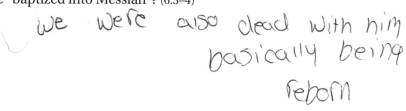

   we were also dead with him basically being reborn

5.  In what ways were we united with Messiah in His death? What part of us died? (6:5–7)

*our old self was crucified with him, our body of sin died*

6.  Whose life do we now live? What has changed? (6:8–11)

*the life of christ, we are dead to sin*

7.  What must we do since sin is no longer our master? (6:12–14) Is this a literal change, or is it only a theological reality, not actually present in our physical lives?

*present our selves as instruments of righteousness. It is a literal change*

8.  What word does Paul use to describe the relationship we had with sin before Messiah? (6:15–16)

*slaves to sin*

9.  According to Paul, we must choose whether to be slaves to ___*sin*___ or slaves to

___*righteousness*___ (6:16)

10. Every believer should consider himself a ___*slave*___ to righteousness. (6:18)

11. Now that we are in Messiah, what are we able to do that we were not able to do before? (6:19–22)

*have eternal life*

12. Based on what Paul teaches, should the believer continue to consider himself a sinner?

*No, but understand that we will sin and that it would be straying away from our new life in christ.*

# Lesson Two – Digging Deeper
## NEW-CREATION THEOLOGY
### ADDITIONAL NOTES, QUOTES, AND SOURCES

When we become believers, we become completely new people. The Bible tells us that we die to our old selves and are raised up as brand-new human beings. Even though we are the same people on the outside, a new identity has been imparted to us. In some ways, this identity is legal in nature. After becoming believers, we have been legally adopted into God's family. We are now sons of God. According to Romans 11, we have been grafted into the olive tree of Israel. We are now, according to Ephesians 2, part of the commonwealth of Israel. We have been declared righteous and justified. Our sins have been forgiven. Records of our guilt have been erased. There is no condemnation. These are the legal aspects of our new identity in Messiah.

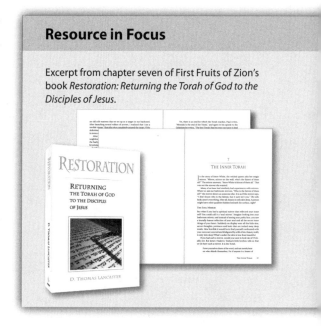

**Resource in Focus**

Excerpt from chapter seven of First Fruits of Zion's book *Restoration: Returning the Torah of God to the Disciples of Jesus*.

*Or do you not know that all of us who have been baptized into Messiah Yeshua have been baptized into His death? Therefore we have been buried with Him through baptism into death, so that as Messiah was raised from the dead through the glory of the Father, so we too might walk in newness of life.* (Romans 6:3–4)

There are also aspects of this new identity that are more mystical than legal. As believers, we are given a portion of God's Holy Spirit to dwell within us. We actually become temples of the Holy Spirit. The Holy Spirit that dwells within us is the same Spirit that dwelled within and anointed Yeshua. Therefore, we say it is the Spirit of Yeshua that dwells within us. Indeed, "Messiah in you [is] the hope of glory" (Colossians 1:27). Messiah is being formed within you. Messiah dwells "in your hearts through faith" (Ephesians 3:17). "Do you not recognize this about yourselves, that Yeshua Messiah is in you?" (2 Corinthians 13:5).

Our new creation identity is premised on the truth that Christ now dwells within us, is being formed within us, and lives through us. This raises a very important implication: There is a Torah-observant, Jewish guy dwelling within you!

To the extent that we surrender our lives to this new inner identity, we succeed in living out our lives in Messiah. When we show the love of Yeshua to others, it is not our love we are manifesting, but the Master's love made manifest through us. Because Messiah dwells within us, our acts of love are actually His acts of love. We become, as it were, the hands and feet of Messiah. Our new nature—our Messianic nature—is revealed.

The same is true for every act of righteousness that we perform. Our good works are credited to Messiah. It is not us but Messiah who lives through us.

When we continue in our old ways, walking in sin and lawlessness, we are living in contradiction to our new nature. Messiah within us is concealed. Our new identity is obscured.

When we keep the Torah, we allow Messiah to live through us. He is righteousness, and Torah is the standard of righteousness. He is the law fulfilled, and He desires to fulfill it through us.

# Lesson Two – Digging Deeper
# WHAT WERE ANIMAL SACRIFICES FOR?
### FURTHER STUDY FROM THIS WEEK'S HAYESOD LESSON

## Korban

The Hebrew word *korban* (קרבן) is translated into English as either "sacrifice" or "offering," but neither of those words accurately expresses the concept. The word "sacrifice" implies that the person bringing it is required to deprive himself of something in order to satisfy someone else's need or caprice, and "offering" implies a form of tribute or gratuity. But God has no satisfaction in inflicting deprivation upon His children, and He is not in need of tribute or gifts.

A *korban* is not merely a sacrifice or an offering. The root of the word *korban* is (קרב, *karav*), which can be translated "to bring near." A *korban* then should be defined as "something brought near." The reason it is so named is that the person bringing an offering does so in order to come closer to God.

The implication is that man himself cannot "come near" to God. God is holy, He is other, distinct and separate from man. Therefore, man must send a substitute in his stead. To "draw near" to God is to enter communion with God. It implies entering His very presence. Inasmuch as His presence resided in the Tabernacle on earth, the worshipper was able to draw near and enter into that presence through the offering of a *korban*—something brought near.

**Resource in Focus**

Excerpt from parashat "Vayikra: And He Called" of First Fruits of Zion's *Torah Club Volume Five: Rejoicing of the Torah*.

## Appeasing an Angry God

This is a very different understanding of sacrifice than we are ordinarily taught. We are normally taught that the Israelites brought sacrifices merely to pay the penalty for their sins. By this reasoning, the sacrifices became a sort of "scapegoat." When a man merited the death penalty, a sacrifice was made for him, and the unfortunate cow or sheep or goat was slaughtered instead of the man. An over-simplification of this concept has it that God was angry with the sinner and demanded punishment, even death. After all, "the wages of sin are death." The sinner then killed an animal, and the death of the animal appeased God. God was no longer angry after the animal was sacrificed. At least something was killed! The angry God was appeased with the blood of the animal. Yet is this really what the Torah teaches? Is this really what the Apostolic Scriptures teach? No, not entirely. Sacrificial substitution and propitiation are far more complex. Furthermore, most of the sacrifices were not offered for sin at all. It is true that there are "sin offerings" and "guilt offerings," but there are other sacrifices which were brought voluntarily by a glad, willing worshipper—not as a ransom for life.

*Korban* means "something brought near." In Torah, the death of the animal is not necessarily a substitution for the death of the sinner. Instead, the death of the animal is a proxy to bring the worshipper near to God. It is not an appeasement of an angry God. It is a method by which God might be approached.

Of course it remains true that the lessons of life and death, sin and punishment are graphically illustrated in the sacrificial system. Without the illustration of sacrifice, we can't appreciate the holiness of God as it pertains to His righteous anger. The price for coming near to God is death. It is a costly affair. It is not something that is entered into haphazardly or casually. Our sin means that blood must be shed if we are to enjoy communion with God. Coming close to God is a very expensive endeavor which must be paid in blood.

The grand words of propitiation, redemption, and atonement are all similar in that they each communicate an aspect of repayment. Payment is never lost sight of in the whole matter of redemption. Thus, even in the voluntary sacrifices, the death of the sacrificial victim is a central issue. At the heart of the sacrificial system is the knowledge that we stand in debt to God.

## Atonement

When offering a sacrifice, the worshipper was to lay his hands upon the animal and offer it in his stead in order that it might make atonement (from the root *kafar*, כפר) for him. But in what sense are we to understand this atonement? One might assume that the sacrifice is meant as an atonement for sin, but this is not exactly accurate. The Torah's use of the term atonement (*kafar*) certainly can imply the forgiveness of sin and removal of guilt, but it is not limited to those applications. The word *kafar* may be used to imply a protective covering.[1] The word *kafar* can be rendered as "ransom" for one's life. Both of the meanings apply in the ritual context of Israel's worship system. During the building of the Tabernacle, we saw that the priesthood, the altar, the furnishings, and even the Tabernacle itself all required *kippur* (from *kafar*) in the sense of "covering." They all need to be covered in order to stand in the presence of God. Without such covering, they would not survive the encounter with the consuming Spirit of the Almighty.

The same is also true for the worshipper that seeks to "draw near" to God. God is dangerous, and to be near Him is to be in jeopardy. The sacrificial system is a means by which those who desire to draw near can do safely, albeit through a surrogate agency. Fragile, mortal flesh cannot survive His presence; the man must send a surrogate on his behalf. Thus we should understand Levitical atonement primarily as a covering in the sense of a protective shelter from the manifest presence of God who occupied the Tabernacle.

## Not For Salvation

Sacrifices were not brought as a means to attain salvation. They were not brought to clear the sinner's conscience. They were not brought to provide forgiveness for sins. The writer of the book of Hebrews makes it clear that the sacrifices were not intended to remove sin or regenerate the sinner when he says, "For it is impossible for the blood of bulls and goats to take away sins" (Hebrews 10:4). In another place he explains that the sacrifices could not cleanse the conscience because they were only intended to relate to matters of the flesh, not the spirit.

> *Gifts and sacrifices are offered which cannot make the worshipper perfect in conscience, since they relate only to food and drink and various washings, regulations for the body.*
> (Hebrews 9:9–10)

Believers misunderstand the sacrificial system because they view it through the grid of "Old Covenant" and "New Covenant" dispensationalist theology. We make the mistake of assuming that prior to the death and resurrection of Yeshua, people's sins were actually forgiven and salvation procured through their participation in the sacrificial rites. We thereby assign efficacy unto eternal salvation to the rites of animal sacrifice—up until Yeshua's death. But if this were actually true, then Yeshua need not have died at all; His sacrifice and death were simply a matter of convenience for us. It is convenient that we no longer need to offer animal sacrifices, but if not for Yeshua, they would suffice us. This is ludicrous thinking.

# What Were Sacrifices For?

But for what then were the sacrifices meant? It is hard for us to understand because there is no Temple in our day; there is no place one can go to enter into a holy space occupied by the manifest presence of God. But if there were, then we would better understand the need for atonement as it pertains to God's presence in this world. The sacrifices and Temple rituals pertained to drawing near to God within His holy precincts. They were rituals for the Temple in this present world. The writer of Hebrews argues that if animal sacrifices were efficacious regarding the flesh, how much more so is the sacrifice of Messiah efficacious regarding the spirit.

> *For if the blood of goats and bulls and the ashes of a heifer sprinkling those who have been defiled sanctify for the cleansing of the flesh, how much more will the blood of Christ, who through the eternal Spirit offered Himself without blemish to God, cleanse your conscience from dead works to serve the living God?* (Hebrews 9:13–14)

Here we learn that the Temple sacrifices were able to "sanctify for the cleansing of the flesh," but they did nothing to cleanse the spirit. That could only be accomplished by faith and repentance.

> *Neither the sin offering, nor the guilt offering, nor the Day of Atonement can bring expiation without repentance.* (t.*Yoma* 5:9)

## Endnotes

1   When the Torah describes how Noah applied pitch to the exterior of his ark, it uses a verb form of the root *kafar*. "You shall cover [*kafar*, כפר] it inside and out with pitch" (Genesis 6:14).

# Notes:

# Lesson Three
# OUR CONNECTION– HIS COVENANTS

THE LAND, THE PEOPLE,
AND THE SCRIPTURES OF ISRAEL

# Lesson Three
## OUR CONNECTION—HIS COVENANTS

*Remember that you were at that time separate from Christ, excluded from the commonwealth of Israel, and strangers to the covenants of promise, having no hope and without God in the world. But now in Christ Jesus you who formerly were far off have been brought near by the blood of Messiah.* (Ephesians 2:12–13)

## Lesson Overview

How often do we use the word "covenant" in our everyday language? To be sure, it is a rare word. But to the people who lived in the world of the Bible, it was an everyday word. The Bible is the story of a series of covenants. The concept of covenant is deeply embedded in the text and fabric of the Bible. It becomes necessary then that we explore the nature of the word "covenant" and the implications that it has on our relationship to God through Messiah. In so doing, we will discover the real meaning of the "New Covenant" and how our personal relationship with God is part of a larger covenant relationship.

Lesson Three will focus on the meaning of covenant and its use in the Scriptures. We will compare the various biblical covenants and consider their implications for believers. Lesson Three gives students an overview of the biblical covenants to see how everything fits together.

## Lesson Purpose

The purpose of this lesson is to:
* ❖ Learn about the meaning of covenants in the biblical text.
* ❖ Compare the Abrahamic, Mosaic, and Davidic covenants with the New Covenant.
* ❖ Discover how later covenants build on the previous ones.
* ❖ Understand that the covenants do not cancel each other out.
* ❖ Define the New Covenant and study its implications.

## Field Trips to the Holy Land

* ❖ Nebi Samwil, North of Jerusalem
* ❖ Tel Beersheva, Negev Region
* ❖ City of David, Jerusalem
* ❖ Southern Steps, Jerusalem Temple Mount

# Lesson Three
# LESSON OUTLINE

## The Need to Study Covenants

A. The Importance That Covenants Play in the Scriptures

B. The Limited Use of the Word "Covenant" in our Society

## Meaning of the Term "Covenant"

A. The Berit

B. Working Definition

## Covenant Basics

A. Ancient Near Eastern Covenants

B. Covenant Principles

C. Covenant Rituals: The Divine Element

D. Covenant Closure: The Shared Meal

E. Covenant Signs

F. The Biblical Covenants

## The Covenant with Abraham

A. The Scripture—Genesis 12, 15 and 17

B. The Covenant Provisions

C. Covenant Obligations
1. Abraham's Faithfulness
2. Faith and Faithfulness

D. The Covenantal Sign

E. Analysis
1. The Perpetuity of this Covenant
2. The Pattern for God's Relationships

## The Covenant at Sinai

A. The Scripture—Exodus 19–24

B. The Covenant Provisions

C. Covenantal Obligations

D. The Covenantal Sign

E. Analysis
1. The Description of the Covenant
2. Comparison with the Covenant of Abraham
3. Confirmation in the Apostolic Writings

## The Covenant with David

A. The Scripture—2 Samuel 7

B. The Covenant Provisions

C. Covenantal Obligations

D. The Covenantal Sign

F. Analysis

## The New Covenant

A. The Scripture—Jeremiah 31; Ezekiel 36
1. New Testament is not the New Covenant
2. The Real New Covenant Scriptures

B. The Covenant Provisions

C. Covenant Obligations

D. The Covenantal Sign

E. Analysis
1. The "Renewed" Covenant
2. The Participants in the Covenant

Key Concepts

*Covenant:* A legally binding relationship between two or more parties. Covenants are binding and inter-generational, and there are penalties for breaking them.

# The Need to Study Covenants

What does it mean to be under the New Covenant? What is the difference between the New Covenant and the New Testament? How is the New Covenant different from the Old Covenant?

### Ⓐ The Importance That Covenants Play in the Scriptures

If you are going to understand the Bible, you have to understand the concept of a covenant. The stories of the Bible are built on a series of covenants.

*Virtually every school of biblical interpretation today has come to appreciate the significance of the covenants for the understanding of the distinctive message of the Scriptures.* (O. Palmer Robertson, *The Christ of the Covenants*)[1]

### Ⓑ The Limited Use of the Word "Covenant" in our Society

The most common form of "covenant" in Western society today is the marriage covenant.

The marriage canopy (*chuppah*)

# Meaning of the Term "Covenant"

**Key Verses**

1 Samuel 25:1
Joshua 9
2 Samuel 21

**Key Words**

*Berit:* Hebrew for "covenant."

*Suzerain:* A feudal lord to whom fealty was due.

*Vassal:* A person, nation, or state dominated by another.

## A  The Berit

> *berit* (ברית) = "covenant"

The Hebrew word for covenant is *berit* (ברית). It is pronounced more like "breet."

*Covenants are permenent*

*Between nations: a treaty, alliance of friendship; between individuals: a pledge or agreement; with obligation between a monarch and subjects: a constitution; between God and man: a covenant accompanied by signs, sacrifices, and a solemn oath that sealed the relationship with promises of blessing for keeping the covenant and curses for breaking it.* (Theological Wordbook of the Old Testament) [2]

## B  Working Definition

Define the word "covenant":

*A legally binding relationship between 2 or more parties*

# Covenant Basics

Four things we learn from the story of the Gibeonites:

1.  *Covenants are Binding*
2.  *Covenants are intergenerational*
3.  *Breaking one has dire consequences*
4.  *Requires atonement*

## A  Ancient Near Eastern Covenants

A common type of covenant was called a "suzerainty treaty."

> **suzerain = a great king**
>
> **vassal = a subordinate or dependent state**

**Your Israel Connection**

**Breaking a Covenant**

*Nebi Samwil, North of Jerusalem* – Nebi Samwil is Arabic for "Samuel the Prophet" and is the traditional location for his tomb. The tomb is located under a mosque/synagogue on top of a high hill north of Jerusalem. Samuel was actually buried in Ramah where he lived most of his life (1 Samuel 25:1), but at some point his burial place became identified with this prominent hill and the tradition has remained. The hill provides a commanding overlook of the Benjamin Plateau, including the ancient sites of Gibeah, Saul's hometown, and Jebus, the city of the Jebusites.

*even if a covenant is made in false pretenses it*

**Refer to Resource**

**Torah Club Volume One: Unrolling the Scroll** "Devarim: Words"

*must be kept*

# 🔍 Treaty Comparison

The book of Deuteronomy can be compared to an ancient suzerainty treaty.

| Suzerainty Treaty | Deuteronomy |
|---|---|
| The nature of the suzerain king | Preamble (Deuteronomy 1:1–5) |
| The acts of the suzerain king | Historical prologue (Deuteronomy 1:6–4:49) |
| The covenant expectations | Stipulations (Deuteronomy 5:1–26:19) |
| The consequences of covenant faithfulness or unfaithfulness | Blessings and curses (Deuteronomy 27–30) |
| Witness to the ratification of the covenant | Witnesses (Deuteronomy 30:19) |
| The continuation of the covenant | Succession (Deuteronomy 31:1–8) |
| Storage and public renewal of the covenant | Deposit/reading (Deuteronomy 31:9–13) |

## ➍ Covenant Principles ✍

A covenant always contains terms and conditions to be fulfilled by both parties. Covenants were supposed to be mutually beneficial for both parties.

The glue of the ancient covenant was a deep sense of fidelity.

A covenant requires for both parties:

1. _Mutual benefit_
2. _terms + conditions_
3. _fidelity + faithfulness_

**Key Concepts**

*Karat berit* : lit. "to cut a covenant." Hebrew term for making a covenant, coming from ancient Near Eastern practices of making sacrifices as part of covenant rituals.

## C  Covenant Rituals: The Divine Element

Ancient Near Eastern (ANE) covenants always had a religious element involving some sort of ceremonial elements like sacrifice or other rituals.

> *karat berit* (כרת ברית) = "to cut a covenant"

The Hebrew term for making a covenant is *karat berit* (כרת ברית) which literally means "to cut a covenant," but idiomatically means "to make a covenant."

"Cutting" a covenant with Abraham

## D  Covenant Closure: The Shared Meal

In the Bible, a covenant was completed with a shared meal between the parties.

*Abraham took sheep and oxen and gave them to Abimelech, and the two of them made a covenant.* (Genesis 21:27)

*Then Jacob offered a sacrifice on the mountain, and called his kinsmen to the meal; and they ate the meal and spent the night on the mountain.* (Genesis 31:54)

*And they saw God, and they ate and drank.* (Exodus 24:11)

## **E** Covenant Signs

*Sometimes the covenant is accompanied by an external sign or token to remind the parties of their obligations. (Encyclopedia Judaica)*[3]

Noah's rainbow

## **F** The Biblical Covenants

Examples:

- ❖ Covenant with Noah: Genesis 8:14–9:17
- ❖ Covenant with Abraham: Genesis 12, 15, 17
- ❖ Covenant with Isaac: Genesis 26
- ❖ Covenant with Jacob: Genesis 28
- ❖ Covenant at Sinai: Exodus 19–20
- ❖ Covenant with Aaron: Numbers 18:19
- ❖ Covenant with Pinchas: Numbers 25:12–13
- ❖ Covenant with David: 2 Samuel 7
- ❖ New Covenant: Jeremiah 31

# Covenant Comparison

| | Scripture | Provisions | Covenantal Obligations | Sign |
|---|---|---|---|---|
| **ABRAHAMIC** | Genesis 12, 15+17 | posterity, inheritance, land, greatnes, blessing + universel blessing | Faith faithfullness | circumcision |
| **SINAI** | Exodus 19-24 | Blessings + curses | Faith + obedience | Sabbath |
| **DAVIDIC** | 2 Samuel 7 | kingdom + Dynasty, posterity, inheritance, peace, greatness + Blessing | obedience | The house |
| **NEW COVENANT** | Jeremiah 31: 31-40 Ezekiel 36: 24-38 | A complete fulfillment of all the covenants | faith + obedience | The holy spirit |

**Key Verses**

Genesis 12:1–3, 7

Genesis 15

Genesis 17:1–14

# The Covenant with Abraham

The covenant God made with Abraham is the foundation on which the rest of the covenants of the Bible are built.

Abraham

## Ⓐ The Scripture – Genesis 12, 15, and 17

❖ Genesis 12:1–3, 7: The initial promises to Abraham

❖ Genesis 15: The ratification of the covenant and covenant ceremony

❖ Genesis 17:1–14: The sign of the Abrahamic covenant

## Ⓑ The Covenant Provisions

*Go forth from your country, and from your relatives and from your father's house, to the land which I will show you; and I will make you a great nation, and I will bless you, and make your name great; and so you shall be a blessing; and I will bless those who bless you, and the one who curses you I will curse. And in you all the families of the earth will be blessed.* (Genesis 12:1–3)

1. God will make of Abraham a great nation.

2. God will bless Abraham.

3. God will make Abraham's name great.

4. God will make Abraham a blessing to others.

5. God will bless the ones who will bless Abraham.

6. God will curse the ones who curse Abraham.

7. God will cause all the families of the earth to be blessed through Abraham.

## C Covenant Obligations

**Key Verses**

Genesis 15:6
Genesis 22:15–18
Genesis 26:3–5
James 1:22
James 2:14
James 2:21–24
Genesis 17:14

From the outset, the promises were conditional; Abraham had to act in faith to receive those promises. Throughout the Abrahamic narratives, that faith was continually tested as God measured Abraham to see if he would prove himself to be faithful to the covenant.

### 1. Abraham's Faithfulness

Did Abraham have any obligations to the covenant?

*[Abraham] believed in the LORD; and He reckoned it to him as righteousness.* (Genesis 15:6)

*Then the angel of the LORD called to Abraham a second time from heaven, and said, "By Myself I have sworn, declares the LORD, <u>because</u> you have done this thing and have not withheld your son, your only son, indeed I will greatly bless you, and I will greatly multiply your seed as the stars of the heavens and as the sand which is on the seashore; and your seed shall possess the gate of their enemies. In your seed all the nations of the earth shall be blessed, <u>because</u> you have obeyed My voice."* (Genesis 22:15–18)

*I will establish the oath which I swore to your father Abraham … <u>because</u> Abraham obeyed Me and kept My charge, My commandments, My statutes and My laws.* (Genesis 26:3–5)

### 2. Faith and Faithfulness

*Prove yourselves doers of the word, and not merely hearers who delude themselves.* (James 1:22)

*What use is it, my brethren, if someone says he has faith but he has no works? Can that faith save him?* (James 2:14)

*Was not Abraham our father justified by works when he offered up Isaac his son on the altar? You see that faith was working with his works, and as a result of the works, faith was perfected; and the Scripture was fulfilled which says, "And Abraham believed God, and it was reckoned to him as righteousness," and he was called the friend of God. You see that a man is justified by works and not by faith alone.* (James 2:21–24; quoting Genesis 15:6)

## D The Covenantal Sign

❖ Circumcision is the sign of the Abrahamic covenant.

*But an uncircumcised male who is not circumcised in the flesh of his foreskin, that person shall be cut off from his people; he has broken My covenant.* (Genesis 17:14)

## E Analysis

### 1. The Perpetuity of this Covenant

The covenant of Abraham is a covenant for all Israel, and it is an ongoing covenant.

A later covenant does not cancel an earlier covenant.

*Brethren, I speak in terms of human relations: even though it is only a man's covenant, yet when it has been ratified, no one sets it aside or adds conditions to it. Now the promises were spoken to Abraham and to his seed. He does not say, "And to seeds," as referring to many, but rather to one, "And to your seed," that is, Christ. What I am saying is this: the [Torah], which came four hundred and thirty years later, does not invalidate a covenant previously ratified by God, so as to nullify the promise.* (Galatians 3:15–17)

### 2. The Pattern for God's Relationships

The Abrahamic covenant establishes the paradigm for all of God's relationships with people, even after Messiah came.

*And he received the sign of circumcision, a seal of the righteousness of the faith which he had while uncircumcised, so that he might be the father of all who believe without being circumcised, that righteousness might be credited to them.* (Romans 4:11)

# The Covenant at Sinai

The covenant at Sinai did not cancel the Abrahamic covenant.

**Your Israel Connection**

**Cutting a Covenant with Abraham**

*Tel Beersheva, Negev Region* – Pictured is a reconstruction of the ancient altar that was found at Tel Beersheva. Contrary to Torah-law, the ancient Israelites honored the home of Abraham by constructing an altar and sacrificing to God at Beersheva, the place where Abraham and the LORD entered into covenant together. This altar was dismantled during one of Israel's returns to Torah. Archaeologists found its stones in secondary use in the walls of buildings.

Moses at Mount Sinai

# Ⓐ The Scripture—Exodus 19–24

❖ Exodus 19: Invitation to enter covenant

❖ Exodus 20–23: Terms and conditions of covenant

❖ Exodus 24: Covenant ratification ceremonies

*Then he took the book of the covenant and read it in the hearing of the people; and they said, "All that the LORD has spoken we will do, and we will be obedient!" So Moses took the blood and sprinkled it on the people, and said, "Behold the blood of the covenant, which the LORD has made with you in accordance with all these words."* (Exodus 24:7–8)

# Ⓑ The Covenant Provisions

❖ Blessings and Curses

❖ Leviticus 24; Deuteronomy 27–29

# Ⓒ Covenantal Obligations

*"Now then, if you will indeed obey My voice and keep My covenant, then you shall be My own possession among all the peoples, for all the earth is Mine; and you shall be to Me a kingdom of priests and a holy nation." These are the words that you shall speak to the sons of Israel.* (Exodus 19:5–6)

❖ The "Old Covenant" (the covenant at Sinai) is NOT the Torah.

❖ The covenant is the AGREEMENT to obey the Torah.

The big "IF" contingency:

*Now it shall be, <u>IF</u> you diligently obey the LORD your God, being careful to do all His commandments which I command you today, the LORD your God will set you high above all the nations of the earth. All these blessings will come upon you and overtake you if you obey the LORD your God.* (Deuteronomy 28:1–2; emphasis added)

*But it shall come about, <u>IF</u> you do not obey the LORD your God, to observe to do all His commandments and His statutes with which I charge you today, that all these curses will come upon you and overtake you.* (Deuteronomy 28:15; emphasis added)

Faith and obedience—a command to believe in God:

*I am the LORD your God, who brought you out of the land of Egypt, out of the house of slavery.* (Exodus 20:2)

**Key Verses**

Exodus 31:16–17
Leviticus 26:41–42

**Key Words**

*Shabbat:* From the root word *shavat* meaning "to cease or to rest;" the Sabbath day.

## **D** The Covenantal Sign

❖ The Sabbath is a perpetual covenant.

> ### *Shabbat* (שבת) = "cease, rest, Sabbath"

*Judaism teaches us to be attached to holiness in time …
The Sabbaths are our great cathedrals … On the Sabbath
we try to become attuned to holiness in time. It is a day
on which we are called upon to share in what is eternal
in time, to turn from the results of creation to the mystery
of creation; from the world of creation to the creation
of the world.* (Abraham Joshua Heschel, *The Sabbath*)[4]

*So the sons of Israel shall observe the sabbath, to celebrate the
sabbath throughout their generations as a perpetual covenant.
It is a sign between Me and the sons of Israel forever; for in six
days the LORD made heaven and earth, but on the seventh day
He ceased from labor, and was refreshed.* (Exodus 31:16–17)

## **E** Analysis

### 1. The Description of the Covenant

If the covenant with Abraham is considered the covenant of promise, the covenant at Sinai may be considered the covenant that begins to fulfill that promise.

### 2. Comparison with the Covenant of Abraham

When the covenant at Sinai failed due to Israel's disobedience, God would fall back on his covenant promises to Abraham.

*If their uncircumcised heart becomes humbled so that they
then make amends for their iniquity, then I will remember
My covenant with Jacob, and I will remember also My
covenant with Isaac, and My covenant with Abraham as
well, and I will remember the land.* (Leviticus 26:41–42)

### 3. Confirmation in the Apostolic Writings

The Torah does not justify a person, because the Torah is contingent upon obedience. When the covenant at Sinai is broken, the covenant with Abraham is like a safety net underneath it, and that is a covenant of faith—Abraham's faith.

*Now that no one is justified by the [Torah] before God is evident; for, "the righteous man shall live by faith." However, the [Torah] is not of faith; on the contrary, "He who practices them shall live by them."* (Galatians 3:11–12)

*Is the [Torah] then contrary to the promises of God? May it never be!* (Galatians 3:21)

**Key Verses**

Galatians 3:11–12
Galatians 3:21
Genesis 22:14
Genesis 14:18
2 Samuel 7:5, 9–16
Psalm 89:3–4
Psalm 102
Jeremiah 33:20–21

# The Covenant with David

God made an exclusive covenant with David and his descendants.

King David

## Ⓐ The Scripture—2 Samuel 7

*I will make you a great name, like the names of the great men who are on the earth. I will also appoint a place for My people Israel and will plant them, that they may live in their own place and not be disturbed again, nor will the wicked afflict them any more as formerly, even from the day that I commanded judges to be over My people Israel; and I will give you rest from all your enemies. The LORD also declares to you that the LORD will make a house for you … I will raise up your descendant after you, who will come forth from you, and I will establish his kingdom. He shall build a house for My name, and I will establish the throne of his kingdom forever. I will be a father to him and he will be a son to Me … Your house and your kingdom shall endure before Me forever; your throne shall be established forever.* (2 Samuel 7:9–16)

## Ⓑ The Covenant Provisions

❖ God promised David the kingdom and a dynasty, posterity, inheritance, peace, greatness, blessing.

📹 **Your Israel Connection**

**The Davidic Covenant**

*City of David, Jerusalem* – The original city of Jerusalem sat on a small hill south of the current Old City walls. On the hill, archaeologists have uncovered inscriptions, seal impressions, and remains from the time of the Judean kings. A 2006–2008 dig revealed foundation stones of what may have been the Davidic palace.

**Key Verses**

2 Samuel 7:9–16
Genesis 12:7
Genesis 12:2
Genesis 17:6, 16
1 Corinthians 6:19

The promises are similar to those given to Abraham:

1. A secure and permanent home for Israel, 2 Samuel 7:10 (cf. Genesis 12:7)

2. Offspring (a dynasty) for David, 2 Samuel 7:11–12 (cf. Genesis 12:2)

3. Kings are to descend from him, 2 Samuel 7:12–16 (cf. Genesis 17:6, 16)

## C Covenantal Obligations

❖ Obedience to Torah

*When [the Davidic king] commits iniquity, I will correct him with the rod of men and the strokes of the sons of men, but My lovingkindness shall not depart from him.* (2 Samuel 7:14–15)

## D The Covenantal Sign

❖ The House:

1. The House of the Davidic dynasty

2. The House of the Temple in Jerusalem

3. The House of the Temple of believers (cf. 1 Corinthians 6:19)

*Or do you not know that your body is a temple of the Holy Spirit who is in you, whom you have from God, and that you are not your own?* (1 Corinthians 6:19)

## E Analysis

The Davidic covenant builds on both the Abrahamic covenant and the Sinai covenant. Both Abraham and David were promised:

1. A great name

2. A piece of real estate

3. Offspring

4. A connection to a throne

5. A special relationship with God

6. An effect upon the Gentiles

7. Great blessing

# The New Covenant

The "New Covenant" includes all previous covenants.

**Key Verses**

Jeremiah 31
Ezekiel 36

The empty tomb

## Ⓐ The Scripture—Jeremiah 31; Ezekiel 36

One might assume that the New Testament is the New Covenant scriptures. Actually the scriptures about the New Covenant are in Jeremiah, Ezekiel, and several other places in the *TaNaK*.

### 1. New Testament is not the New Covenant

The New Testament is a collection of scriptures that tell about how the gospel brought about the New Covenant, but it is not actually the New Covenant itself.

**The Apostolic Scriptures**

| | |
|---|---|
| **Gospels** | Narratives and teachings about Yeshua |
| **Acts of the Apostles** | Historical narratives about the apostolic community |
| **Epistles** | Personal communication from apostles to believing communities |
| **Revelation** | Apocalyptic vision of end times |

**Refer to Resource**

*HaYesod Student Workbook*
"The New Covenant"
Pages 3.28–3.30

### 2. The Real New Covenant Scriptures

*"Behold, days are coming," declares the LORD, "when I will make a new covenant with the house of Israel and with the house of Judah, not like the covenant which I made with their fathers in the day I took them by the hand to bring them out of the land of Egypt, My covenant which*

# The Apostolic Scriptures

- Matthew
- Mark
- Luke
- John

**Gospels**

- Acts

**Acts**

- Romans
- 1 Corinthians
- 2 Corinthians
- Galatians
- Ephesians
- Philippians
- Colossians
- 1 Thessalonians
- 2 Thessalonians
- 1 Timothy
- 2 Timothy
- Titus
- Philemon
- Hebrews
- James
- 1 Peter
- 2 Peter
- 1 John
- 2 John
- 3 John
- Jude

**Epistles**

- Revelation

**Revelation**

*they broke, although I was a husband to them," declares the LORD. "But this is the covenant which I will make with the house of Israel after those days," declares the LORD, "I will put My [Torah] within them and on their heart I will write it; and I will be their God, and they shall be My people. They will not teach again, each man his neighbor and each man his brother, saying, 'Know the LORD,' for they will all know Me, from the least of them to the greatest of them," declares the LORD, "for I will forgive their iniquity, and their sin I will remember no more."* (Jeremiah 31:31–34)

*For I will take you from the nations, gather you from all the lands and bring you into your own land. Then I will sprinkle clean water on you, and you will be clean; I will cleanse you from all your filthiness and from all your idols. Moreover, I will give you a new heart and put a new spirit within you; and I will remove the heart of stone from your flesh and give you a heart of flesh. I will put My Spirit within you and cause you to walk in My statutes, and you will be careful to observe My ordinances. You will live in the land that I gave to your forefathers; so you will be My people, and I will be your God.* (Ezekiel 36:24–28)

## Ⓑ The Covenant Provisions

A list of New Covenant promises that are found in Jeremiah 31 and Ezekiel 36:

❖ God will write His Torah on their hearts (Jeremiah 31:33).

❖ The LORD will be their God (Jeremiah 31:33).

❖ Israel and Judah shall be God's people (Jeremiah 31:33).

❖ They shall all know the LORD (Jeremiah 31:34).

❖ God will forgive their sin (Jeremiah 31:34).

❖ God will regather the people of Israel to their Land (Ezekiel 36:24).

❖ God will spiritually cleanse Israel (Ezekiel 36:25).

❖ God will give the nation a new heart (Ezekiel 36:26).

❖ God will put His Spirit within them (Ezekiel 36:27).

❖ They will be faithful to the covenant of Torah (Ezekiel 36:27).

## **C** Covenant Obligations

❖  Faith and Obedience

*I will put My [Torah] within them and on their heart I will write it and I will be their God, and they shall be My people. They will not teach again, each man his neighbor and each man his brother, saying, "Know the LORD," for they will all know Me, from the least of them to the greatest of them.* (Jeremiah 31:33–34)

## 🔍 The New Covenant

**Jeremiah 31:33**
God will write His Torah on their hearts. The LORD will be their God.

**Jeremiah 31:33**
Israel and Judah shall be God's people.

**Jeremiah 31:34**
They shall all know the LORD.

**Jeremiah 31:34**
God will forgive their sin.

**Ezekiel 36:24**
God will regather the people of Israel to their Land.

**Ezekiel 36:25**
God will spiritually cleanse Israel.

**Ezekiel 36:26**
God will give the nation a new heart.

**Ezekiel 36:27**
God will put His Spirit within them.

**Ezekiel 36:27**
They will be faithful to the covenant of Torah.

*I will put My Spirit within you and cause you to walk in My statutes, and you will be careful to observe My ordinances.* (Ezekiel 36:27)

## Ⓓ The Covenantal Sign

❖ The Holy Spirit

*[God has] sealed us and gave us the Spirit in our hearts as a pledge.* (2 Corinthians 1:22)

*[God] gave us the Spirit as a pledge.* (2 Corinthians 5:5)

*You were sealed in Him with the Holy Spirit of promise, who is given as a pledge of our inheritance.* (Ephesians 1:13–14)

## Ⓔ Analysis

The New Covenant was instituted by Messiah's death and resurrection, but it has not yet been fully implemented.

1. **The "Renewed" Covenant**

> *chadash* (חדש) = "new" or "renewed"
>
> *Berit Chadashah* (ברית חדשה) = "New Covenant"

Some prefer the term "Renewed Covenant."

*For if that first covenant had been faultless, there would have been no occasion sought for a second.* (Hebrews 8:7)

2. **The Participants in the Covenant** 🖋

*Behold, days are coming … when I will make a new covenant with the house of Israel and with the house of Judah.* (Jeremiah 31:31)

The New Covenant is a covenant only with the:

 People of Israel

### Key Verses

Ezekiel 36:27
2 Corinthians 1:22
2 Corinthians 5:5
Ephesians 1:13–14
Acts 2
Exodus 19–20
Genesis 15:17
Psalm 119:43
John 16:13
Hebrews 8:7
Jeremiah 31:31

### Key Words

*Chadash:* Hebrew word meaning "new" or "renewed."

*Berit Chadashah:* Hebrew for "New Covenant."

**🎥 Your Israel Connection**

**The Day of Pentecost and the Temple**

*Southern Steps, Jerusalem Temple Mount –* Christian tradition places the apostles in an upper room in Jerusalem when the Holy Spirit was poured out in Acts 2, but internal evidence in the narrative points toward the Temple as the location of the miracle. From that day on, the apostles congregated in the Temple courts daily.

**Refer to Resource**

*HaYesod Student Workbook*
"The Letter and the Spirit"
Pages 3.31–3.33

Our Connection—His Covenants    **3.21**

Grafted in

What about Gentiles?

*Remember that you were at that time separate from Messiah, excluded from the commonwealth of Israel, and <u>strangers to the covenants of promise</u>, having no hope and without God in the world. But now in Messiah Yeshua you who formerly were far off have been brought near by the blood of Christ.* (Ephesians 2:12–13)

### Endnotes

1   O. Palmer Robertson, *The Christ of the Covenants* (Phillipsburg, NJ: Presbyterian and Reformed Publishing Co., 1980), vii.

2   R. Laird Harris, Gleason L. Archer, Jr., Bruce K. Waltke, *Theological Wordbook of the Old Testament* (2 vols.; Chicago: Moody Press, 1980), 1:128.

3   Moshe Weinfeld, "Covenant," *Encyclopedia Judaica* (1st Edition) 5:1013.

4   Abraham Joshua Heschel, *The Sabbath, Its Meaning for Modern Man* (New York: Farrar, Straus, and Giroux, 2005), 8–10.

# Lesson Three
# LESSON SUMMARY

## First …

We introduced the need to study the concept of the covenant within its historical, biblical context.

- ❖ We took note of the importance that covenants play in the Scriptures.
- ❖ We saw marriage as a modern equivalent of covenant making.
- ❖ We defined the term "covenant" (*berit*, ברית) as a legally binding relationship between two or more parties.

## Then …

We looked briefly at the historical context of covenants in the ancient Near East because the Bible is an ancient Near-Eastern covenantal document. We listed and examined the elements involved in covenants:

- ❖ Covenant Principles
- ❖ Covenant Rituals: The Divine Element
- ❖ Covenant Closure: The Shared Meal
- ❖ Covenant Signs

## Next …

We discussed four key biblical covenants and compared them with one another to determine their relationship. We discovered that each covenant includes and builds upon the previous covenants. Those covenants were:

- ❖ The Covenant with Abraham
- ❖ The Covenant at Sinai
- ❖ The Covenant with David
- ❖ The New Covenant

## After that …

We learned that the "New Covenant" is not the "New Testament," and it does not replace the Torah. The Torah is actually a part of the New Covenant; that is why the New Covenant could be called the "Renewed Covenant."

## Finally …

We learned that the New Covenant was made only with God's chosen people Israel. Gentiles who want to have a share in the New Covenant must do so by participation in Israel through the Messiah of Israel.

# Lesson Three
## LESSON REVIEW – Q&A

1. What is a covenant? What is the most common type of covenant in Western society today?

2. What are some common elements that covenants share? How many biblical covenants can you name off the top of your head? Which one is foundational to the rest of the covenants?

3. What was the "sign" of the covenant with Noah? With Abraham? At Sinai? With David? Of the New Covenant?

4. What are some of the promises that the Abrahamic and Davidic covenants shared?

5. How do the covenants work together? Do they cancel or build?

6. What is the difference between the "New Covenant" and the "New Testament"? Where is the New Covenant found in the Bible? What does God do with the Torah in the New Covenant?

7. List the promises of the New Covenant.

8. With whom does God make the New Covenant?

# Lesson Three
# EXTRA CREDIT
### SUPPLEMENTAL MATERIAL FOR THIS HAYESOD LESSON

**Extra Credit Instructions:**

1. This material is not mandatory, but it will serve as a helpful tool for further study.
2. Provide answers to each question based upon the passages indicated.

## God's Covenants in the Torah

### The Covenant with Noah

*Read Genesis 8:14–9:17.*

1. With whom did God make His rainbow covenant? (See 9:12)

2. What terms did God agree to keep? (See 9:14–15)

3. What terms did the covenant impose on man? (See 9:1–7)

### The Covenant with Abraham

*Read Genesis 12:1–3 and Genesis 15.*

1. Why did Abraham want a son? (See 15:3)

2. To what did God compare the promised number of Abraham's children? (See 15:5)

3. What did God promise to give to Abraham's children? (See 15:18)

4. Does this covenant cancel the covenant with Noah?

## The Covenant with Isaac

*Read Genesis 26:1–5.*

1. What condition did God impose on Isaac? (See 26:2)

2. How were these covenant promises similar to those given to Abraham?

3. Why did God pass the covenant to Isaac? (See 26:5)

4. Does this covenant cancel the ones with Noah and/or the one with Abraham?

## The Covenant with Jacob

*Read Genesis 28:13–15.*

1. How did God identify Himself to Jacob? (See 28:13)

2. Which promises are similar to those given to Abraham and Isaac?

3. Are there any new promises?

4. Does this covenant cancel either the covenants with Noah, Abraham, or Isaac?

## Covenant at Sinai

*Read Exodus 19:3–8.*

1. What was the covenant condition God imposed on Israel? (See 19:5)

2. What are the three incentives God offered Israel? (See 19:5–6)

3. What did Israel answer? (See 19:8)

4. Does the Sinai covenant cancel either the covenant with Noah or the covenants with the fathers?

## Covenant with Aaron

*Read Exodus 28:43; Numbers 18:19; Deuteronomy 18:5.*

1.  How long is God's covenant with the Aaronic priesthood in Exodus 28:43?

2.  How long is God's covenant with the Aaronic priesthood in Numbers 18:19?

3.  How long is God's covenant with the Aaronic priesthood in Deuteronomy 18:5?

4   Does this covenant in any way cancel the ones with Noah, the forefathers, or at Sinai?


## Covenant with Phinehas

*Read Numbers 25:11–13.*

1.  What kind of covenant does God give Phinehas?

2.  What does God promise to Phinehas?

3.  How long will this covenant last?

4.  Does this covenant in any way cancel the covenant with Aaron?

# Lesson Three – Digging Deeper
# THE NEW COVENANT
### ADDITIONAL NOTES, QUOTES, AND SOURCES

## Resource in Focus

Excerpt from parashat "Ki Tisa: When You Take" from First Fruits of Zion's *Torah Club Volume Five: Rejoicing of the Torah.*

## New Covenant and Old Covenant: Jeremiah 31

In any discussion of the New Covenant some preliminary statements are necessary. There are three primary misconceptions about the New Covenant which must be immediately dispelled. First of all, we must agree that the New Testament canon (Matthew–Revelation) does not constitute the New Covenant. Referring to the New Testament as the New Covenant is a misnomer. While it is certainly true that the Apostolic Scriptures speak about the New Covenant and the central figure of the New Covenant (i.e., Messiah), the New Testament is not the New Covenant. Neither is the Old Covenant God's covenant with the Jews while the New Covenant is His covenant with the Christians. This kind of thinking is anachronistic. Finally, the Old Covenant is not a covenant of works while the New Covenant is a covenant of grace. This last error strikes closer to the truth than the other two misconceptions, but as we will see, it is an oversimplification.

In the Hebrew Scriptures, the Torah, the Prophets, and the Writings allude to the New Covenant, but only Jeremiah 31 speaks explicitly about the New Covenant. Thus if we hope to understand the New Covenant, we must begin there and study the words of Jeremiah.

| Common Misconceptions about the New Covenant | |
| --- | --- |
| Old Testament vs. New Testament | Mistaken identity |
| Judaism vs. Christianity | Anachronism |
| Grace vs. Works | Oversimplification |

## Jeremiah 31 and the New Covenant

Jeremiah lived at a turbulent time in Jewish history, just before the Babylonian destruction of Jerusalem. Sometime near the year 586 BCE, he was prophesying to the people, "You have broken God's covenant and this city is going to be destroyed! This Temple is going to be destroyed. Judgment is coming." That was the main thrust of his message, but in Jeremiah 31, he speaks of a time of future hope.

> *"Behold, days are coming," declares the LORD, "when I will make a new covenant with the house of Israel and with the house of Judah, not like the covenant which I made with their fathers in the day I took them by the hand to bring them out of the land of Egypt, My covenant which they broke, although I was a husband to them," declares the LORD. "But this is the covenant which I will make with the house of Israel after those days," declares the LORD, "I will put My Torah within them and on their heart I will*

*write it; and I will be their God, and they shall be My people. They will not teach again, each man his neighbor and each man his brother, saying, 'Know the LORD,' for they will all know Me, from the least of them to the greatest of them," declares the LORD, "for I will forgive their iniquity, and their sin I will remember no more."* (Jeremiah 31:31–34)

## Old Covenant and Torah

The most common mistake we make in parsing this passage is equating Torah and Old Covenant as if they are the same thing. Jeremiah says that the New Covenant is not like the old one made at Sinai. Therefore, we assume this means the New Covenant is not like the Torah. But Old Covenant does not equal Torah. They are not the same.

The Old Covenant is easily confused with the Torah because the Old Covenant is predicated upon obedience to the Torah—the Law. The Torah is interrelated with the covenant at Sinai because the Torah tells the story of the covenant and presents its laws and instructions in covenantal format. The Torah is written in covenantal language; it comes with covenant curses and blessings for keeping or breaking its laws, and is covenantal in form and function. The Law of God—the Torah—was presented to Israel as a covenant, inasmuch as the covenant at Sinai was an agreement to obey the Law.

Yet, there is a critical distinction to be made: The Torah is not the Covenant. The Covenant is the agreement to keep the Torah. You may think that I am nitpicking, but these are important nits to pick. The covenant and the Torah are so intermeshed that they are not completely separable, but for purposes of understanding the difference between "Old Covenant" and "New Covenant," we must make the distinction.

The Torah is more than just a covenant. It is a record of numerous covenants, starting with Noah and ending with Israel's covenant renewal in Deuteronomy. The Torah is God's instruction and law. The covenant at Sinai is Israel's agreement to abide by the Torah. In Exodus 24, Moses read aloud from the "Book of the Covenant," and all Israel agreed to keep God's laws:

> *Then he took the book of the covenant and read it in the hearing of the people; and they said, "All that the LORD has spoken we will do, and we will be obedient!"* (Exodus 24:7)

At that moment, the Torah became the covenant document, but the Torah itself is not the covenant. The covenant is Israel's agreement to keep the Torah.

## The Broken Covenant

The covenant lasted only forty days. When Israel made the golden calf, they broke the covenant. Thus Jeremiah says of the New Covenant that it is "not like the covenant which I made with their fathers in the day I took them by the hand to bring them out of the land of Egypt, My covenant which they broke" (Jeremiah 31:32). To symbolize the broken covenant, Moses broke the tablets of the Ten Commandments.

After the golden calf, Moses interceded for Israel and implored God to be merciful. God was gracious and offered Israel a new covenant. The new covenant even came with new tablets. But notice that this new covenant did not come with a different law. The covenant stipulations were the same.

Israel broke the covenant at Mount Sinai. God renewed it. He made a new covenant (a "new agreement") based upon His mercy and grace, but the Torah of God remained unchanged.

# New Covenant

Jeremiah lived in a time when Judah was practicing apostasy and suffering punishment, much like Israel had experienced at Mount Sinai when they broke the covenant. He invoked Exodus 34's new covenant imagery as he described the coming time of reprieve when Judah and Israel will be reconciled to their God. The people of Israel will be reconciled to God just as they were reconciled at Mount Sinai after Moses successfully interceded on their behalf:

> *"This is the covenant which I will make with the house of Israel after those days,"* declares the LORD, *"I will put My Torah within them and on their heart I will write it; and I will be their God, and they shall be My people."* (Jeremiah 31:33)

According to Jeremiah, the New Covenant will be different from the Old Covenant primarily in this respect: The Torah, which was previously written on tablets of stone, will now be written on the heart. It aims for the same goal: "I will be their God, and they shall be My people." It is not a different Torah; it is the same Torah, but it is in a different place.

Jeremiah 31:31–40 lists seven promises of the New Covenant. They are as follows:

1.  God will forgive Israel's wickedness. (31:34)

2.  God will not remember Israel's sins. (31:34)

3.  All Israel will know the LORD. (31:34)

4.  Israel will never cease to be a nation before God. (31:36)

5.  God will never reject the seed of Israel. (31:37)

6.  God will rebuild Jerusalem as an eternal structure. (31:38–40)

7.  The entire city of Jerusalem will be holy to the LORD (31:40)

The astute Torah student will quickly notice that most of these promises have not yet been fulfilled. We are not there yet. The Torah is not written on our hearts yet—not completely. The process has begun, but it is not yet complete. Not all Israel knows the LORD. Jerusalem has not been rebuilt as an eternal city; in fact, it was destroyed just 40 years after Yeshua instituted the New Covenant over the cup saying "This is my blood of the New Covenant." So the New Covenant is not yet here in its fullness.

Rather, it is a contract for the Messianic Age and the World to Come. When Messiah comes, these things will be accomplished.

The Old Covenant is part of this present world. The New Covenant is the covenant of the restored world of the Messianic Age. The Torah is the same in both covenants, but our relationship to it changes. In the Old, it was a matter of "if you obey me" and in the New it is a matter of "this Torah will be written on your heart." Thus the New Covenant is not an abrogation of the Torah but rather a new agreement changing our relationship to the Torah.

If so, when did the New Covenant begin? Did it begin with Messiah or with Moses? The death and resurrection of Messiah is the propitiating sacrifice which seals and accomplishes the New Covenant, but we should not delude ourselves into supposing that His death and resurrection were the beginning of the New Covenant era. We are still waiting for the dawning of the era when every man will know the LORD and Jerusalem will be rebuilt as an eternal structure.

# Lesson Three – Digging Deeper
# THE LETTER AND THE SPIRIT
### FURTHER STUDY FROM THIS WEEK'S HAYESOD LESSON

## Old Covenant and New Covenant: 2 Corinthians 3

The difference between the Old Covenant and the New Covenant is better explained by Paul; in 2 Corinthians 3:6, he says, "[God] also made us adequate as servants of a new covenant, not of the letter but of the Spirit; for the letter kills, but the Spirit gives life."

**Resource in Focus**

Excerpt from parashat "Ki Tisa: When You Take" from First Fruits of Zion's *Torah Club Volume Five: Rejoicing of the Torah.*

When Paul contrasts the letter that kills and the Spirit that gives life, he contrasts the condemnation wrought by sin with the restoration wrought by God's Spirit. It is erroneous to equate the "letter" with the Torah's mandates. Rather, Paul uses the term "letter of the law" similar to the way he uses the phrase "under the law," that is to be "under the condemnation of the Torah." The consequences of breaking the Torah are certainly death. "The wages of sin is death,"[1] and "All have sinned and fallen short of the glory of God."[2] Thus it is rightly said, "The letter kills." Paul speaks of the Old Covenant agreement in similar terms. Because Torah condemns sin absolutely and because all men sin, Paul speaks of the Old Covenant relationship to Torah as "the ministry of death, in letters engraved on stone" (2 Corinthians 3:7).

The Spirit, however, gives life, because under the New Covenant the Spirit is writing the Torah upon our hearts. Life is no longer contingent upon our obedience to Torah. In the New Covenant God says, "I will forgive their iniquity, and their sin I will remember no more" (Jeremiah 31:34). This process results in changed lives, as evidenced among the Corinthians. Paul points to the redeemed lives of the Corinthian community as evidence of the efficacy of his ministry in the New Covenant.

> *You are our letter [of commendation], written in our hearts, known and read by all men;*
> *being manifested that you are a letter of Christ, cared for by us, written not with ink but*
> *with the Spirit of the living God, not on tablets of stone but on tablets of human hearts.*
> (2 Corinthians 3:2–3)

Thus "the letter kills, but the Spirit gives life" (2 Corinthians 3:6) because "the free gift of God is eternal life in Messiah Yeshua our Lord" (Romans 6:23).

## The Face of Moses

As Paul compares the Old Covenant and the New Covenant, he personifies them by making an interpretation of Moses' glowing visage. When Moses descended bearing the tablets of the renewed covenant in his arms, his face was alight with glory of God. Henceforth, Moses covered his face with a veil except when in the presence of God or when speaking God's commandments directly to the people. The Torah does not tell us *why* he covered his face, only that it was covered.

Moses was at times veiled, concealing the glory of God, and at times he was unveiled, revealing the glory of God. To understand Paul's interpretation, one must keep in mind that Moses is a metonymy for Torah.

When the Torah is read without faith and the revelation of Messiah, it is like Moses with his face veiled. The glory lies within it, but it is concealed from view. This is likened to the Old Covenant. When the Torah is read with faith and one sees in it the revelation of Messiah, however, it is like Moses with his face uncovered. The resplendent glory is revealed. This is likened to the New Covenant:

> *But if the ministry of death, in letters engraved on stones, came with glory, so that the sons of Israel could not look intently at the face of Moses because of the glory of his face, fading as it was, how will the ministry of the Spirit fail to be even more with glory? For if the ministry of condemnation has glory [i.e., the Old Covenant], much more does the ministry of righteousness [i.e., the New Covenant] abound in glory.*

> *For indeed what had glory, in this case has no glory because of the glory that surpasses it. For if that which fades away [was rendered ineffective] was with glory, much more that which remains is in glory.*

> *Therefore having such a hope, we use great boldness in our speech, and are not like Moses, who used to put a veil over his face so that the sons of Israel would not look intently at the end of what was fading away. But their minds were hardened; for until this very day at the reading of the old covenant the same veil remains unlifted, because it is removed in Messiah. But to this day whenever Moses is read, a veil lies over their heart; but whenever a person turns to the Lord, the veil is taken away.* (2 Corinthians 3:7–16)

According to this passage, the difference between the Old Covenant and the New Covenant is not a difference in the Torah. Both the veiled and the unveiled are reading the same Torah! The difference is that the participant in the New Covenant beholds Messiah in the Torah; the participant in the Old Covenant does not. The participant in the New Covenant "turns to the Lord" (i.e., repents), while the participant in the Old Covenant does not. Those who are unveiled and participate in the New Covenant are those who have found faith, repentance, and Messiah in the Torah. Thus they see Messiah—the Glory of God—with eyes unveiled.

## Both New and Old are in the Torah

According to Paul, then, both the Old Covenant and the New Covenant are expressed in the same Torah. The difference between the two is the people doing the reading. For those who read it, find Messiah, repent, and turn to the LORD, the Torah is a Tree of Life; it is the Spirit. To those who read it and do not, the Torah is condemnation. Thus the New Covenant is available, and always has been available. It was there for Moses; he surely saw it and understood it, and turned to the Lord in anticipation of Messiah. Moses will be in the Kingdom. He is part of the New Covenant. King David, or any Israelite who looked into the Torah with heart unveiled and placed faith in God entered the New Covenant.

But none of us have as yet entered its fullness. One day, we will all gaze into the mirror of perfect liberty with faces unveiled:

> *Now the Lord is the Spirit, and where the Spirit of the Lord is, there is liberty. But we all, with unveiled face, beholding as in a mirror the glory of the Lord, are being transformed into the same image from glory to glory, just as from the Lord, the Spirit.*
> (2 Corinthians 3:17–18)

## Summary of the New Covenant

The New Covenant is the discovery of God's gracious character as expressed in Torah through Messiah. We access this covenant through faith, by which we are reborn through the Holy Spirit, who writes God's eternal Torah on our hearts. One day we will enter the eternal New Jerusalem, and in that day, all mankind will know the LORD. The New Covenant does not result in a new Torah. It results in new creations.

### Endnotes

1   Romans 6:23.
2   Romans 3:23.

# Notes:

# Lesson Four
# OUR RABBI–
# HIS TEACHINGS

THE LAND, THE PEOPLE,
AND THE SCRIPTURES OF ISRAEL

# Lesson Four
# OUR RABBI—HIS TEACHINGS

*Do not think that I came to abolish the [Torah] or the Prophets;
I did not come to abolish but to fulfill. For truly I say to you, until
heaven and earth pass away, not the smallest letter or stroke
shall pass from the Law until all is accomplished. Whoever then
annuls one of the least of these commandments, and teaches
others to do the same, shall be called least in the kingdom
of heaven; but whoever keeps and teaches them, he shall be
called great in the kingdom of heaven.* (Matthew 5:17–19)

## Lesson Overview

In the previous three HaYesod lessons, we have learned about the believer's connection to the Land, the People, and the Scriptures of Israel. We have learned about the role of Torah, our need for salvation, and the function of the biblical covenant. In lesson four, we turn our attention to the Gospels to try to better understand Jesus of Nazareth in His Jewish context: in the Land, as part of the People, and teaching the Scriptures of Israel. We are primarily interested in those passages which Christianity has traditionally used to teach that Jesus was against Judaism and the observance of the Torah. On closer examination, each of these passages proves just the opposite. Instead, we learn that in order to be "sinless," Jesus had to be Torah observant.

## Lesson Purpose

Here are the main points that you should learn in this lesson:

❖ Yeshua came to properly interpret the Torah—
not to cancel it or replace it.

❖ Yeshua is the Living Torah.

❖ Yeshua did not teach against Torah, Sabbath, or kosher laws.

❖ Yeshua's law of love does not replace the Torah.

## Field Trips to the Holy Land

❖ Mount of Beatitudes, Sea of Galilee

❖ Capernaum Synagogue, Sea of Galilee

❖ Docks of Capernaum, Sea of Galilee

❖ Caesarea Maritima, Mediterranean Coast

## Yeshua—Jesus

A. Joshua

B. Salvation

C. Yah-Shua

D. Is "Jesus" a Pagan Name?

E. Christ

## Master and Rabbi

A. Lord

B. Rabbi

C. Teacher and Disciples

## The Torah Made Flesh

A. Logos

B. The Living Torah

## Torah-Sermon on the Mount

A. The Rabbi on the Mountain

B. Matthew 5:17
  1. Teaching Halachah
  2. Abolish and Fulfill
     a. In Greek
     b. In Hebrew/Aramaic
  3. Jot and Tittle
  4. Fences on the Mount

## The Sabbath Breaker?

A. Melachah

B. The Grain Fields
  1. They Did Break the Sabbath
  2. Saving a Life

C. Healing on the Sabbath
  1. To Save a Life
  2. To Do Good or to Do Harm

## Yeshua and Kosher Food

A. Ritual Hand-Washing
  1. Tradition, not Torah
  2. Some of His Disciples

B. The Conflict
  1. The Accusation
  2. The Defense

C. He Declared All Foods Clean?

D. Moral Defilement

E. Minutia vs. Weighty Matters

## Loving God and Loving Neighbor

A. The Man Who Stood on One Foot

B. Summing Up the Torah
  1. And You Shall Love …
  2. Love Cancels the Torah?

C. The Whole Torah Hangs on These

## The Sinless Messiah

# Yeshua—Jesus

**Key Verse**

Matthew 1:21

**Key Words**

*Yeshua:* "Jesus" in Hebrew, literally meaning "salvation."

*Yoshia:* Hebrew for "he will save."

Jesus' Hebrew name is "Yeshua" and is pronounced "*Yei-shu-ah.*"

Jesus = Yeshua (ישוע)

First-century "Yeshua" inscription

## Ⓐ Joshua

Yeshua is the Aramaic form of the Hebrew Joshua (Yehoshua, יהושע). In first-century Galilean Aramaic, it was shortened further: "*Yeshu.*"

## Ⓑ Salvation ✍

**Yeshua means "salvation."**

*You shall call His name* ___Salvaton___ [Yeshua, ישוע],

*for He will* ___save___ [yoshia, יושיע] *His people from*

*their sins.* (Matthew 1:21)

**Refer to Resource**

*Hallowed Be Your Name*

"Jesus, Yeshua or Yahshua: Which is Correct?"
Pages 49–56

## Ⓒ Yah-Shua

His name is not and never was pronounced as "Yah-Shua." This is a common mistake made by people who do not have a firm grasp of Hebrew.

## D  Is "Jesus" a Pagan Name?

Misinformed people sometimes assert that the name "Jesus" is pagan in origin. This is not true.

"Jesus" is an English transliteration of a Greek transliteration of His Hebrew name, *Yeshua*.

When the name Yeshua is translated into the Greek language, the closest phonetic approximation is "*ee-YAY-soos*" (Ιησους). The translators of the Septuagint (LXX) were already translating the OT biblical Hebrew names *Yehoshua* and *Yeshua* as *Iesous*. The "*oos*" ending on a Greek name indicates a masculine subject. Further phonetic changes occurred as the church translated the Greek to Latin and the Latin to English, eventually emerging as "Jesus."

**Key Verses**
1 Samuel 16:13

**Key Words**
*Christos*: Original Greek word from which we get our word "Christ."
*Mashiach*: Original Hebrew word from which we get our word "Messiah." Messiah and Christ both mean "Anointed One."

Names of God

## E  Christ

> **Christ = *Christos* (Χριστος) = "Anointed One"**
>
> **Messiah = *Mashiach* (משיח) = "Anointed One"**

*Then Samuel took the horn of oil and anointed him in the midst of his brothers; and the Spirit of the LORD came mightily upon David from that day forward.* (1 Samuel 16:13)

"Anointed One" means ___king___ .

**Key Words**

*Kurios:* Greek word meaning "Lord," "Master," or "Sir."

*Adon:* Hebrew word meaning "Lord," "Master," or "Sir."

*Mar:* Aramaic word meaning "Lord," "Master," or "Sir."

*Rabbi:* Hebrew word meaning "teacher;" literally "my great one" or "my honorable sir."

*Didaskalos:* Greek word usually translated as "teacher." In the Gospels, the Hebrew term "rabbi" probably lies behind this greek word.

*Logos:* Greek word meaning "word." In Hebrew, "word" signified Torah.

# Master and Rabbi

Disciples of a sage rarely called their teacher by first name but rather addressed them by titles: "Lord" and "Rabbi."

**Ⓐ Lord** 🖎

> *Kurios* (Κυριος) = *Adon* (אדון) or *Mar* (מר) = "Lord," "Master," or "Sir"

"Lord" or "Master" = _a title of respect_

**Ⓑ Rabbi**

> *rabbi* (רבי) = "teacher;" literally "my great one" or "my honorable sir"

While today this is usually reserved as a title for someone who has received official rabbinic ordination, in the Master's time it simply referred to someone who was a respected teacher of the Scriptures.

**Ⓒ Teacher and Disciples** 🖎

The job of a rabbi was _to teach + interpret_.

The job of a disciple was _learn the rabbi's teachings_.

# The Torah Made Flesh

*In the beginning was the Word, and the Word was with God, and the Word was God. He was in the beginning with God ... And the Word became flesh, and dwelt among us, and we saw His glory, glory as of the only begotten from the Father, full of grace and truth.* (John 1:1–2, 14)

**Refer to Resource**

*Torah Club Volume Four: The Good News of Messiah*
"Bamidbar: In the Wilderness"

**Ⓐ Logos**

What does it mean that the "Word became flesh"?

> *Logos* (Λογος) = "Word"

"Word" was a Jewish term for "Torah."

*Deal bountifully with Your servant, that I may live and keep
Your <u>word</u>. Open my eyes, that I may behold wonderful things
from Your <u>law</u>.* (Psalm 119:17–18)

**Key Verses**
Psalm 119:17–18

## Yeshua, the Living Mishkan

| Definition | Transliteration | Hebrew Word/Root | | | |
|---|---|---|---|---|---|
| He dwelt | *shachan* | ן | כ | שׁ | |
| Place of dwelling | *mishkan* | ן | כ | שׁ | מ |
| Dwelling glory | *shechinah* | ינה | כ | שׁ | |

**Key Verses**

Deuteronomy 33:4

John 1:14

Mark 1:35

Matthew 5:1–2

Exodus 19:3

**Key Words**

*Hayah yoshev vedoresh:* Hebrew expression appearing in rabbinic literature meaning "he sat down and interpreted," which implies giving instruction in an authoritative manner.

*And <u>law</u> is nothing else but the <u>word (logos)</u> of God, enjoining what is right and forbidding what is not right, as he bears witness, where he says, "He received the law from his words [Deuteronomy 33:4 (LXX)]."* (Philo, *On the Migration of Abraham* 130)

*And the Torah emerged as flesh and tabernacled among us— and we beheld the glory of it, glory as of an only one from Father— [it—the Torah—was] full of grace-and-truth.* (Jacobus Schoneveld, "Torah in the Flesh")[1]

## B The Living Torah

❖ The Word, the Torah, became alive in the person of Messiah Yeshua.

❖ The disciples of Rabbi Eliezer referred to their teacher as "the Scroll of the Torah."[2]

❖ The generation of Jewish believers in Yeshua following the death of the apostles called Yeshua "The Torah."[3]

# Torah-Sermon on the Mount

The entire discourse of the Sermon on the Mount centers on proper interpretation of the Torah.

**Your Israel Connection**

**Introduction to the Sermon on the Mount**

*Mount of Beatitudes, Sea of Galilee –* Christian tradition identifies a sloping hillside overlooking the site of Tabgha on the north shore of the Sea of Galilee as the location at which Yeshua delivered the Sermon on the Mount. It is also remembered as the place He used to pray at, as in Mark 1:35: "In the early morning, while it was still dark, Jesus got up, left the house, and went away to a secluded place, and was praying there."

The Sermon on the Mount

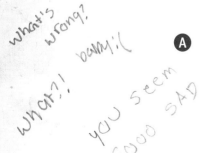

## A The Rabbi on the Mountain

*When Jesus saw the crowds, He went up on the mountain; and after He sat down, His disciples came to Him. He opened His mouth and began to teach them.* (Matthew 5:1–2)

## B Matthew 5:17

*Do not think that I came to abolish the Law or the Prophets;*
*I did not come to abolish but to fulfill.* (Matthew 5:17)

a. _____ I did not come to abolish it but to abolish it.

b. _____ I did not come to abolish it but to cancel it.

c.   ✓   I did not come to abolish it but to keep it.

d. _____ I did not come to abolish it but to make it obsolete.

### 1. Teaching Halachah

> ### *bati* (באתי) = "I came to," indicates purpose and intention

"Don't think my intention is to abolish the Torah, My intent isn't to abolish but to fulfill it."

> ### *halachah* (הלכה) = "path, way"

*Halachah* is the legal judgments of Judaism that define the way in which the Torah is applied, how Torah is practically walked out in everyday life.

### 2. Abolish and Fulfill

What does Jesus mean when He says He does not intend to abolish but to fulfill the Torah?

**a. *In Greek***

> ### *pleroo* (πληροω) = "fulfill"

*Pleroo: To make full, to fill, to fill up … Hebraistically,*
*with the accusative of the thing in which one abounds …*
*to cause God's will (as known in the law) to be obeyed as it*
*should be.* (Thayer's Greek-English Lexicon)[4]

To fulfill the Torah is to ___Obey___ the Torah.

**Key Verses**

Matthew 5:17
Matthew 3:15

**Key Words**

*Bati:* Hebrew word meaning "I came to," indicates purpose and intention.

*Halachah:* The legal judgments of Judaism that define the way in which the Torah is applied, how Torah is practically walked out in everyday life.

*Pleroo:* Greek word meaning "fulfill."

**b.** *In Hebrew/Aramaic*

> *batel* (בטל) = "abolish"
>
> *kiyem* (קיים) = "fulfill"

In relationship to Torah, "abolish" and "fulfill" are technical terms relating to improper and proper interpretations of the Torah.

*Whoever fulfills [kiyem] the Torah in poverty, will fulfill it later on in wealth; and whoever abolishes [batel] the Torah in wealth, will abolish it later in poverty.* (m.*Avot* 4:9)

*If, however, they ruled that a part [of a commandment] was to be annulled [batel] and a part retained [kiyem], they are liable.* (m.*Horayot* 1:3)

## 🔍 Jots and Tittles

**Tittle**

The "horn" or "crown" used to decorate a Hebrew letter.

**Jot**

A reference to the *yod,* the smallest letter in the Hebrew alphabet.

Mezuzah parchment

*For assuredly, I say to you, till heaven and earth pass away, one jot or one tittle will by no means pass from the law till all is fulfilled.* (Matthew 5:18, NKJV)

*Levi ben Sisi ... took a scroll of the Torah and went up to the roof and said, "Lord of the ages! If I have neglected [batel] a single word of this scroll of the Torah, let them come up against us, and if not. Let them go their way."* (y.Ta'anit 3:8 [Neusner])

*It is therefore exceedingly clear that the Nazarene never dreamed of destroying the Torah.* (Rabbi Jacob Emden)[5]

### 3. Jot and Tittle

*For truly I say to you, until heaven and earth pass away, not the smallest letter or stroke shall pass from the Law until all is accomplished. Whoever then annuls one of the least of these commandments, and teaches others to do the same, shall be called least in the kingdom of heaven; but whoever keeps and teaches them, he shall be called great in the kingdom of heaven.* (Matthew 5:18–19)

### 4. Fences on the Mount

*[The men of the great synagogue] used to say three things: Be patient in [the administration of] justice, rear many disciples, and make a fence around the Torah.* (m.Avot 1:1)

Protective fence

*ne'emar* (נאמר) = **"it is written (said)," technical term employed when citing a verse from the *TaNaK***

Yeshua did not contradict the Torah; instead He made a fence around the commandments.

**Key Verses**

Matthew 5:18–19
Luke 4:16–20
Leviticus 23:3
Psalm 92
Deuteronomy 6, 11
Numbers 15
Numbers 6:24–26

**Key Words**

*Ne'emar:* Hebrew word meaning "it is written (said)."

*Melachah:* Creative work.

📷 **Your Israel Connection**

**Yeshua in the Synagogue on the Sabbath**

*Capernaum Synagogue, Sea of Galilee* – A partially reconstructed, fourth-century limestone synagogue in Capernaum stands astride the basalt foundation stones of an earlier synagogue which may date from the days of the Master. Only a few paces from the traditional house of Simon Peter, the fourth-century synagogue probably preserves the location of the Capernaum synagogue in which Yeshua once taught and worshiped.

# The 39 Prohibitions

The Hebrew word for prohibited work on Shabbat, *melachah*, is a bit ambiguous (Exodus 20:10). The rabbis found a clue to help define *melachah* in Exodus chapter 31. There God reiterates the commandment to rest on Shabbat, emphasizing the fact that it even overrides the injunction to build the Tabernacle. Since Tabernacle construction could not take place on Shabbat, the sages specified 39 categories of work related to building the Tabernacle and then used that list to help define what work was prohibited on the Shabbat. Although an exact list of prohibited activities is not spelled out in the Bible, this list offers helpful principles that enable us to cease from labor on Shabbat.

As we approach these more detailed issues, keep in mind that even this list is subject to interpretation. It invites legalism, division, and obsession with minutia. We must not fall into any of those traps. However, we can use the list as a tool to consider Shabbat and to make distinctions between what seems to be a violation of Shabbat and what does not. For a complete discussion of these and other commandments pertaining to Shabbat see parashat "Vayakhel: And He Assembled" of *Torah Club Volume Five: The Rejoicing of the Torah*.

| | | |
|---|---|---|
| 1. Planting | 14. Combing | 28. Tanning |
| 2. Plowing | 15. Dyeing | 29. Marking |
| 3. Reaping | 16. Spinning | 30. Smoothing (polishing) |
| 4. Harvesting | 17. Chainstitching | 31. Shaping |
| 5. Threshing | 18. Warping | 32. Writing |
| 6. Winnowing | 19. Weaving | 33. Erasing |
| 7. Selecting | 20. Unraveling | 34. Building |
| 8. Grinding | 21. Knotting | 35. Demolishing |
| 9. Sifting | 22. Untying | 36. Extinguishing |
| 10. Kneading | 23. Sewing | 37. Burning |
| 11. Cooking (boiling, baking, melting) | 24. Tearing | 38. Completing |
| 12. Shearing | 25. Trapping | 39. Carrying (which includes buying and selling) |
| 13. Washing | 26. Slaughtering | |
| | 27. Skinning | |

# The Sabbath Breaker?

*Six days you shall labor and do all your work, but the seventh day is a sabbath of the LORD your God; in it you shall not do any work, you or your son or your daughter, your male or your female servant or your cattle or your sojourner who stays with you. For in six days the LORD made the heavens and the earth, the sea and all that is in them, and rested on the seventh day; therefore the LORD blessed the sabbath day and made it holy.* (Exodus 20:9–11)

**Key Verses**

Exodus 20:9–11
Genesis 2:2
Exodus 31:15
Matthew 12:1–8
Hosea 6:6

## Ⓐ Melachah

Creative work is prohibited on the Sabbath.

> ***melachah*** (מלאכה) **= creative work, which is prohibited on the Sabbath**

*By the seventh day God completed His* [melachah] *which He had done, and He rested on the seventh day from all His* [melachah] *which He had done.* (Genesis 2:2)

*For six days* [melachah] *may be done, but on the seventh day there is a sabbath of complete rest, holy to the LORD.* (Exodus 31:15)

The term is used in the Bible in two contexts: the creation narrative and the construction of the Tabernacle, such as sewing or building. Jewish law identifies thirty-nine general categories of prohibited labor.

## Ⓑ The Grain Fields

*At that time Yeshua went through the grain fields on the Sabbath, and His disciples became hungry and began to pick the heads of grain and eat. But when the Pharisees saw this, they said to Him, "Look, Your disciples do what is not lawful to do on a Sabbath." But He said to them, "Have you not read what David did when he became hungry, he and his companions, how he entered the house of God, and they ate the consecrated bread, which was not lawful for him to eat nor for those with him, but for the priests alone? Or have you not read in the Law, that on the Sabbath the priests in the temple break the Sabbath and are innocent? But I say to you that something greater than the temple is here. But if you had known what this means, 'I desire compassion, and not sacrifice,' you would not have condemned the innocent. For the Son of Man is Lord of the Sabbath."* (Matthew 12:1–8; quoting Hosea 6:6)

**Refer to Resource**

*Guarding Shabbat Card*
*Kiddush Shabbat Card*
*Closing Shabbat Card*

**Key Verses**

Exodus 34:21

Leviticus 18:5

1 Samuel 21

Matthew 12:6

Mark 3:1–5

**Key Words**

*Pikkuach nefesh:* Hebrew for "saving a life"

1. **They did break the Sabbath**

   Picking heads of grain is a type of harvesting, a form of *melachah* the Bible forbids on the Sabbath.

   *You shall work six days, but on the seventh day you shall rest; even during plowing time and harvest you shall rest.*
   (Exodus 34:21)

2. **Saving a Life**

   It is permissible to break the Sabbath to "save a life."

   > *pikkuach nefesh* (פקוח נפש) = "saving a life"

   *So you shall keep My statutes and My judgments, by which a man may live if he does them; I am the Lord.* (Leviticus 18:5)

   *"Because [David] found only the bread of the presence there [in the house of God], David said to him, 'Give me some to eat, so that we will not die of hunger. The preservation of life takes precedence over the Sabbath.'" (Yalkut Shemeoni 2:130 on 1 Samuel 21:5) … In Jewish oral tradition [not found in the Tanakh], the episode about David's escape refers to the Sabbath and eating food to preserve life. (Brad Young, Jesus the Jewish Theologian)[5]*

   *But I say to you that something greater than the temple is here.* (Matthew 12:6)

   Saving a life is greater than the ___Sabbath___ and the ___temple___.

## C  Healing on the Sabbath

**Refer to Resource**

*HaYesod Student Workbook*

"A Look at Matthew 12:1–8"

Pages 4.29–4.32

*He entered again into a synagogue; and a man was there whose hand was withered. They were watching Him to see if He would heal him on the Sabbath, so that they might accuse Him. He said to the man with the withered hand, "Get up and come forward!" And He said to them, "Is it lawful to do good or to do harm on the Sabbath, to save a life or to kill?" But they kept silent. After looking around at them with anger, grieved at their hardness of heart, He said to the man, "Stretch out your hand." And he stretched it out, and his hand was restored.* (Mark 3:1–5)

1. **To Save a Life**

In rabbinic law healing would only be an issue if medicine had to be made because of the prohibition on grinding the medicine; but even then saving life took precedent.

*Moreover, in the case of any lingering doubt concerning the potential severity of an illness, legal presumption favours intervention and the Mishnah ([in] Yoma 8.6) cites the principle: "Whenever there is doubt concerning life being in danger (the case discussed is a sore throat!), this overrides the Sabbath."* (Geza Vermes, *The Religion of Jesus the Jew*)[7]

2. **To Do Good or to Do Harm**

If it is prohibited to slaughter/kill on Sabbath then shouldn't saving and restoring the fullness of one's life be permitted?

Yeshua does not come against the rabbinic oral tradition but works within it.

# Yeshua and Kosher Food

Did Yeshua topple the Torah's dietary laws?

*You are not to eat of these among those … they are unclean for you.* (Deuteronomy 14:7)

*Thus He declared all foods clean.* (Mark 7:19)

*Purity broke out among Israel.* (t.Shabbat 1:14)

## Ⓐ Ritual Hand-Washing ✍

*The Pharisees and some of the scribes gathered around Him when they had come from Jerusalem, and had seen that some of His disciples were eating their bread with impure hands, that is, unwashed.* (Mark 7:1–2)

1. **Tradition, not Torah**

Ritual hand-washing before eating bread is a ___tradition___,

not a ___command ment___.

2. **Some of His Disciples**

*Some of His disciples were eating their bread with impure hands, that is, unwashed.* (Mark 7:2)

**Key Verses**

Luke 8:43–44
Numbers 15:38
Malachi 4:2
Mark 6:56
Matthew 23:5
Deuteronomy 6:8
Deuteronomy 14:7
Mark 7:19
Mark 7:1–2

📹 **Your Israel Connection**

**Yeshua and Tzitzit**

*Docks of Capernaum, Sea of Galilee* – The fishing village of Capernaum on the northern shore of the Sea of Galilee was Yeshua's base of operation. He stayed in Peter's home there, taught in the local synagogue, and performed many of His miracles there, including the famous healing of the woman with the issue of blood.

**Key Verses**

Mark 7:5–9

Isaiah 29:13

Mark 7:8

Mark 7:18–19

## Ⓑ The Conflict

*The Pharisees and the scribes asked Him, "Why do Your disciples not walk according to the tradition of the elders, but eat their bread with impure hands?" And He said to them, "Rightly did Isaiah prophesy of you hypocrites, as it is written: 'This people honors me with their lips, but their heart is far away from me. But in vain do they worship me, teaching as doctrines the precepts of men.' Neglecting the commandment of God, you hold to the tradition of men." He was also saying to them, "You are experts at setting aside the commandment of God in order to keep your tradition."* (Mark 7:5–9; quoting Isaiah 29:13)

### 1. The Accusation

The Pharisees accused the disciples of eating ___bread___ with unwashed hands, not of eating ___unclean meats___.

### 2. The Defense

Washing hands before bread is a tradition, not a commandment.

*Neglecting the commandment of God, you hold to the tradition of men.* (Mark 7:8)

## Ⓒ He Declared All Foods Clean?

**Mark 7:18–19 Translation Comparison**

| New American Standard | Young's Literal Translation |
| --- | --- |
| Do you not understand that whatever goes into the man from outside cannot defile him, because it does not go into his heart, but into his stomach, and is eliminated? (Thus He declared all foods clean.) | Do ye not perceive that nothing from without entering into the man is able to defile him? Because it doth not enter into his heart, but into the belly, and into the drain it doth go out, purifying all the meats. |

*what?*

| Thus He Declared | All Foods | Clean |
| --- | --- | --- |
| not greek | all foods | purging out other end |

*Jesus criticizes the Pharisees for being concerned with problems of food purity, important as they might be, and less concerned (in his view) with moral purity which is the "weightier matter of law."* (Menahem Kister, "Law, Rhetoric in Some Sayings of Jesus")[8]

**Refer to Resource**

*Holy Cow!*

"There's More on Mark 7:1–23"
Pages 99–104

## D Moral Defilement

**Key Verses**

Mark 7:21–23
Matthew 23:23
Luke 13:31
Matthew 22:40

Yeshua taught that moral defilement is a greater danger than ritual defilement.

*For from within, out of the heart of men, proceed the evil thoughts, fornications, thefts, murders, adulteries, deeds of coveting and wickedness, as well as deceit, sensuality, envy, slander, pride and foolishness. All these evil things proceed from within and defile the man.* (Mark 7:21–23)

## E Minutia vs. Weighty Matters

*Woe to you, scribes and Pharisees, hypocrites! For you tithe mint and dill and cummin, and have neglected the weightier provisions of the law: justice and mercy and faithfulness; but these are the things you should have done without neglecting the others.* (Matthew 23:23)

*Jesus' displeasure is directed against those who regard the ceremonial laws as of greater importance than the moral laws: he is far from annulling the former … This verse proves in the strongest possible fashion that never did Jesus think of annulling the Law (or even the ceremonial laws which it contained) and setting up a new law of his own.* (Joseph Klausner, *Jesus of Nazareth*)[9]

# Loving God and Loving Neighbor

*On these two commandments depend the whole Law and the Prophets.* (Matthew 22:40)

## A The Man Who Stood on One Foot

*A certain Gentile came to Shammai and said to him, "Make me a convert, on condition that you teach me the whole Torah while I stand on one foot." Immediately Shammai drove him away with the measuring stick which was in his hand. When the same Gentile went before Hillel [with the same proposition] Hillel said to him, "What is hateful to you, do not do to your neighbor: that is the whole Torah, while the rest is the commentary thereof; go and learn it."* (b.Shabbat 31a)

**Your Israel Connection**

**Are All Pharisees Hypocrites?**

*Caesarea Maritima, Mediterranean Coast* – In the days of the apostles, Judea was occupied and controlled by the Roman Empire. They governed the province out of the coastal city of Caesarea, a city in the land of Israel complete with idolatrous temples and the worship of Roman gods. The religious sect of the Pharisees resisted assimilation with Roman Hellenism. They were the fundamentalists who defended the Word of God and maintained a clear distinction between the holy and the profane.

## שמאי ❖ Shammai the Elder

An important rabbi of the late first century BCE and early first century CE whose Torah academy was known as Beit Shammai ("The House of Shammai"). Jewish tradition records that he was the president of the Sanhedrin, along with his contemporary Hillel. Although both were Pharisees, they disagreed on almost every issue of *halachah*, with Shammai often taking the stricter view. Shammai's views were mostly rejected in favor of Hillel's during the post-Temple era. Although Yeshua's teachings usually bear more similarity to those of Hillel, they sometimes reflect Shammai's position, such as his teaching on grounds for divorce.

## הלל ❖ Hillel the Elder

A well-known, prominent rabbi of the late first century BCE and early first century CE, perhaps the most influential rabbi, whose Torah academy was known as Beit Hillel ("The House of Hillel"). Jewish tradition records that he was the head of the Sanhedrin, along with his contemporary Shammai. Although both were Pharisees, they disagreed on almost every issue of *halachah*, with Hillel often taking the more lenient view. Hillel's views mostly prevailed over Shammai's and became the basis for post-Temple Judaism. Yeshua's teachings bear more similarity to the lenient views of Hillel.

## Ⓑ Summing Up the Torah

**Key Verses**

Matthew 22:35–40
Deuteronomy 6:5
Leviticus 19:18

**Key Words**

*Gezerah shevah:* Hebrew words meaning "equivalent decrees," or "verbal analogy."

*And one of them, a lawyer, asked Him a question, testing Him, "Teacher, which is the great commandment in the Law?" And He said to him, "'You shall love the LORD your God with all your heart, and with all your soul, and with all your mind.' This is the great and foremost commandment. The second is like it, 'You shall love your neighbor as yourself.' On these two commandments depend the whole Law and the Prophets."*
(Matthew 22:35–40; quoting Deuteronomy 6:5 and Leviticus 19:18)

*The dialectic discussion between Jesus and the scholar was not characterized by hostility or confrontation, as many NT scholars have assumed. The question is a genuine inquiry. Jewish learning involved asking questions and answering questions with more questions.* (Brad Young, *The Parables*)[10]

### 1. And You Shall Love …

> *gezerah shevah* (גזרה שוה) = "verbal analogy" or "equivalent decrees"

A rabbinic method of interpretation where similar words used in different contexts are connected to expound upon one another.

***Gezerah shevah* with "And you shall love …"**

Both verses begin with the same Hebrew word.

# "*Ve'ahavta*"

ואהבת

**And you shall love** the Lord your God with all your heart and with all your soul and with all your might. (Deuteronomy 6:5)

ואהבת

**And you shall love** your neighbor as yourself; I am the LORD. (Leviticus 19:18)

### 2. Love Cancels the Torah?

Summarizing the Torah as love of God and love for one's neighbor was a common teaching among the rabbis.

*Really great moral teachers never do introduce new moralities: it is quacks and cranks who do that.* (C.S. Lewis, *Mere Christianity*)[11]

*The questioner perhaps expected Him to say something new and startling. Instead, Jesus reiterates the central features of Judaism, emphasizing the importance of love above all.* (Paul P. Levertoff, *St. Matthew*)[12]

*What is hateful to you, do not do to your neighbor: that is the whole Torah, while the rest is the commentary thereof; go and learn it.* (b.Shabbat 31a)

*"You shall love your neighbor like yourself," —this is the greatest principle of the Torah.* (Genesis Rabbah 24:7)

### ⓒ The Whole Torah Hangs on These

Loving God and loving one's fellow is like the tree and its branches. The fruit hanging from the tree is the rest of the Torah. The whole Torah hangs on those commandments.

*On these two commandments hang all the law and the prophets.* (Matthew 22:40, KJV)

The tree of commandments

# The Sinless Messiah

**Key Verses**

1 Peter 1:18–19
1 John 3:4

**Key Words**

*Tzaddik gamur:* Hebrew words meaning "perfectly righteous."

In order for Yeshua to be the spotless lamb, He must have perfectly kept the Torah.

*Knowing that you were not redeemed with perishable things like silver or gold from your futile way of life inherited from your forefathers, but with precious blood, as of a lamb unblemished and spotless, the blood of Messiah.* (1 Peter 1:18–19)

*Everyone who practices sin also practices lawlessness; and sin is lawlessness.* (1 John 3:4)

> ***tzaddik gamur*** (צדיק גמור) = **"perfectly righteous"**

## Endnotes

1   Jacobus Schoneveld, "Torah in the Flesh," *Immanuel* 24/25 (1990): 77–94.

2   b.*Sanhedrin* 101a.

3   Found in the 2nd century *Preaching of Peter* as quoted in Clement of Alexandria, *Stromata* 1:29, 2:15.

4   Thayer, "πληροω," *Thayer's Greek-English Lexicon* 517–518.

5   Harvey Falk, *Jesus the Pharisee* (Eugene, Oregon: Wipf and Stock Publishers, 2002), 19.

6   Brad Young, *Jesus the Jewish Theologian* (Peabody, MA: Hendrickson, 1996), 107.

7   Geza Vermes, *The Religion of Jesus the Jew* (Minneapolis: Fortress, 1993), 22–23.

8   Menahem Kister, "Law, Rhetoric in Some Sayings of Jesus", in *Studies in Ancient Midrash* (Harvard University Press, 2001), 153.

9   Joseph Klausner, *Jesus of Nazareth: His Life, Times, and Teaching* (New York: Bloch Publishing Company, 1989), 367.

10  Brad Young, *The Parables: Jewish Tradition and Christian Interpretation* (Peabody, MA: Hendrickson, 1998), 103.

11  C.S. Lewis, *Mere Christianity* (San Francisco, CA: Harper Collins, 2001), 82.

12  Paul P. Levertoff, *St. Matthew: With Introduction, Maps, and Explanatory Notes* (London: Thomas Murby & Co, 1940), 70–71.

# Lesson Four
# LESSON SUMMARY

## First ...

We learned that Jesus' Hebrew name is "Yeshua" and that "Christ" means "Anointed One." We also learned that Yeshua is:

* ❖ Our Master and Rabbi
* ❖ The Torah made flesh
* ❖ The Living Torah

## Then ...

We began to study the Sermon on the Mount, where we discovered that Yeshua's teaching did not overturn the Torah; instead He made fences around the commandments to keep the Torah from being broken.

## After that ...

We looked at some of His conflicts with the religious authorities of His day. One conflict was over the interpretation of Sabbath:

* ❖ Yeshua considered it permissible to break the Sabbath in order to save a life—this was in accord with Jewish law.
* ❖ Yeshua believed it permissible to heal on the Sabbath—this was also in accord with Jewish law.
* ❖ Yeshua kept the Sabbath.

Another conflict involved placing Jewish tradition above the commandments of God. Yeshua did not declare all foods clean, instead Yeshua taught that:

* ❖ God's commands are weightier than Jewish tradition.
* ❖ Eating bread with unwashed hands does not make a person unclean.
* ❖ Moral defilement is a more serious matter than supposed ritual defilement.

## Finally ...

We learned that Yeshua did not replace the laws of the Torah with the commandments of loving God and loving our neighbors. Instead, those two commandments are:

* ❖ Summaries of the Torah used by other rabbis in Yeshua's day
* ❖ The commands on which the whole Torah and prophets hang

# Lesson Four
# LESSON REVIEW – Q&A

1. "Yeshua" is the short Aramaic version of what common Hebrew name? What does the name "Yeshua" mean? What does "Christ" mean? What does the word "rabbi" mean?

2. What does it mean to say that "the Word became flesh"?

3. What did it mean to "abolish" the Torah? What did it mean to "fulfill" the Torah? Explain the concept of making a "fence" around the Torah.

4. Define the word *melachah*. Did Yeshua's disciples break the Sabbath when they plucked the grain? How did Yeshua justify this?

5. On what basis did Yeshua argue that it is permissible to heal on the Sabbath?

6. Does eating bread with unwashed hands break a commandment of the Torah? Did Yeshua declare all foods clean? Where does this misunderstanding come from?

7. Does loving God and loving one's neighbor replace the Torah? How did other sages in the days of the apostles teach the same concept?

8. The sages also taught that, if Yeshua broke the Torah or taught others to break the Torah, He could not be our sinless Messiah. Why?

# Lesson Four
# EXTRA CREDIT
### SUPPLEMENTAL MATERIAL FOR THIS HAYESOD LESSON

---

**Extra Credit Instructions:**

1. This material is not mandatory, but it will serve as a helpful tool for further study.
2. First read the maxim of Yeshua in the left-hand column, and then compare it to the rabbinic parallel in the right-hand column.

## Rabbinic Parallels to the Sermon on the Mount

In this week's lesson, we learned that Yeshua did not come to abolish the Torah but to fulfill it. We also learned that He did not come to abolish Judaism. The following chart compares Yeshua's teachings from the Sermon on the Mount with those of the sages and rabbis of classical Judaism. You can study the chart for personal meditation, or use it as a basis for discussion with other HaYesod students.

| Yeshua said ... | The Sages said ... |
| --- | --- |
| Blessed are the gentle, for they shall inherit the earth. (Matthew 5:5) | Great is the peace of the meek, as it is written [in Psalm 37:11], "But the meek shall inherit the land and delight themselves in abundant peace." (*Sifre Numbers* 42) |
| Blessed are the merciful, for they shall receive mercy. (Matthew 5:7) | He who is merciful to men, toward him God is merciful in heaven. (b.*Shabbat* 151b) |
| You are the salt of the earth; but if the salt has become tasteless, how can it be made salty again? It is no longer good for anything, except to be thrown out and trampled under foot by men. (Matthew 5:13) | The Sages asked Rabbi Yehoshua, "When salt becomes unsavory, how can it be made salty?" He replied, "With the afterbirth of a mule." They asked, "And does a mule have an afterbirth?" He replied, "And can salt become unsavory?" (b.*Bechorot* 8b) |
| Nor does anyone light a lamp and put it under a basket, but on the lampstand, and it gives light to all who are in the house. (Matthew 5:15) | To what may Moses be compared at that time? To a light which is set upon a lampstand. (*Sifre Numbers* 93) |
| For truly I say to you, until heaven and earth pass away, not the smallest letter or stroke shall pass from the Law until all is accomplished. (Matthew 5:18) | At that time, the letter *yod* went up on high and prostrated itself before God and said: "Master of the Universe! Hast thou not said that no letter shall ever be abolished from the Torah? Behold, Solomon has now arisen and abolished one. Who knows? Today he has abolished one letter, tomorrow he will abolish another until the whole Torah will be nullified!" God replied: "Solomon and a thousand like him will pass away, but the smallest tittle will not be erased from thee." (*Exodus Rabbah* 6:1) |

| Yeshua said ... | The Sages said ... |
|---|---|
| But I say to you that everyone who is angry with his brother shall be guilty before the court; and whoever says to his brother, "You good-for-nothing," shall be guilty before the supreme court; and whoever says, "You fool," shall be guilty enough to go into the fiery hell. (Matthew 5:22) | R. Eliezer said: "He who hates his brother belongs to the shedders of blood!" (*Sifre* Deuteronomy)<br><br>He who publicly shames his neighbor is as though he shed blood. (b.*Bava Metzia* 58b) |
| But I say to you that everyone who looks at a woman with lust for her has already committed adultery with her in his heart. (Matthew 5:28) | Reish Lakish expounded: "You must not suppose that only he who has committed the crime with his body is called an adulterer, if he commits adultery with his eyes he is also called an adulterer." (*Leviticus Rabbah* 23:12) |
| If your right hand makes you stumble, cut it off and throw it from you; for it is better for you to lose one of the parts of your body, than for your whole body to go into hell. (Matthew 5:30) | R. Tarfon said, "If his hand fondled the private member, let his hand be cut off … It is preferable that his [hand be cut off] than that he should go down into the pit of destruction." (b.*Niddah* 13b) |
| But let your statement be, "Yes, yes " or "No, no"; anything beyond these is of evil. (Matthew 5:37) | Rabbi Huna said in the name of Rabbi Shmuel ben Yitzchak, "The 'Yes' of the righteous is a yes, and the 'No' of the righteous is no." (*Ruth Rabbah* 7:6)<br><br>R. Eleazar said, "'No' is an oath and 'Yes' is an oath." … But Raba said [contradicting Eleazar], "It is an oath only if he said, 'No! No!' twice, or he said, 'Yes! Yes!' twice." (b.*Shevuot* 36a) |
| But I say to you, do not resist an evil person; but whoever slaps you on your right cheek, turn the other to him also. If anyone wants to sue you and take your shirt, let him have your coat also. Whoever forces you to go one mile, go with him two. Give to him who asks of you, and do not turn away from him who wants to borrow from you … love your enemies and pray for those who persecute you, so that you may be sons of your Father who is in heaven. (Matthew 5:39–45) | Regarding those who are insulted but do not return an insult, those who are rebuked without replying, they are the ones who do good out of love of God and rejoice in their sufferings. (b.*Yoma* 23a)<br><br>Those who are insulted but do not insult, who hear themselves reviled without retaliating, who act with love and rejoice in suffering, of them the Scripture says [in Judges 5:31], "But let those who love Him be like the rising of the sun in its might." (b.*Shabbat* 88b) |
| But I say to you, love your enemies and pray for those who persecute you. (Matthew 5:44) | Reb Meir prayed that [the wicked that vexed him] should die. His wife Beruria said to him, "What makes you think a prayer like that is permissible? … Instead you should pray for them that they will repent, and then there will be no more wicked." (b.*Berachot* 10a) |
| He causes His sun to rise on the evil and the good, and sends rain on the righteous and the unrighteous. (Matthew 5:45) | R. Abbahu said: "The day when rain falls is greater than the day of the resurrection, for the resurrection is for the righteous only whereas rainfall is both for the righteous and for the wicked." (b.*Ta'anit* 7a) |
| If you greet only your brothers, what more are you doing than others? Do not even the Gentiles do the same? (Matthew 5:47) | It was related of R. Yochanon ben Zakkai that no man ever gave him greeting first, even a heathen in the street. (b.*Berachot* 17a)<br><br>Shammai used to say, "Greet all men with a cheerful face." (m.*Avot* 1:15) |
| Give us this day our daily bread. (Matthew 6:11) | He who has bread in his basket today but worries, "What will I eat tomorrow?"—that man is of little faith. (b.*Sotah* 48b) |

| Yeshua said … | The Sages said … |
|---|---|
| And do not lead us into temptation, but deliver us from evil. (Matthew 6:13) | Do not lead us into the power of sin, nor into the power of trespass or iniquity, nor into the power of temptation … Rescue me from an evil man, an evil friend, and an evil neighbor, an evil encounter and from Satan the destroyer. (Morning Prayers, *Siddur*) |
| For if you forgive others for their transgressions, your heavenly Father will also forgive you. (Matthew 6:14) | Whoever refrains from exacting his measure, the heavenly court forgives his sins, as it is written [in Micah 7:18], "He pardons sin and forgives the transgression." Whose sin does he forgive? One who passes over sins. (b.*Rosh Hashanah* 17a) <br><br> He who passes over an opportunity to retaliate has all his transgressions passed over. (b.*Yoma* 23a) <br><br> He who is merciful to others, mercy is shown to him by Heaven, while he who is not merciful to others, mercy is not shown to him by Heaven. (b.*Shabbat* 151b) |
| Do not store up for yourselves treasures on earth, where moth and rust destroy, and where thieves break in and steal. But store up for yourselves treasures in heaven, where neither moth nor rust destroys, and where thieves do not break in or steal; for where your treasure is, there your heart will be also. (Matthew 6:19–21) | My fathers stored up below and I am storing above … My fathers stored in a place which can be tampered with, but I have stored in a place which cannot be tampered with … My fathers stored something which produces no fruits, but I have stored something which does produce fruits … My fathers gathered for this world, but I have gathered for the future world. (b.*Bava Batra* 11a) |
| Look at the birds of the air, that they do not sow, nor reap nor gather into barns, and yet your heavenly Father feeds them. Are you not worth much more than they? (Matthew 6:26) | Simeon b. Eliezer says, "Have you ever seen an animal or bird practicing a craft? Yet they have their food without care … How much more then ought I to have my food without care." (m.*Kiddushin* 4:14) |
| So do not worry about tomorrow; for tomorrow will care for itself. Each day has enough trouble of its own. (Matthew 6:34) | Do not worry about tomorrow's trouble, for you do not know what the day will bring. Tomorrow may come and a man will be no more so he has worried about a world which never belonged to him. (b.*Yevamot* 63b) <br><br> Sufficient is the evil in the time thereof. (b.*Berachot* 9b) |
| Do not judge so that you will not be judged. (Matthew 7:1) | Hillel said, "Do not judge your neighbor until you have reached his place." (m.*Avot* 2:5) |
| For in the way you judge, you will be judged; and by your standard of measure, it will be measured to you. (Matthew 7:2) | With the measure with which one measures on earth it will be measured to him in heaven. (*Jerusalem Targum* on Genesis 38:26) <br><br> By the same measure with which a man measures out to others, [Heaven] measures it out it him. (m.*Sotah* 1:7) |
| You hypocrite, first take the log out of your own eye, and then you will see clearly to take the speck out of your brother's eye. (Matthew 7:5) | If one say to him, "Take the speck from between your eyes," he will answer, "Take the log from between your eyes!" (b.*Arachin* 16b) |
| Do not give what is holy to dogs, and do not throw your pearls before swine, or they will trample them under their feet, and turn and tear you to pieces. (Matthew 7:6) | A treasure must not be revealed to everyone, so also with the precious words of Torah. One must not go into the deeper meaning of them, except in the presence of those individuals who are suitably trained. (y.*Avodah Zarah* 2:7)[1] |

| Yeshua said ... | The Sages said ... |
|---|---|
| Ask, and it will be given to you; seek, and you will find; knock, and it will be opened to you. For everyone who asks receives, and he who seeks finds, and to him who knocks it will be opened. (Matthew 7:7–8) | Rabbi Isaac also said, "If a man tells you, 'I have sought hard but I have not found,' do not believe him … If he says, 'I have sought hard and I have found, you may believe him.'" (b.*Megillah* 6b)<br><br>He knocked at the gates of mercy and they were opened to him. (b.*Megillah* 12b) |
| In everything, therefore, treat people the same way you want them to treat you, for this is the Law and the Prophets. (Matthew 7:12) | Hillel said to him, "What is hateful to you, do not do to your neighbor. That is the whole Torah, while the rest is the commentary on it. Now go and study it." (b.*Shabbat* 31a)<br><br>What you hate for yourself, do not do to your neighbor. (*Avot d. Rabbi Natan* 26) |
| Therefore everyone who hears these words of Mine and acts on them, may be compared to a wise man who built his house on the rock. And the rain fell, and the floods came, and the winds blew and slammed against that house; and yet it did not fall, for it had been founded on the rock. Everyone who hears these words of Mine and does not act on them, will be like a foolish man who built his house on the sand. The rain fell, and the floods came, and the winds blew and slammed against that house; and it fell—and great was its fall. (Matthew 7:24–27) | Rabbi Elazar ben Azariah used to say: "He whose learning is greater than his good deeds, to what can he be compared? He is like a tree with many branches but few roots. The wind blows and uproots the tree … But he whose good deeds are greater than his learning, to what can he be compared? He is compared to a tree with only a few branches but with many roots. Even if all the wind in the world was blowing against it, it could not be uprooted." (m.*Avot* 3:22) |

## Endnotes

1 Brad Young, *Meet the Rabbis: Rabbinic Thought and the Teachings of Jesus* (Peabody, MA: Hendrickson Publishers, 2007), 75.

# Lesson Four – Digging Deeper
## A Look at Matthew 12:1–8
### Further study from this week's HaYesod Lesson

## Matthew 12:1–8

Matthew relates the story of the disciples in the grain fields. Certain Pharisees criticize Yeshua's disciples for picking grain and husking it in their hands on the Sabbath. Yeshua Himself is not the subject of the criticism; nevertheless He comes to the defense of His disciples by engaging in a *halachic* argument with the Pharisees. The opinion of the critics is that by picking grain and husking it, the disciples are working on the Sabbath. According to the codification of the *halachah*, the disciples were indeed violating the Sabbath, but in the days of Yeshua, the specifics of those issues were not necessarily practiced by the common people of the land. The oral tradition was still oral and various schools within Judaism had different interpretations and practices. According to the yoke (*halachic* interpretation of Torah) of the Pharisees, it was a clear violation of Shabbat, but according to the yoke of Yeshua, the issue was not so cut and dry.

**Resource in Focus**

Excerpt from parashat "Chayei Sarah: Life of Sarah" of First Fruits of Zion's *Torah Club Volume Four: The Good News of the Messiah*.

Yeshua defends His disciples by appealing to the commandment of the bread of the presence that is made and eaten by the priesthood on the Sabbath day. He retells the story of David who impinged upon both the Sabbath and the Priesthood by taking the bread of the presence (which was supposed to be eaten only by the priesthood) and eating it on the Sabbath. What is the connection? What is the relationship between David and the disciples? Both were hungry. A midrash in *Yalkut Shimoni* provides the context for the story's rhetorical punch in the Matthew 12 debate. In the midrashic version of the story, David tells the priest at Nob, "Give me some bread to eat so that we will not die of hunger. The preservation of life takes precedence over the Sabbath."

That the preservation of life takes precedence over the Sabbath is true and well attested in rabbinic literature. But are Yeshua's disciples so hungry that their lives are in danger? Probably not, but Yeshua uses the story as a precedent to exonerate the disciples. Still speaking of the bread of the presence, He brings a second example from the priesthood ministering in the Temple. By making bread of the presence on the Sabbath, the priesthood violates the Biblical prohibition against preparing food on the Sabbath. Slaughtering animals, tending the altar pyre, lighting the menorah, baking bread are all Sabbath violations, but they are also positive commandments in the Torah. From this and many similar examples the sages derived the following axiom:

> *Wherever you find a positive commandment and a negative commandment contradicting, if you can fulfill both of them, it is preferable; but if not, let the positive command come and supersede the negative command.* (b.*Shabbat* 133a)

Regarding the priesthood, the positive commands of the Temple service supersede the prohibitions of Sabbath. But how does this relate to Yeshua's disciples? What is the positive command that allows His disciples to break a Sabbath prohibition?

In tractate *Yoma*, the same pattern of argumentation is used to defend the use of medical treatments on the Sabbath:

*If the service in the Temple supersedes the Sabbath, how much more should the saving of human life supersede the Sabbath laws!* (b.*Yoma* 85b)

Yeshua's argument is based upon simple, clear rabbinic logic. If it was permissible for David and his men to eat what was ordinarily forbidden (and on the Sabbath day) because they were hungry, how much more so is it permitted for the Son of David and His men? Likewise, if it is permitted for the priests ministering in the Temple to break the Sabbath—baking bread and making sacrifices—how much more so is it permissible to break the Sabbath in order to alleviate human suffering? The principle of "I desire compassion, and not a sacrifice," is "something greater than the Temple" (Matthew 12:6–7).

The story is meant to illustrate Yeshua's prioritization of compassion for human beings. His yoke is easy, and His burden is light. "After all," He quips, "the Sabbath was made for man, not man for the Sabbath." It is a sentiment that is not unique to Him. Yeshua was not expressing an idea in contradiction to Judaism. Rather, He was invoking established interpretive principles in the defense of His disciples. For example, consider the following parallel statement:

> *The Sabbath has been given over to you, but you have not been given over to the Sabbath.*
> (b.*Yoma* 85b)

The term "son of man," as used in the statement "the son of man is Lord of the Sabbath," should probably be understood in the more general Hebrew usage as "human beings" rather than as a reference to Himself. But perhaps the traditional reading is correct and we should understand the statement to mean, "The Messiah is Lord of the Sabbath." This too is a sentiment consistent with Jewish theology. Rabbinic literature commonly refers to the anticipated Messianic reign as the ultimate Sabbath. The redemption and the World to Come are likened to the Sabbath, whereas the waiting for redemption and this present age are related to the other days of the week.

In either case, we should not let ourselves be tempted into thinking that Yeshua meant to trivialize the Sabbath. On the contrary, He is concerned with restoring a balanced perspective regarding Sabbath observance. His conflict with the Pharisees over the particulars of how one ought to observe the Shabbat proves that the Sabbath was an important institution to Him, one which He was not lightly dismissing or telling His disciples to disregard; rather, He is concerned that it be kept according to the spirit in which God gave it. The numerous stories told of His healing work on Shabbat show us that Sabbath-related issues were still very relevant to the believers for whom the Gospels were originally written.

## Mark 3:1–6

Mark relates an incident in which Yeshua encounters a man with a withered hand in a synagogue on the Sabbath day. Some of the disciples of the sages were carefully watching Him to see what He would do. The arguments of the *Talmud* make it clear that the application and ingestion of medicines on the Sabbath day for the purpose of healing was a point of *halachah* still being debated centuries after the ministry of Yeshua. The variety of opinions and legal maneuvers represented in the *Talmud* suggest that there could not have been clear consensus on the issue of Sabbath healing in the days of the Master. It is more likely that there were those who allowed it and those who forbade it.

Yeshua defended His decision to heal on the Sabbath with the rhetorical question, "Is it lawful to do good or to do harm on the Sabbath, to save a life or to kill?" (Mark 3:4). Regarding the first question, yes, it is lawful to do good on the Sabbath. To "do good" refers to the performance of a positive commandment. As we saw, b.*Shabbat* 133a taught that when there is a command to do good, the performance of that commandment supersedes a prohibition which would impede it.

But is there a commandment to heal? Regarding His second question, whether it is permissible to save life or to kill, consensus does emerge when a medical condition is regarded as constituting a threat to life. The Sabbath laws may be breached in any situation where one's life is at risk, even if it is an uncertain risk. The *Mishnah* cites the principle of danger to life overriding the Sabbath as a general rule of thumb. The *Talmud* makes various arguments to try to justify the principle:

> *Rabbi Mattiyah Ben Charash said, "He who has a sore throat—they administer medicine to him even on the Sabbath because it is uncertain if [the sore throat] might be a danger to life, and any case in which life might be endangered overrides the prohibitions of the Sabbath."* (m.*Yoma* 8:6)

Had Yeshua's clients been in any distress that constituted a danger to life, He would have been able to heal them with impunity. It is lawful on the Sabbath to save life, not to destroy it. A shriveled hand, however, does not constitute a danger to life. As the *chazan* of the synagogue in Luke 13 said, "There are six days for work. So come and be healed on those days, not on the Sabbath!"

Had He been concerned over issues of healing on the Sabbath, Yeshua certainly could have waited until sunset to heal the man's hand. It is not the threat to life that Yeshua invokes as His legal precedent for healing. As Matthew related the same story to us, Yeshua defended His decision to heal the man with the withered hand by asking a hypothetical question:

> *What man is there among you who has a sheep, and if it falls into a pit on the Sabbath, will he not take hold of it and lift it out? How much more valuable then is a man than a sheep! So then, it is lawful to do good on the Sabbath.* (Matthew 12:11–12)

A later argument in the *Talmud* takes up the same question. It must have been a typical rhetorical scenario for discussing Sabbath prohibitions. In any case, notice the justification the *Talmud* brings for assisting an animal that has fallen into a pit:

> *Rabbi Yehudah said in Rab's name, "If an animal falls into a pit, one may bring cushions and blankets to put under the animal, and if it climbs out, it climbs out." Another opinion objects, "If an animal falls into a pit, provisions may be made in the pit to keep it alive." … Preventing the suffering of animals is a biblical law. The biblical law comes and supersedes the authority of the rabbis.* (b.*Shabbat* 128b)

According to the *Talmud*, it is necessary to violate rabbinic prohibitions in order to alleviate or prevent the suffering of animals because showing kindness to animals is a biblical law, whereas the various categories of Sabbath prohibitions were only rabbinic mandates. Biblical law, in theory at least, trumps rabbinic mandates. Therefore it was permissible to bring provisions to an animal, to enable it to climb out of a pit, or (as in Luke 13:15) to untie one's ox or donkey from the stall and lead it out to give it water all on the Sabbath day. All of these fall into the category of "doing good" on the Sabbath because it is a positive, biblical commandment to show mercy to animals.

Yeshua's argument is based upon simple rabbinic logic: "If it is permissible to violate Shabbat in order to do good to animals and alleviate their suffering, how much more so is it permissible to do the same for human beings?"

In the end, Jewish law came to similar conclusions. Under *halachah*, Jewish doctors are required to work over the Sabbath (when necessary) without raising questions of Sabbath prohibitions. Theoretically, this is because the potential for saving a life is always there when a doctor is on duty, but the doctor is allowed to conduct all medical procedures whether life is threatened or not.

**Notes:**

## Lesson Five

# OUR CALL–
# HIS YOKE

THE LAND, THE PEOPLE,
AND THE SCRIPTURES OF ISRAEL

# Lesson Five
# OUR CALL—HIS YOKE

*By this we know that we are in Him: the one who says he abides in Him ought himself to walk in the same manner as He walked. Every disciple fully trained will be like his teacher.* (1 John 2:5–6; Luke 6:40)

## Lesson Overview

Thus far in our HaYesod studies, we have learned that a believer's connection to Israel and Torah is foundational to our faith. The previous lesson introduced Yeshua of Nazareth within that context: in the Land of Israel, as one of the People of Israel, and teaching the Scriptures of Israel. This week, we will learn about the high calling of discipleship and how discipleship was a part of Jewish life and learning in the days of the apostles. Discipleship to Yeshua requires the believer to take on the commandments of God and learn to identify himself with the Land, the People, and the Scriptures of Israel.

## Lesson Purpose

Here are the main points that you can expect to learn in this lesson:

❖ Discipleship is the art of imitation.
❖ Discipleship is a relationship with a teacher.
❖ Discipleship to Yeshua includes Torah.
❖ Discipleship to Yeshua is a high and difficult calling.

## Field Trips to the Holy Land

❖ Tabgha, Sea of Galilee
❖ Tel Aviv, Mediterranean Coast
❖ Mount of Beatitudes, Sea of Galilee

# Lesson Five
## LESSON OUTLINE

## What is a Disciple?

A. The Art of Imitation

B. Higher Education

C. The Disciple-Teacher Relationship

D. Radical Dedication

E. Devekut-Connection
   1. How Do You Cling to God?
   2. Clinging to a Teacher
   3. Clinging to God through Yeshua

F. The Four Jobs of a Disciple
   1. Memorization
   2. Tradition
   3. Imitation
   4. Raise Many Disciples

## His Yoke

A. The Yoke of Discipleship

B. The Cost of Discipleship
   1. Count the Cost
   2. Higher than Family
   3. Taking Up Your Cross
   4. Laying Down Your Life

## The Kingdom of Heaven

A. The Gospel in a Nutshell
   1. Repent
   2. The Kingdom
      a. Kingdom of Heaven in Rabbinic Sources
      b. Accepting the Kingdom of Heaven
   3. At Hand

B. The Kingdom and the Commandments

## Keep My Commandments

A. Love One Another
   1. All We Need is Love
   2. The New Commandment

B. Biblical Love

C. Keep My Commandments

## The Great Commission

A. Make Disciples

B. Being a Light

C. Priorities

# What is a Disciple?

**Key Verses**

Luke 6:40
1 John 2:5–6
Matthew 10:24
2 Timothy 1:2
Luke 11:19
Ephesians 5:23

**Key Words**

*Talmid:* Hebrew word meaning "student."

**Key Concepts**

*Discipleship:* Dedication or loyalty to a teacher; attachment. It is the art of imitation.

Discipleship was a well-established institution within Jewish culture.

> *talmid* (תלמיד) = "student"

A disciple is a ___Student___ ☺ .

## Ⓐ The Art of Imitation

*Every disciple fully trained will be like his teacher.* (Luke 6:40)

Discipleship is the art of imitation.

*By this we know that we are in Him: the one who says he abides in Him ought himself to walk in the same manner as He walked.* (1 John 2:5–6)

*Every Christian is to become a little Christ. The whole purpose of becoming a Christian is simply nothing else.* (C.S. Lewis, *Mere Christianity*)[1]

## Ⓑ Higher Education

Discipleship—apprenticeship to a Torah-teacher—was the primary institution of higher religious education in the days of the Master.

*Some Disciples Viewed the Rabbi higher than there Fathers*

## Ⓒ The Disciple-Teacher Relationship

### The Rabbi and the Disciple

| | The Rabbi | The Disciple | |
|---|---|---|---|
| 1. | Teacher | Student | A [student] is not above his teacher, nor a slave above his master. (Matthew 10:24) |
| 2. | Master | Slave | |
| 3. | Father | Son | To Timothy, my beloved son. (2 Timothy 1:2) By whom do your sons cast them out? (Luke 11:19) |
| 4. | husband | wife | For the husband is the head of the wife, as the Messiah also is the head of the church. (Ephesians 5:23) |

**Refer to Resource**

*King of the Jews*
"The Great Omission"
Pages 49–58

## D Radical Dedication

Disciples had absolute dedication and loyalty for their teachers.

*Rabbi Akiba said, "Once I followed Rabbi Joshua into a privy and I learned three things from him …" Ben Azzai said to him, "How did you dare to take such liberties with your master?" Akiba answered, "It was a matter of Torah, and I am required to learn."* (b.Berachot 62a)

## E Devekut-Connection

*You shall fear the LORD your God; you shall serve Him and cling* [davak, דבק] *to Him, and you shall swear by His name.* (Deuteronomy 10:20)

> *devekut* (דבקות) = "attachment"
>
> *davak* (דבק) = "to cling, cleave, keep close"

### 1. How Do You Cling to God?

Clinging to God is problematic:

*The LORD your God is a consuming fire.* (Deuteronomy 4:24)

### 2. Clinging to a Teacher

One must cling to a worthy sage, and this clinging would in turn be counted as clinging to the Almighty.

*By this injunction we are commanded to mix and associate with wise men, to be always in their company, and to join with them in every possible manner of fellowship: in eating, drinking, and business affairs, to the end that we may succeed in becoming like them in respect of their actions and in acquiring true opinions from their words.* (Rambam, *Sefer HaMitzvot* [Chaval])

**Key Verses**

Deuteronomy 10:20
Deuteronomy 4:24

**Key Words**

*Devekut:* Hebrew word meaning "attachment" or "connection."

*Davak:* Hebrew word meaning "to cling," "cleave," or "keep close."

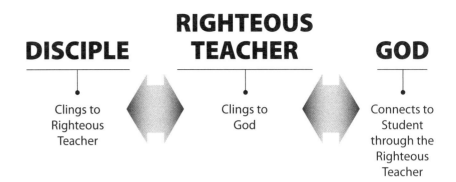

*Devekut* (דבקות) = "Clinging to God"

---

**DISCIPLE** — **RIGHTEOUS TEACHER** — **GOD**

| DISCIPLE | RIGHTEOUS TEACHER | GOD |
|---|---|---|
| Clings to Righteous Teacher | Clings to God | Connects to Student through the Righteous Teacher |

*[Handwritten margin note:]* The better Israel clung to moses the better they clung to God

*I was standing between the LORD and you at that time, to declare to you the word of the LORD; for you were afraid because of the fire and did not go up the mountain.* (Deuteronomy 5:5)

### 3. Clinging to God through Yeshua

We cling to God by clinging to His Son.

*I am the way, and the truth, and the life; no one comes to the Father but through Me. If you had known Me, you would have known My Father also; from now on you know Him, and have seen Him.* (John 14:6–7)

*In that day you will know that I am in My Father, and you in Me, and I in you.* (John 14:20)

*[Handwritten margin note:]* Do you wub me?!!

## F  The Four Jobs of a Disciple

In first-century Judaism, the disciple of a sage had four major tasks to perform.

**The Four Jobs of a Disciple**

| Job | Description |
|---|---|
| Job Number One | *To memorize his teachers words* |
| Job Number Two | *Learn teachers traditions* |
| Job Number Three | *immitate teachers actions* |
| Job Number Four | *Raise up Deciples* |

## 1. Memorization

The oral transmission process was the only intergenerational communication practiced among the sages.

*For I transmitted to you as of first importance what I also received.* (1 Corinthians 15:3)

"Transmitted" (*masorah*, מסורה) and "received" (*kabbalah*, קבלה) are technical terms used in rabbinic literature for the detailed process of the oral transmission.

*The student that repeats his lesson a hundred times is not to be compared with the one who repeats it a hundred and one times.* (b.*Chagigah* 9b)

The Master teaching His disciples

## 2. Tradition

A disciple was responsible for learning the traditions of how his teacher kept the commands of God and interpreted the Scriptures.

*To you it has been granted to know the mysteries of the kingdom of God.* (Luke 8:10)

*The use of the mishnaic Hebrew word* מסתורין [mistorin] *("mysteries") in rabbinic literature refers to the unique Oral Torah.* (Chana Safrai, "The Kingdom of Heaven and the Study of Torah")[2]

**Key Verses**

1 Corinthians 15:3
Luke 8:10

**Key Words**

*Masorah:* Hebrew word meaning "transmitted."

*Kabbalah:* Hebrew word meaning "received."

**Key Words**

*Shema:* From the root word *shama,* meaning "listen" or "obey."

*Ol:* Hebrew word meaning "yoke."

### Your Israel Connection

**Calling of the Disciples**

*Tabgha, Sea of Galilee* – Tabgha is Christianity's traditional location of the multiplication of the fish and loaves. The word Tabgha is an Arabic form of the Greek word *heptapegon* which means "seven springs." At Tabgha, seven springs empty into the Sea of Galilee. The warm water of the springs attracts fish, making Tabgha an ideal fishing spot for fisherman trying to fill their nets. It was probably at Tabgha that Yeshua found His first disciples.

*[handwritten note:] Not everyone was called to be a full time disciple but the ones who did had to make it their #1*

## 3. Imitation

A disciple's highest calling was to be a reflection of his teacher.

*Everyone who hears these words of Mine and acts on them, may be compared to a wise man who built his house on the rock.* (Matthew 7:24)

> *shema* (שמע) = "listen, obey"

## 4. Raise Many Disciples

When fully trained, a disciple was to become a teacher and raise up his own disciples.

*[The men of the great synagogue] used to say three things: Be patient in [the administration of] justice, raise up many disciples and make a fence around the Torah.* (m.*Avot* 1:1)

*Go therefore and make disciples of all the nations.* (Matthew 28:19)

Instead of raising up disciples for ourselves, we are to raise up disciples for Yeshua.

# His Yoke

For Yeshua's followers, the yoke of discipleship is a free choice but one that comes with responsibility and requires submission.

*Come to Me, all who are weary and heavy-laden, and I will give you rest. Take My yoke upon you and learn from Me, for I am gentle and humble in heart, and you will find rest for your souls. For My yoke is easy and My burden is light.* (Matthew 11:28–30)

> *ol* (על) = "yoke"

*For He was in the habit of working as a carpenter when among men, making ploughs and yokes.* (Justin Martyr, *Dialogue with Trypho* 88)

*Rabbi Nehunia ben Hakkanah said: "Whoever takes upon himself the yoke of Torah, they remove from him the yoke of government and the yoke of worldly concerns, and whoever breaks off from himself the yoke of Torah, they place upon himself the yoke of government and the yoke of worldly concerns."* (m.*Avot* 3:5)

**Key Words**

*Kaval:* Hebrew word meaning "receive, accept, to take obligation upon one's self."

In rabbinic literature:

yoke = torah

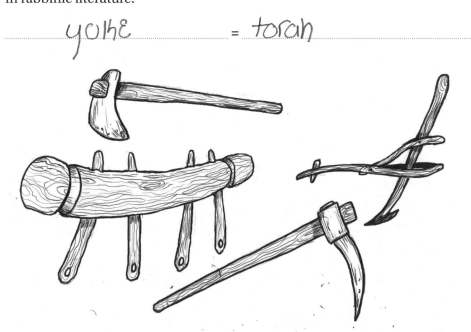

Ancient agricultural tools

## A The Yoke of Discipleship

> ***kaval*** (קבל) = "receive, accept, to take obligation upon one's self"[3]

*Draw near to me, you who are untaught, and lodge in my school. Why do you say you are lacking in these things, and why are your souls very thirsty? I opened my mouth and said, "Get these things for yourselves without money. Put your neck under the yoke, and let your souls receive instruction; it is to be found close by. See with your eyes that I have labored little and found myself much rest. Get instruction with a large sum of silver, and you will gain by it much gold."* (The Wisdom of Ben Sira 51:23–28, RSV)

*Probably, like the passages in [Ben Sira], Matthew 11:28–30 refers to the context of learning. This suggests that Jesus was likely not contrasting his burden to the burden of the Pharisees to which he referred elsewhere (Mt. 23:4), but rather, as he extended an invitation to prospective students to join his band of traveling students, he was alluding to the burden, or cost of discipleship.* (David Bivin, *New Light on the Difficult Words of Jesus*)[4]

**B** **The Cost of Discipleship**

Yeshua warned His followers to count the cost of discipleship before taking it on.

1. **Count the Cost**

   *For which one of you, when he wants to build a tower, does not first sit down and calculate the cost to see if he has enough to complete it? Otherwise, when he has laid a foundation and is not able to finish, all who observe it begin to ridicule him, saying, "This man began to build and was not able to finish."* (Luke 14:28–30)

*He wants us to consider full discipleship before just doing it*

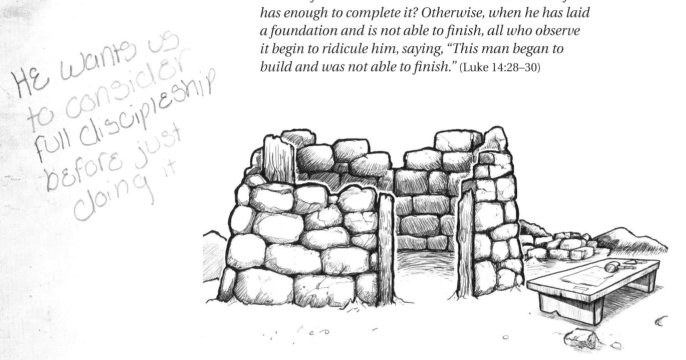

Building a tower

   Counting the cost means:

   *measuring demands of discipleship before commiting*

2. **Higher than Family**

   To "hate" one's family and life is a Hebraic idiom which means to show an order of preference.

   *If anyone comes to Me, and does not hate his own father and mother and wife and children and brothers and sisters, yes, and even his own life, he cannot be My disciple.* (Luke 14:26)

   *He who loves father or mother more than Me is not worthy of Me; and he who loves son or daughter more than Me is not worthy of Me.* (Matthew 10:37)

**Refer to Resource**

*Torah Club Volume Four:*
*The Good News of Messiah*
"Acharei Mot: After the Death"

*When one is searching for the lost property both of his father and of his teacher, his teacher's loss takes precedence over that of his father since his father brought him only into the life of this world, whereas his teacher, who taught him wisdom [i.e., Torah], has brought him into the life of the World to Come. But if his father is no less a scholar than his teacher, then his father's loss takes precedence.* (m.*Bava Metzia* 2:11)

Counting the cost means:

*Prioritizing yeshua above all*

3. **Taking Up Your Cross**

Observance of Torah often led to martyrdom.

*And he who does not take his cross and follow after Me is not worthy of Me.* (Matthew 10:38)

*R. Nathan says: "Of them that love Me and keep My commandments"[Exodus 20:6], refers to those who dwell in the land of Israel and risk their lives for the sake of the commandments. "Why are you being led out to be decapitated?" "Because I circumcised my son to be an Israelite." "Why are you being led out to be burned?" "Because I read the Torah." "Why are you being led out to be crucified?" "Because I ate the unleavened bread."* (*Mekhilta, BaChodesh* [Lauterbach])

Counting the cost means:

*Being willing to die for the kingdom*

Taking up your cross

**Key Verses**

Matthew 10:39
Mark 1:14–15
Matthew 3:1–2

**Key Words**

*Teshuvah:* Hebrew word meaning "repentance" or "turning back."

**4. Laying Down Your Life**

Yeshua is calling His disciples to make the ultimate sacrifice for the sake of the gospel and discipleship.

*He who has found his life will lose it, and he who has lost his life for My sake will find it.* (Matthew 10:39)

*He said to them: "What shall a man do to live?" They replied: "Let him kill himself (with study and hard work)." "What should a man do to kill himself?" They replied: "Let him keep himself alive."* (b.Tamid 32a)

Counting the cost means:

*Being willing to sacrifice everything*

# The Kingdom of Heaven

The message of the gospel is intimately connected with the concept of the kingdom of heaven.

## Ⓐ The Gospel in a Nutshell

The gospel in a nutshell is: "Repent for the kingdom of heaven is at hand."

*Now after John had been taken into custody, Jesus came into Galilee, preaching the gospel of God, and saying, "The time is fulfilled, and the kingdom of [heaven] is at hand; repent and believe in the gospel."* (Mark 1:14–15)

*Now in those days John the Baptist came, preaching in the wilderness of Judea, saying, "Repent, for the kingdom of heaven is at hand."* (Matthew 3:1–2)

The message of the gospel is:

*Repent the kingdom of Heaven is at hand*

**1. Repent**

> ***teshuvah*** (תשובה) = "repentance, turning back"

**Your Israel Connection**

**Introduction to the Twelve Disciples**

*Tabgha, Sea of Galilee* – Peter, Andrew, James, John, and probably Philip too, were all professional fishermen on the Sea of Galilee before they encountered Yeshua of Nazareth who called them to leave their nets, embark on a life of discipleship, and become "fishers of men."

*He wants ordinary people!!!*

**Refer to Resource**

*King of the Jews*
"The Kingmaker and the Kingdom"
Pages 29–37

Repentance (*teshuvah*) literally means to "turn around"—in other words turning around from the life of sin that we have been leading and walking the other way.

**Key Words**

*Malchut hashamayim:* Hebrew phrase meaning "kingdom of heaven," referring to the Messianic Age.

*Shamayim:* Hebrew word meaning "heaven," or "sky." It is also commonly used as a circumlocution for God's name.

Repentance

## 2. The Kingdom

> *malchut hashamayim* (מלכות השמים) = "kingdom of heaven"
>
> *shamayim* (שמים) = "heaven, sky;" also a circumlocution for God's Name

Kingdom of heaven means the "rule and reign of God" and refers to the Messianic Age, now and in the future.

### a. *Kingdom of Heaven in Rabbinic Sources*

In rabbinic literature, the sages equated accepting the "kingdom of heaven" with the acceptance of God's Torah.

*In essence [the Sages] meant by [kingdom of heaven] that any Jew who would seriously follow the Torah (the Law) had accepted the Lordship of God, that is, was prepared to do whatever the Law demanded of him … They meant that any Jew who began to keep the Torah and the rabbinic interpretations of the Torah had come under the rule of Law and was now in God's rule or Kingdom. He had taken upon himself "the yoke of the Kingdom of God," or simply, "the Kingdom of God."* (Robert Lindsey, *Jesus Rabbi and Lord*)[5]

**Refer to Resource**

*Hallowed Be Your Name*
"The Master's Use of Evasive Synonyms"
Pages 25–33

*For them, this Kingdom was, in essence, the rule of God, most often described as equal to the personal acceptance of God's reigning over a given person.* (Robert Lindsey, *Jesus Rabbi and Lord*)[6]

*The LORD shall <u>reign forever and ever</u>.* (Exodus 15:18)

**b.  *Accepting the Kingdom of Heaven***

In its original Jewish context, accepting "the yoke of the kingdom of heaven" means submitting to God's authority in our lives, and this leads us naturally to accepting "the yoke of the commandments."

| The Yoke of the Kingdom of Heaven | The Yoke of the Commandments |
|---|---|
| "Hear, O Israel! The LORD is our God, the LORD is one!" (Deuteronomy 6:4) | "It shall come about, if you listen obediently to my commandments which I am commanding you today." (Deuteronomy 11:13) |

*Rabbi Joshua ben Korhah said, "Why was the section of 'Hear' [Deuteronomy 6:4] placed before that of 'And it shall come to pass' [Deuteronomy 11:13]? So that one should first accept upon himself the yoke of the kingdom of heaven and then take upon himself the yoke of the commandments."* (m.Berachot 2:2)

*It's a place not a status!*

Ancient yoke

**Refer to Resource**

*Love and the Messianic Age*
"Knowledge and Love"
Pages 31–42

**3.  At Hand**

When the Master says the kingdom of heaven is "at hand," He means that it is here now. Even though the Messianic Age has not yet begun, we can begin living in it right now.

## B The Kingdom and the Commandments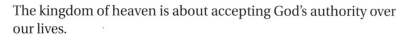

The kingdom of heaven is about accepting God's authority over our lives.

*Whoever then annuls one of the least of these commandments, and teaches others to do the same, shall be called least in the kingdom of heaven: but whoever keeps and teaches them, he shall be called great in the kingdom of heaven.* (Matthew 5:19)

*Not everyone who says to Me, "Lord, Lord," will enter the kingdom of heaven, but he who does the will of My Father who is in heaven will enter. Many will say to Me on that day, "Lord, Lord, did we not prophesy in Your name, and in Your name cast out demons, and in Your name perform many miracles?" And then I will declare to them, "I never knew you; depart from Me, you who practice lawlessness* [anomia]." (Matthew 7:21–23)

> ### *anomia* (ανομια) = "against law, without Torah"

The message of the gospel in plain language:

Repent, ~~Turn around, quit sinning~~, and ~~start doing good~~ as defined by God's righteous standard, the Torah, for God's kingdom is here now.

# Keep My Commandments

Love is closely bound up with keeping the commandments.

## A Love One Another

Love is the mark of discipleship to Yeshua.

*A new commandment I give to you, that you love one another, even as I have loved you, that you also love one another. By this all men will know that you are My disciples, if you have love for one another.* (John 13:34–35)

**Key Verses**

Matthew 5:19
Matthew 7:21–23
2 Peter 3:11
John 13:34–35

**Key Words**

*Anomia:* Greek word meaning "against law" or "without Torah."

**Your Israel Connection**

**Shaliach**

*Tel Aviv, Mediterranean Coast* – The coastal city of Tel Aviv is the second-largest city in Israel. Half a million people live in Tel Aviv, and over two-and-a-half million in the surrounding metropolitan. Tel Aviv is not the capital of Israel, but it is the center of Israel's secular culture. A drive through Tel Aviv today demonstrates that the average Israeli is very much in need of God.

**Refer to Resource**

*HaYesod Student Workbook*
"Repent, for the Kingdom of Heaven is at Hand"
Pages 5.27–5.29

**Key Verses**

John 13:1

Multiple-Choice Question (choose one answer)

People will know we are Yeshua's disciples if:

a. ............... we keep the Sabbath.

b. ............... we eat kosher.

b. ............... we use Hebrew terms.

c. ✓............ we love one another.

d. ............... we despise one another.

### 1. All We Need is Love

<u>If we love one another, it is enough.</u>

*The blessed evangelist John, when he delayed at Ephesus up to the highest old age and could scarcely be carried to congregation in the hands of disciples and was not able to put together a statement of several words, used to offer in different sayings nothing but: "Little children, love one another." At last the disciples and brethren who were present, tired of the fact that they always heard the same thing, said, "Teacher, why do you always say this?" John made a worthy response: "<u>Because it was the Lord's precept, and if it alone is done, it is enough.</u>"* (Jerome, *Commentary on Galatians*)[7]

### 2. The New Commandment

The Master's "new commandment" is not a completely "new" commandment.

*[The Master] explained the matter more clearly when he said "that you should love each other just as I have loved you. There is no love greater than someone giving his life for his friends." By this it is a new commandment, for Moses only said, "love your neighbor as yourself," meaning, "and not more than this." Therefore R. Akiva ruled in the Talmud (b.Baba Metzia 62a), "Your life has precedence over your friend's life," but in the view of the Master and as shown in his deeds, the life of your friend has precedence.* (Rabbi Lichtenstein, *Commentary on the New Testament*)[8]

*The consummation of His "giving Himself" is His death. It is not only the highest expression of His love, it is its perfection. "He loved us perfectly" [John 13:1].* (Paul P. Levertoff, *Love and the Messianic Age*)[9]

**The New Commandment of Love**

| | | The Difference |
|---|---|---|
| **The "Old" Commandment** | You shall love your neighbor as yourself; I am the LORD. (Leviticus 19:18) | "As Yourself." |
| **The "New" Commandment** | A new commandment I give to you, that you love one another, even as I have loved you, that you also love one another. (John 13:34) | "As I have loved you." |

**Key Verses**

Leviticus 19:18
John 13:34
John 14:15, 21
John 15:10
1 John 2:3–4
Matthew 28:18–20
Matthew 5:17–19

## B  Biblical Love

In the biblical sense, love is about action, not feelings.

*You shall love your neighbor as yourself; I am the LORD.* (Leviticus 19:18)

*The Hebrew reads, "V'ahavta l'reiacha kamocha." This is translated correctly to "Love to your neighbor as yourself" and not "Love your neighbor as yourself." This is as awkward in Hebrew as it is in English and requires explanation. The Ramban (d. 1270) … interprets the grammatical peculiarity thus: "Do [acts of] love to your neighbor as you would have him do to you."* (Avigdor Bonchek, *Studying the Torah*)[10]

## C  Keep My Commandments

Our love for Yeshua is ultimately expressed by the keeping of His commandments.

*If you love Me, you will keep My commandments … He who has My commandments and keeps them is the one who loves Me; and he who loves Me will be loved by My Father, and I will love him and will disclose Myself to him.* (John 14:15, 21)

*If you keep My commandments, you will abide in My love; just as I have kept My Father's commandments and abide in His love.* (John 15:10)

*By this we know that we have come to know Him, if we keep His commandments. The one who says, "I have come to know Him," and does not keep His commandments, is a liar, and the truth is not in him.* (1 John 2:3–4)

**◉◀ Your Israel Connection**

**The Great Omission**

*Mount of Beatitudes, Sea of Galilee –* The Mount of the Beatitudes is traditionally identified as the hill on which Yeshua delivered the "Sermon on the Mount." In Matthew 28, the eleven disciples encountered the risen Messiah on the same hill, and He charged them with the great commission.

**Refer to Resource**

*Love and the Messianic Age*
"Epilogue: Love and the Fourth Gospel"
Pages 73–80

# The Great Commission

The Great Commission consists of four imperatives.

*Go therefore and make disciples of all the nations, baptizing them in the name of the Father and the Son and the Holy Spirit, teaching them to observe all that I commanded you; and lo, I am with you always, even to the end of the age.* (Matthew 28:19–20)

The Four Imperatives:

1. Go
2. make disciples
3. immerse
4. teach commandments

## Ⓐ Make Disciples

Yeshua urges His followers to go unto the nations—the Gentiles—and make disciples.

## Ⓑ Being a Light

*You are the light of the world. A city set on a hill cannot be hidden; nor does anyone light a lamp and put it under a basket, but on the lampstand, and it gives light to all who are in the house. Let your light shine before men in such a way that they may see your good works, and glorify your Father who is in heaven.* (Matthew 5:14–16)

The city of Sefat sits high on a hill

*I will also make You a light of the nations so that My salvation may reach to the end of the earth.* (Isaiah 49:6)

*Our Rabbis taught: "Four things require to be done with energy, namely, [study of] the Torah, good works, praying, and one's worldly occupation. Whence do we know this of Torah and good works? Because it says, 'Only be strong and very courageous to observe to do according to all the law' (Joshua 1:7)."* (b.Berachot 32b)

Good Works = _Commandments of toran_

Ancient oil lamp

## C Priorities

The Master encourages us to keep our priorities straight and not to get so into the Torah's physical side that we neglect the ethical virtues.

*Woe to you, scribes and Pharisees, hypocrites! For you tithe mint and dill and cummin, and have neglected the weightier provisions of the law: justice and mercy and faithfulness; but these are the things you should have done without neglecting the others.*
(Matthew 23:23)

## Endnotes

1   C.S. Lewis, *Mere Christianity* (San Francisco, CA: Harper Collins, 2001), 177.

2   Chana Safrai, "The Kingdom of Heaven and the Study of Torah," in *Jesus' Last Week* (ed. R. Steven Notley, Marc Turnage, and Brian Becker; Boston, MA: Brill, 2006), 175.

3   Marcus Jastrow, "קבל," *A Dictionary of the Targumim, the Talmud Babli and Yerushalmi, and the Midrashic Literature* (2 vols.; New York: Pardes Publishing House, 1950), 2:1308.

4   David Bivin, *New Light on the Difficult Words of Jesus: Insights from His Jewish Context* (Holland, MI: En-Gedi Resource Center, 2005), 25.

5   Robert A. Lindsey, *Jesus Rabbi and Lord* (Oak Creek, WI: Cornerstone Publishing, 1990), 24.

6   Ibid., 55.

7   Jerome in his commentary on Galatians 6:10, see R. Alan Culpepper, *John, the Son of Zebedee* (Columbia, SC: University of South Carolina Press, 1994), 165.

8   Rabbi Yechiel Lichtenstein, *Commentary on the New Testament: John* (trans. Robert Morris; Marshfield, MO: Vine of David, forthcoming) to John 13:34.

9   Paul P. Levertoff, *Love and the Messianic Age* (Marshfield, MO: Vine of David, 2009), 77.

10  Avigdor Bonchek, *Studying the Torah: A Guide to In-Depth Interpretation* (Northvale, NJ: Jason Aronson Inc, 1997), 106.

# Lesson Five
# LESSON SUMMARY

## First …

We learned that a "disciple" was a student who apprenticed himself to a rabbi or sage. We saw that a disciple would try to cling to God by clinging to his teacher, a relationship which was like that of:

❖ Disciple to rabbi

❖ Slave to master

❖ Son to father

❖ Wife to husband

## Then …

We learned that disciples had four primary jobs:

❖ To memorize the teacher's words

❖ To learn the teacher's traditions

❖ To imitate the teacher's actions

❖ To raise up more disciples

## After that …

We learned about Yeshua's yoke of discipleship and that "yoke" was a rabbinic metaphor for "Torah." Yeshua warned us to count the cost before taking up His yoke.

## Then …

We learned the message of the gospel which Yeshua was teaching His disciples: "Repent, for the kingdom of heaven is at hand."

❖ "Repent" means to turn around.

❖ The "kingdom of heaven" refers to the reign and rule of God.

❖ "At hand" means "already present."

This led us to realize that keeping the commandments is an act of love toward Messiah, toward God, and toward others.

## Finally …

We learned that Yeshua sent out His disciples telling them

❖ Go!

❖ Make disciples of all nations.

❖ Immerse them in the name of the Father, Son, and Spirit.

❖ Teach them everything Yeshua commanded.

# Lesson Five
## LESSON REVIEW – Q&A

1. What is a disciple?

2. What is the concept of *devekut*? How does it apply to our relationship to God through His Son?

3. List and explain the four jobs of being a disciple. How do those four jobs apply to our relationship to Yeshua?

4. In rabbinic literature, what does a "yoke" ordinarily represent?

5. What are the "costs" of discipleship that Yeshua encourages us to count?

6. What is the message of the gospel as found in the mouth of Yeshua? Explain the concept.

7. How do we show our love for Yeshua and for the Father?

8. What are the four imperatives of the Great Commission? Which one is the "Great Omission?"

# Lesson Five
# EXTRA CREDIT
### SUPPLEMENTAL MATERIAL FOR THIS HAYESOD LESSON

Are you ready to take up the yoke of discipleship? Here's an opportunity to meet some of your colleagues among the disciples of Yeshua. Welcome to the team!

1. The roster of twelve disciples appears three times in the Gospels and also in the book of Acts. Begin by reading the text of Matthew 10:2–4 and record each of the disciples' names in the first column—one name on each of the twelve lines. Do the same for the other three passages in their respective columns. Do your best to match the names, reordering them when necessary to keep the same disciple consistent across the same line.

| Scripture Reference | Matthew 10:2–4 | Mark 3:16–19 | Luke 6:13–16 | Acts 1:13 |
|---|---|---|---|---|
| 1 | Simon called Peter | Simon named Peter | Simon named Peter | Peter |
| 2 | | | | |
| 3 | | | | |
| 4 | | | | |
| 5 | | | | |
| 6 | | | | |
| 7 | | | | |
| 8 | | | | |
| 9 | | | | |

| Scripture Reference | Matthew 10:2–4 | Mark 3:16–19 | Luke 6:13–16 | Acts 1:13 |
|---|---|---|---|---|
| 10 | | | | |
| 11 | | | | |
| 12 | | | | |

2.  Several women were disciples and "followed Jesus" along with the Twelve. Which are identified by name in Scripture? (Matthew 27:55–56; Mark 15:40–41; Luke 8:1–3)

3.  The mothers of two of Yeshua's disciples were also disciples. What were their names and the disciples' names? (Matthew 27:55–56; Mark 15:40–41; Luke 8:1–3)

4.  How many of the Master's disciples were formerly disciples of John the Baptist? What is one of their names? (John 1:35–40)

5.  How many of the twelve disciples had been baptized by John? (Acts 1:22)

6.  Who were the two choices brought forward to replace Judas Iscariot? What was the criterion for their appointment, and who won out? (Acts 1:21–26)

7.  What is the relationship between Simon Peter and Andrew? (Matthew 4:18; Mark 1:16, 29; Luke 6:14)

8.  Which disciples were from Bethsaida? (John 1:44)

9. How do we know that Peter was married? Where was Peter living when he became a disciple? (Matthew 8:14; Mark 1:21–30; Luke 4:38; 1 Corinthians 9:5)

10. Who are the two male disciples who visit the empty tomb first? (John 20:1–8)

11. To which of the Twelve did the Master appear first after His resurrection? (1 Corinthians 15:5)

12. Which disciples were fisherman? (Matthew 4:18, 21; Mark 1:19–20; Luke 5:10)

13. Which disciple was a Levite? What was his occupation? (Matthew 9:9; Mark 2:14; Luke 5:27)

14. Which of the disciples might have been of priestly descent? (Leviticus 21:1–41; John 18:15–16, 20:4–5)

15. The rabbis liked to teach "under a fig tree." Which of the Master's disciples might have been a Torah scholar? (John 1:48)

16. Who is referred to as the disciple whom the Master loved? (John 19:26, 21:20)

17. Who tells Peter about the Messiah? (John 1:40–41)

18. Who tells Nathaniel about the Messiah? (John 1:45)

19. Which disciples constituted Yeshua's inner court of three? In what three Gospel events are they singled out? (Matthew 17:1; Mark 5:37, 9:2, 14:33; Luke 8:51, 9:28)

20. Which of the four disciples questioned the Master privately on the Mount of Olives about the end of the age? (Mark 13:3)

21. The Apostolic Scriptures single out one disciple as preeminent: "His disciples and ........................," "........................ and his companions," and "the apostles and the brothers of the Lord and ........................." Who was he? (Matthew 16:18; Mark 16:7; Mark 16:20; 1 Corinthians 9:5)

22. How many disciples does Yeshua send out the first time? The second? (Matthew 10:5; Luke 9:1, 10:1)

# Lesson Five – Digging Deeper
## REPENT, FOR THE KINGDOM OF HEAVEN IS AT HAND
### FURTHER STUDY FROM THIS WEEK'S HAYESOD LESSON

John only had one sermon. He probably had many different versions of it, but the message was always the same: "Repent, for the kingdom of heaven is at hand" (Matthew 3:2). Those nine words are the gospel message in a nutshell.

**Resource in Focus**

Excerpt from chapter one of First Fruits of Zion's book *King of the Jews: Resurrecting the Jewish Jesus.*

When He was teaching the crowds, Yeshua never preached a sermon presenting the plan of salvation. Nor did He ever bother to share a tract. We never hear Yeshua ask anyone, "If you died today, do you know for sure that you would go to heaven?" We never hear Him ask, "Do you have Me in your heart?" or "Are you saved?" But if those clichés were not the gospel message taught by Yeshua and His disciples, what *was* the message? What was He preaching? He was preaching John's nine-word sermon.[1] When He sent out His disciples, He told them to preach the same thing.[2]

John's sermon was: "Repent, for the kingdom of heaven is at hand." Yeshua's sermon was: "Repent, for the kingdom of heaven is at hand." The apostles' sermon was "Repent, for the kingdom of heaven is at hand." The message of the gospel is: "Repent, for the kingdom of heaven is at hand." But what do those words really mean?

## Repent

In Hebrew, the word for "repent" is *shuv* (שוב). It means "to turn around." Repentance (*teshuvah*, תשובה), in the noun form, is a foundational concept in Judaism. It means "to return." Unlike the Greek equivalent that implies a change of mind, *teshuvah* means "to turn around and go back the other direction." The call to repent is an imperative to turn one's life in the opposite direction. In the mouths of the prophets, it meant "quit sinning, turn around: and start doing good." It is more than just a change of mind; *teshuvah* demands a change of behavior. In Judaism, "to return" means "to return to the covenant norms of Torah." Sin is defined as a transgression of Torah.[3] Therefore, the call to repent is the call to quit sinning, turn around, and return to obedience to God's commandments.

## The Kingdom

When we think of a kingdom, we tend to think of a geographic territory with political borders under the domain of a sovereign. When we think of the kingdom of heaven, we tend to think of the same thing but somewhere beyond the sky (perhaps with pearly gates and streets of gold) or in the future when heaven is on earth.

The Hebrew word *malchut* (מלכות) is the word John and Yeshua would have used for "kingdom." While it might be understood to refer to a territorial domain, it is better understood as the active rule and reign of a sovereign. To be in the *malchut*, one must be under the reign of the *melech* (מלך). To be in the kingdom, one must be under the reign of the king.

The sages of Second-Temple Judaism understood the kingdom of heaven to be lives lived in obedience to God. They spoke of the recitation of the *Shema* (Deuteronomy 6:4–9) as "taking on the yoke of the kingdom." Yeshua described the kingdom in these terms when He said, "The kingdom of God is not coming with signs to be observed; nor will they say, 'Look, here it is!' or, 'There it is!' For behold, the kingdom of God is in your midst" (Luke 17:20–21).

In this perspective, the kingdom of heaven is not a place; it is a status. Those who choose to obey the king are under the reign of the king—that is to say, in the kingdom.

But there is a visible aspect to the kingdom of heaven as well, and that is the literal presence of a reigning king on earth. The ancient prophets of Israel promised that one day God's anointed king, a descendant of the house of David, would reign over Israel and the entire world. To make a kingdom, you need a king. Yeshua came as that promised King, and John the Immerser fully expected Him to establish His kingdom in short order.

## Kingdom of Heaven

John and Yeshua referred to the coming kingdom as the kingdom of heaven (*shamayim*, שמים). We are a long way from their intended meaning if we think of pearly gates and streets of gold. In the days of the Master, the Jewish people had ceased using the name of God for fear of breaking the third commandment. Instead of pronouncing God's name as it is spelled, they employed circumlocutions. These evasive synonyms were understood to be just that, even as they are to this day. For example, our English translations of the Bible employ such circumlocutions by translating the holy and unspeakable name of God (Y/H/V/H) as LORD. Yeshua Himself used evasive synonyms like this to speak of God. In all the Scriptures, neither He nor His disciples ever pronounced the name of God. Instead, by all appearances, they reverenced and sanctified His name, setting it apart from common use. When speaking of God, Yeshua referred to Him as "the Father," "my Father," "the Spirit," "the Mighty One," "God," and "Lord of heaven and earth." The word "heaven," as used in the term "kingdom of heaven," functions as such a circumlocution, just as it does in the common English term of exasperation, "Oh, for heaven's sake!"

The Gospel writers Luke and Mark understood that the subtlety of this idiom would be lost on readers unfamiliar with the Jewish context, so in their Gospels they translated the term as "kingdom of God." The terms "kingdom of heaven" and "kingdom of God" are actually synonymous.

## Is at Hand

The gospel message of "the kingdom of heaven is at hand" seems to imply that the kingdom of heaven is very close but has not yet arrived or that it is about to begin but has not yet begun. Bivin and Blizzard point out that in Hebrew the connotation of the phrase has the opposite meaning:

> *The Hebrew word for near* (karav, ברק) *"does not imply that there necessarily has to be any distance at all between that which is coming near and that which is being approached. … We can see how the Greek or English leaves the wrong concept of Kingdom of God: futuristic. The Hebrew leaves the correct concept: present tense—NOW! The Kingdom of Heaven … is always present tense, 'right now,' according to Jesus' understanding, and in rabbinic usage as well."*[4]

It follows that where there is a king, there is a kingdom. The message of John, Yeshua, and the disciples was consistent. The king is here! The kingdom is now because the king is here! If we translate the terminology back to Hebrew, we can see the heightened sense of urgency with which John, Yeshua, and the disciples all delivered the gospel message. Repent quickly, because the kingdom of heaven is already here!

If we put it all together, the meaning of this central message of the gospel comes through loud and clear: "Quit sinning, turn around and start obeying God, because the King is already here and the reign of God is starting right now!" The good news of the gospel is that the King has arrived. The demand of the gospel is repentance.

## Endnotes

1     Matthew 4:17.

2     Matthew 10:7.

3     1 John 3:4.

4     David Bivin and Roy Blizzard, *Understanding the Difficult Words of Jesus: New Insights from a Hebraic Perspective* (Dayton, OH: Center for Judaic-Christian Studies, 1994), 63.

**Notes:**

Notes:

Lesson Six

# OUR IDENTITY– HIS APOSTLE

THE LAND, THE PEOPLE,
AND THE SCRIPTURES OF ISRAEL

# Lesson Six
# OUR IDENTITY—HIS APOSTLE

*I am a Jew, born in Tarsus of Cilicia, but brought up in this city, educated under Gamaliel, strictly according to the law of our fathers, being zealous for God just as you all are today … I am a Pharisee, a son of Pharisees; I am on trial for the hope and resurrection of the dead!* (Acts 22:3, 23:6)

## Lesson Overview

In our HaYesod lessons thus far, we have been learning about the believer's connection to the Land, the People, and the Scriptures of Israel. We have learned about the role of Torah, salvation, covenant, and discipleship in the believer's life. We have learned about Yeshua and His connection to the Torah. But what about Paul? Many Christians have difficulty accepting the idea of the ongoing roles of Torah and Israel because of the writings of the Apostle Paul. Christian identity is based upon our understanding of the apostle Paul. Paul's renunciation of Judaism, conversion to Christianity, and ongoing campaign against "the Law" is axiomatic in Christian theology. Therefore, it is important for us to examine Paul—the man and his message—in order to see if, in fact, his teachings are actually incompatible with the Land, the People, and the Scriptures of Israel.

## Lesson Purpose

Here are the main points that you can expect to learn in this lesson:

- ❖ Acquire a biblical view of Paul's background and relationship with Judaism.
- ❖ Learn the context of Paul's ministry and letters.
- ❖ Understand Paul's relationship to Torah and Israel before and after coming to faith in Yeshua.
- ❖ Dispel misunderstandings about Paul.

## Field Trips to the Holy Land

- ❖ Damascus Gate, Old City Jerusalem
- ❖ The Great Synagogue, Jerusalem
- ❖ Jewish Quarter, Old City Jerusalem
- ❖ Caesarea Maritima, Mediterranean Coast

# Lesson Six
# LESSON OUTLINE

## Saul vs. Paul

A. Paul's Credentials
1. Confidence in the Flesh
2. Circumcised on the Eighth Day
3. An Israelite
4. A Benjamite
5. Hebrew of Hebrews
6. A Pharisee
   a. Doctrines of the Pharisees
   b. Paul's Education as Pharisee
      1. Zealous
      2. Torah Observant
B. Jewish Rubbish?

## Paul the Torah-Observant Jew

A. Paul's Last Trip to Jerusalem
B. Zealous for the Torah
C. Allegations about Paul
D. Paul's Nazirite Vow
E. Was Paul an Apostate?

## Paul's Gospel

A. The Gentile Inclusion
B. An Unpopular Message

## The Argument in Antioch

A. The Challenge
B. Dissension and Debate

## Jerusalem Council

A. Council of the Elders
B. The Formal Charge
C. Peter's Rebuttal
D. The Proof Text
E. The Decision
F. The Four Essentials
G. The Rest of the Torah

## Paul on Trial

A. In the Temple
B. Before the Sanhedrin
C. Before Felix
D. Before Festus
E. Before Agrippa
F. Before the Jewish Community of Rome

# Saul vs. Paul

Saul the Jew vs. Paul the Christian

> **Saul = *Shaul* (שָׁאוּל)**
>
> **Paul = *Paulos* (Παυλος)**

## Ⓐ Paul's Credentials

Paul provides an autobiographical statement in Philippians 3:4–8.

### 1. Confidence in the Flesh

*Although I myself might have confidence even in the flesh. If anyone else has a mind to put confidence in the flesh, I far more.* (Philippians 3:4)

"Confidence in the flesh" = <u>Status & Prestige</u>

"If anyone has good credentials for being an apostle and teacher, I have better credentials."

### 2. Circumcised on the Eighth Day

*Circumcised the eighth day.* (Philippians 3:5)

Paul was not a convert to Judaism; he was born into it as a covenant member since birth.

*On the eighth day the flesh of his foreskin shall be circumcised.* (Leviticus 12:3)

### 3. An Israelite

*Of the nation of Israel.* (Philippians 3:5)

Paul's parents were not converts; he came from a pure Israelite lineage.

### 4. A Benjamite

*Of the tribe of Benjamin.* (Philippians 3:5)

Paul was from a Benjamite family, which explains why he was named after the first king of Israel: Saul the Benjamite.

### 5. Hebrew of Hebrews

*A Hebrew of Hebrews.* (Philippians 3:5)

Hebrew pedigree back to Abraham; Hebrew language skills; affiliation with conservative, Hebraic Judaism.

Saul vs. Paul

### 6. A Pharisee

*As to the [Torah], a Pharisee.* (Philippians 3:5)

The term Pharisee does not mean "hypocrite."

*[The Pharisees] believe that souls have an immortal vigor in them, and that under the earth there will be rewards or punishments, according as they have lived virtuously or viciously in this life, and the latter are to be detained in an everlasting prison, but that the former shall have power to revive and live again.* (Josephus, *Antiquities of the Jews* 18:1:3)

**Refer to Resource**

*Torah Club Volume Four:*
*The Good News of the Messiah*
"Re'eh: Behold"

a. *Doctrines of the Pharisees:*

The Pharisees believed in:

1. immortal soul
2. reward & punishment in afterli
3. resurrection of the Dead
4. coming of messiah
5. existence of angels and Demons
6. tradition interpretation of bible

b. *Paul's Education as a Pharisee*

A disciple of the famous sage Gamaliel (the grandson of Hillel)

*I am a Jew, born in Tarsus of Cilicia, but brought up in this city, educated under Gamaliel, strictly according to the law of our fathers.* (Acts 22:3)

YESHIVAT RABBAN GAMALIEL
YERUSHALAYIM
ישיבת רבן גמליאל

THIS IS TO CERTIFY THAT

**SHAUL OF TARSUS**

HAS SATISFACTORILY COMPLETED
THE COURSE OF STUDIES.

רב גמליאל
SIGNED

*Rabban Gamaliel used to say, "Take a teacher for yourself and remove all uncertainty, and do not make a habit of approximating your tithes."* (m.Avot 1:16)

Rabban Gamaliel used to say, "Take a teacher for yourself and remove all uncertainty, and do not make a habit of approximating your tithes." (m.*Avot* 1:16)

**The Road to Damascus**

*Damascus Gate, Old City Jerusalem* – The Damascus Gate is the main north-facing gate of old city Jerusalem. It is referred to as Damascus Gate because travelers leaving for Damascus would have left the city from that direction. The current gate was built in 1542, but it stands above the remains of a Hadrianic-era gate in front of which the Romans erected a victory column dedicated to Hadrian. The Arabic name for the gate *Bab-al-Amud* translates to "Gate of the Column."

## 7. Zealous

*As to zeal, a persecutor of the church.* (Philippians 3:6)

Paul was so passionate about his faith that he even went so far as to campaign against those he at first perceived to be heretics.

## 8. Torah Observant

*As to the righteousness which is in the Law [Torah], found blameless.* (Philippians 3:6)

Paul was scrupulously Torah observant and did not neglect any of the commandments.

## B  Jewish Rubbish?

*But whatever things were gain to me, those things I have counted as loss for the sake of Messiah. More than that, I count all things to be loss in view of the surpassing value of knowing Messiah Yeshua my Lord, for whom I have suffered the loss of all things, and count them but rubbish so that I may gain Messiah.* (Philippians 3:7–8)

When Saul became a believer, did he renounce Judaism and walk away from Torah?

# Paul the Torah-Observant Jew

*A thoroughly Jewish Paul, functioning entirely within the context of Judaism, giving priority to Israel, even willing to give his life in place of the Jewish people … This study finds the Paul behind the text … to be a practicing Jew—"a good Jew" albeit a Jew shaped by his conviction in Jesus as Israel's Christ, who did not break with the essential truths of Judaism(s) of his day.* (Mark Nanos, *The Mystery of Romans*)[1]

## A  Paul's Last Trip to Jerusalem

Acts 21 tells the story of Paul's last trip to Jerusalem.

*After we arrived in Jerusalem, the brethren received us gladly. And the following day Paul went in with us to James, and all the elders were present.* (Acts 21:17–18)

Paul's dual citizenship

## B Zealous for the Torah

The Jewish believers of the apostolic community in Jerusalem were all Torah observant.

*They said to him, "You see, brother, how many thousands there are among the Jews of those who have believed, and they are all zealous for the [Torah]."* (Acts 21:20)

## C Allegations about Paul

The Jewish believers of apostolic Jerusalem had heard allegations about Paul.

*And [the Jewish believers] have been told about you, that you are teaching all the Jews who are among the Gentiles to forsake Moses, telling them not to circumcise their children nor to walk according to the customs.* (Acts 21:21)

Paul allegedly was teaching Jews living outside of Israel:

1. Forsake Moses
2. not to circumsize kids
3. Not to keep the customs

*What, then, is to be done? They will certainly hear that you have come.* (Acts 21:22)

**Key Verses**

Acts 21:24

Numbers 6:13–21

Acts 11

Romans 2:16

Romans 16:25

2 Timothy 2:8

## ⓓ Paul's Nazirite Vow

*All will know that there is nothing to the things which
they have been told about you, but that you yourself
also walk orderly, keeping the [Torah].* (Acts 21:24)

To prove that Paul was walking according to Torah and keeping the Torah,
James and the apostles proposed that Paul not only fulfill his own Nazirite
vow but that he pay the expenses of four other Jewish believers who were
also completing their Nazirite vows.

### Expenses for Five Nazirites Completing Their Vows (Numbers 6:13–21)

| Item | Sacrifice |
| --- | --- |
| 5 unblemished yearling lambs | Burnt Offerings |
| 5 unblemished yearling ewe lambs | Sin Offerings |
| 5 unblemished rams | Fellowship Offerings |
| 33 liters (nearly 2 bushels) of fine flour mixed with oil | Supplementary Grain Offerings |
| 8 liters (2 gallons) of wine | Wine Libations |
| 5 additional baskets of unleavened bread with oil | Grain Offerings |

**📷❚ Your Israel Connection**

**Synagogue of the Christianos**

*The Great Synagogue, Jerusalem* – The
Great Synagogue at 58 King George
Street in Jerusalem was inaugurated
in 1982 and consecrated in memory
of the six million Jews who perished in
the holocaust and in memory of fallen
IDF soldiers. The architecture is meant
to be reminiscent of the Temple. The
synagogue seats 1,400 and is a popular
Sabbath service for visitors to Jerusalem.

## ⓔ Was Paul an Apostate?

When Saul became a believer, did he renounce Judaism and walk away
from Torah to become a Christian? According to James, the other apostles
and Paul's own testimony in Acts 21, the answer is "No."

# Paul's Gospel

**Refer to Resource**

*HaYesod Student Workbook*
"Paul's Nazirite Vow"
Pages 6.27–6.29

What makes "Paul's gospel" different than everyone else's gospel?

*According to my gospel, God will judge the secrets of
men through the Messiah Yeshua.* (Romans 2:16)

*Now to Him who is able to establish you according to my gospel
and the preaching of Yeshua the Messiah.* (Romans 16:25)

*Remember Yeshua the Messiah, risen from the dead, descendant
of David, according to my gospel.* (2 Timothy 2:8)

## A The Gentile Inclusion

*That by revelation there was made known to me the mystery … the mystery of Messiah, which in other generations was not made known to the sons of men, as it has now been revealed to His holy apostles and prophets in the Spirit; to be specific, that the Gentiles are fellow heirs and fellow members of the body, and fellow partakers of the promise in Messiah Yeshua through the gospel, of which I was made a minister, according to the gift of God's grace which was given to me according to the working of His power.* (Ephesians 3:3–7)

What made Paul's message of the gospel unique?

inclusion of gentils

## B An Unpopular Message

Not only was this an unpopular message with the Jewish people, it was not a popular message with the Jewish believers in Yeshua either. Most of the other Jewish believers thought that if Gentiles wanted to become believers and part of the religion, they needed to convert to Judaism.

# The Argument in Antioch

*Some men came down from Judea and began teaching the brethren, "Unless you are circumcised according to the custom of Moses, you cannot be saved." And when Paul and Barnabas had great dissension and debate with them, the brethren determined that Paul and Barnabas and some others of them should go up to Jerusalem to the apostles and elders concerning this issue.* (Acts 15:1–2)

## A The Challenge

Jewish believers from Jerusalem charged that for a Gentile to be saved, he had to be "circumcised according to the custom of Moses" (Acts 15:1).

"To be saved, you must be Jewish."

## B Dissension and Debate

Paul argued that Gentiles did not need to go through conversion and become Jewish before they could be saved. He believed that God could save both Jews and Gentiles, and that Gentiles needed only to have faith in Yeshua for salvation.

**Key Verses**

Ephesians 3:3–7
Acts 15:1–2
Galatians 2:11–14

**Your Israel Connection**

**The Argument in Antioch**

*Jewish Quarter, Old City Jerusalem* – The Jewish Quarter of Jerusalem's old city was seized during the Arab-Israeli war of 1948. The Jewish residents were forced out and the area was demolished. It remained in Jordanian control until its liberation during the Six-Day War of 1967. Today, tourists can visit, purchase Judaica, and eat falafels.

**Refer to Resource**

*HaYesod Student Workbook*
"The Offense of the Cross"
Pages 6.24–6.26

**Key Verses**

Acts 15:1
Acts 15:5
Acts 15:8–11
Amos 9:11–12
Acts 15:16–21

# Jerusalem Council

Jewish opinion was that only Jews had a place in the world-to-come since God had made the covenant of blessing with Israel and no other nation. A Gentile could secure a place in the world-to-come only by becoming a Jew. Paul and Barnabas were of the opinion that salvation had been extended to the Gentiles through faith in Yeshua alone. To settle the matter, Paul brought the question to James and the court of the apostles in Jerusalem.

| Overview of Jerusalem Council | |
| --- | --- |
| **The Original Question** | Must the Gentiles become Jewish (circumcised) in order to be saved? (Acts 15:1) |
| **The Charge** | The Gentiles must become Jewish (circumcised) and be required to obey the Torah of Moses in order to be saved. (Acts 15:5) |
| **The Rebuttal** | Why do you put God to the test by placing upon the neck of the disciples a yoke which neither our fathers nor we have been able to bear? But we believe that we are saved through the grace of the Lord Yeshua, in the same way as they also are. (Acts 15:8–11) |
| **The Proof Text** | Amos 9:11–12 (David's Fallen Tabernacle) (Acts 15:16–18) |
| **The Decision** | Therefore it is my judgment that we do not trouble those who are turning to God from among the Gentiles, but that we write to them that they abstain from things contaminated by idols and from fornication and from what is strangled and from blood. (Acts 15:19–20) |
| **The Explanation of the Decision** | For Moses from ancient generations has in every city those who preach him, since he is read in the synagogues every Sabbath. (Acts 15:21) |

## Ⓐ Council of the Elders

The Council of Elders consisted of all the survivors among the Master's disciples. This believer's version of the Sanhedrin was presided over by James the Righteous, the brother of Yeshua.

## Ⓑ The Formal Charge

The Gentiles must be circumcised (become Jewish) and required to obey the Torah of Moses in order to be saved:

*Some of the sect of the Pharisees who had believed stood up, saying, "It is necessary to circumcise them and to direct them to observe the [Torah] of Moses."* (Acts 15:5)

Peter's rebuttal

## C  Peter's Rebuttal

Jews and Gentiles are both saved by grace, not by keeping the Torah or being Jewish.

*Brethren, you know that in the early days God made a choice among you, that by my mouth the Gentiles would hear the word of the gospel and believe. And God, who knows the heart, testified to them giving them the Holy Spirit, just as He also did to us; and He made no distinction between us and them, cleansing their hearts by faith. Now therefore why do you put God to the test by placing upon the neck of the disciples a yoke which neither our fathers nor we have been able to bear? But we believe that we are saved through the grace of the Lord Jesus, in the same way as they also are.* (Acts 15:7–11)

## D  James' Proof Text

*After these things I will return, and I will rebuild the tabernacle of David which has fallen, and I will rebuild its ruins, and I will restore it, so that the rest of mankind may seek the LORD, and all the Gentiles who are called by my name.* (Acts 15:16–17; quoting the LXX of Amos 9:11–12)

**Refer to Resource**

*Boundary Stones*
"Divine Invitation: The Spiritual Life of a Gentile"
Pages 93–99

James' proof text

*if you dont believe me the first time I say it then why do you ask*

*Rav Nahman said to Rabbi Isaac: "Have you heard when [Bar-Nafli] The Son of the Fallen will come?" "Who is [Bar-Nafli] The Son of the Fallen?" he asked. "Messiah," he answered. "Why do you call Messiah [Bar-Nafli] 'The Son of the Fallen'?" "Because," he answered, "It is written [in Amos 9:11], 'in that day I will raise up the fallen tabernacle of David.'"* (b.Sanhedrin 96b–97a)

The "tabernacle of David which has fallen" refers to the Davidic throne and Messiah, the Davidic king.

The Amos 9 prophecy clearly speaks of God-seeking Gentiles in the days of Messiah. Therefore, in the days of Messiah, there must be both Jews and Gentiles—an impossibility if all Gentiles are forced to be circumcised and become Jewish.

## **E** The Decision

*It is my judgment that we do not trouble those who are turning to God from among the Gentiles.* (Acts 15:19)

Gentiles should not be required to become Jewish or even Torah observant as a prerequisite for salvation.

**Refer to Resource**

*Grafted In*
"David's Fallen Sukkah"
Pages 105–114

## **F** The Four Essentials

*It seemed good to the Holy Spirit and to us to lay upon you no greater burden than these essentials: that you abstain from things sacrificed to idols and from blood and from things strangled and from fornication; if you keep yourselves free from such things, you will do well.* (Acts 15:28–29)

The Gentile believers are to abstain from:

1. *Things sacrificed to idols*
   (Exodus 34:15–16)

2. *Blood*
   (Genesis 9:4; Leviticus 17:10–14)

3. *things strangled*
   (Genesis 9:4; Exodus 22:31; Leviticus 17:15; Deuteronomy 12:15–16)

4. *Fornication*
   (Leviticus 18; Deuteronomy 22:20–24)

**Key Verses**

Exodus 34:15–16
Genesis 9:4
Leviticus 17:10–15
Exodus 22:31
Deuteronomy 12:15–16
Leviticus 18
Deuteronomy 22:20–24
Acts 15:21
Acts 21

## Ⓖ The Rest of the Torah

*For Moses from ancient generations has in every city those who preach him, since he is read in the synagogues every Sabbath.*
(Acts 15:21)

At the time of the Jerusalem council, Jewish and Gentile believers were still assembling in the local synagogue every Shabbat. And in those synagogues, the Torah was read every week.

**Your Israel Connection**

**Paul in Caesarea**

*Caesarea Maritima , Mediterranean Coast* – In the days of the apostles, Caesarea was the Roman capital of Judea from which Roman officials like Pilate, Felix, and Festus administered the government. It was a harbor city built by Herod the Great to rival the great cities of the classical world. In the apostolic era, it was a home to Cornelius the centurion and Philip the deacon. Paul was held under arrest for over two years in Caesarea.

The decision

*Paul has thus, wrongly, I believe, been seen as disregarding the Law and customs of his Jewish past as he developed entirely new, Christian solutions. He has, mistakenly, been made the creator of a Gentile Christianity that rejected Judaism and the Law as operative, rather than the champion of the restoration of Israel who fought for the inclusion of "righteous gentiles" in this new community as equals … as understood by James and the Council.* (Mark Nanos, *The Mystery of Romans*)[2]

# Paul on Trial

| | Scripture | Venue | Accusation | Paul's Defense |
|---|---|---|---|---|
| 1. | Acts 22 | Temple | Anti jewish, torah, temple | Jew gamliels stud. torah obse prays in temp |
| 2. | Acts 23 | sanhedrin | | good conscience before god  I am pharisee |
| 3. | Acts 24 | court of felix | Trouble maker descrat ing temple | non trouble maker nonors temple believes torah |
| 4. | Acts 25 | court of festis | false alligations | no off against torah temple roma |
| 5. | Acts 26 | court of Agrippa | — | teaches nothing but prophet torah |
| 6. | Acts 28 | Roman — Jewish community | | Nothing against jews or customs |

Can I shave your legs + w/ the hair make a blanket?

## Ⓐ In the Temple

❖ Acts 22

**Key Verses**

Acts 22
Acts 21:28
Acts 23

An angry mob attempted to accost Paul on the charges that he was anti-Jewish, anti-Torah, and anti-Temple:

*This is the man who preaches to all men everywhere against our people and the Law and this place.* (Acts 21:28)

Paul replied that he was a Jew, Gamaliel's student, Torah observant, and prayed in the Temple.

*I am a Jew, born in Tarsus of Cilicia, but brought up in this city, educated under Gamaliel, strictly according to the law of our fathers, being zealous for God just as you all are today.* (Acts 22:3)

Paul on trial

## Ⓑ Before the Sanhedrin

❖ Acts 23

Paul stood trial before the Sanhedrin on the charge that he is anti-Jewish, anti-Torah, and anti-Temple.

*Brethren, I have lived my life with a perfectly good conscience before God up to this day.* (Acts 23:1)

Paul replied that he kept Torah with good conscience before God and was a Pharisee.

*Brethren, I am a Pharisee, a son of Pharisees; I am on trial for the hope and resurrection of the dead!* (Acts 23:6)

**Refer to Resource**

*Torah Club Volume Four: The Good News of Messiah*
"Ha'azinu: Give Ear"

## ❶ Before Felix

❖ Acts 24

Paul stood trial before Felix on the charges that he was a troublemaker, disturbing the peace, and desecrating the Temple.

*For we have found this man a real pest and a fellow who stirs up dissension among all the Jews throughout the world, and a ringleader of the sect of the Nazarenes. And he even tried to desecrate the temple; and then we arrested him.* (Acts 24:5–6)

*I went up to Jerusalem to worship. Neither in the temple, nor in the synagogues, nor in the city itself did they find me carrying on a discussion with anyone or causing a riot. Nor can they prove to you the charges of which they now accuse me. But this I admit to you, that according to the Way which they call a sect I do serve the God of our fathers, believing everything that is in accordance with the [Torah] and that is written in the Prophets … I came to bring alms to my nation and to present offerings; in which they found me occupied in the temple, having been purified, without any crowd or uproar.* (Acts 24:11–18)

Paul replied that he does not stir up riots, he believes everything in the Torah, and he came to Jerusalem to offer sacrifices in the Temple, not defile it.

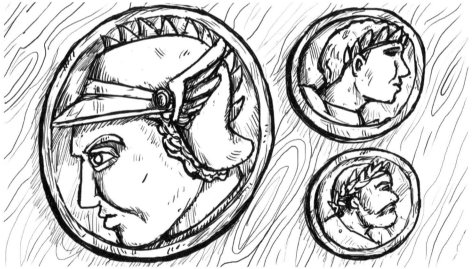

Roman coins

## D   Before Festus

**Key Verses**
Acts 25
Acts 26
Acts 28

❖   Acts 25

Paul stood trial before Festus on the serious and unproven charges simi-lar to those brought to Felix.

*After Paul arrived, the Jews who had come down from Jerusalem stood around him, bringing many and serious charges against him which they could not prove.* (Acts 25:7)

Paul replied that he had not broken the Torah or Roman law.

*I have committed no offense either against the [Torah] of the Jews or against the temple or against Caesar.* (Acts 25:8)

## E   Before Agrippa

❖   Acts 26

Paul testified before Agrippa and Bernice that his teaching was consistent with Torah.

*So, having obtained help from God, I stand to this day testifying both to small and great, stating nothing but what the Prophets and Moses said was going to take place.* (Acts 26:22)

King Agrippa declared that Paul had not broken Torah, Jewish law, or Roman law.

*This man is not doing anything worthy of death or imprisonment … This man might have been set free if he had not appealed to Caesar.* (Acts 26:31–32)

## F   Before the Jewish Community of Rome

❖   Acts 28

Paul testified before the Jewish community in Rome that he had not even broken the "customs of our fathers," that is, the oral traditions of Torah.

*I had done nothing against our people or the customs of our fathers.* (Acts 28:17)

**Refer to Resource**

*Restoration*
"Paul and the Torah"
Pages 147–158

## Endnotes

1   Mark Nanos, *The Mystery of Romans: The Jewish Context of Paul's Letters* (Minneapolis: Fortress Press, 1996), 9.

2   Ibid., 175.

# Lesson Six
# LESSON SUMMARY

## First …

We acknowledged that our interpretation of Paul and his message shapes our religious identity, so we took a look at Saul of Tarsus through his own autobiographical remarks.

- ❖ We learned that he was a native-born Jew of the tribe of Benjamin.
- ❖ He was a disciple of the famous Rabbi Gamaliel and a Pharisee.
- ❖ He was zealous for Torah and faultless in his observance.

## Then …

We learned that Saul's name was not changed to Paul on the road to Damascus, and he did not forsake Judaism and Torah after becoming a believer.

## After that …

We followed the story of his last trip to Jerusalem and saw that:

- ❖ There were already rumors about Paul that he taught against Torah.
- ❖ Paul brought sacrifices to the Temple to dispel those rumors.
- ❖ The other apostles testified that Paul walked according to the Torah.

## Next …

We looked into the context of Paul's arguments and discovered that he was the champion of an unpopular doctrine: Gentile inclusion in the kingdom. We followed Paul to the Jerusalem Council of Acts 15 where the apostles decided that:

- ❖ Gentiles do not need to become Jewish to be saved.
- ❖ Gentiles are required to keep four essential standards.
- ❖ The rest of the Torah is open to Gentiles, and is taught in the synagogue every week.

## Finally …

We followed Paul through six trials to hear his own testimony in defense of himself and his message. In every instance Paul insisted that:

- ❖ He had done nothing against Roman law.
- ❖ He had done nothing against Torah law.
- ❖ He taught only what the Torah taught.
- ❖ He was a Pharisee.
- ❖ He kept the traditions of the fathers.

# Lesson Six
## LESSON REVIEW – Q&A

1. What are some of Paul's credentials? Did Paul cease to be Jewish or Torah observant after becoming a believer? Did Yeshua change Saul's name to Paul on the road to Damascus?

2. What are the six beliefs of the Pharisees? Do you agree with the beliefs of the Pharisees?

3. In Acts 21, what were the false allegations that the Jewish believers in Jerusalem had heard about Paul? How did Paul refute those charges?

4. What made "Paul's gospel" unique?

5. What was the argument in Antioch that led to the Jerusalem Council of Acts 15?

6. What were the four essentials that the apostles required of the Gentile believers? Do those four essentials replace the whole Torah for Gentile believers?

7. What was Paul charged with when he stood before the crowd in the Temple, before the Sanhedrin, before Felix, Festus, and Agrippa, and before the Jewish community in Rome? How did Paul answer those charges?

8. Did Paul convert out of Judaism to become a Christian? Did he quit being Jewish or keeping Torah after becoming a believer?

# Lesson Six
# EXTRA CREDIT
### SUPPLEMENTAL MATERIAL FOR THIS HAYESOD LESSON

## In His Own Words: Paul's Opinion About Torah

In this week's lesson, we have seen that Paul remained a faithful, Torah-keeping Jew, even after becoming a believer. However, his writings are often cited as evidence that Paul taught against the Torah. Let's take a look at some of Paul's statements about the Torah from his own words. Paul's own words on the subject indicate his high regard for Torah.

1. Romans 2:13 – According to Paul, who is justified before God?

2. Romans 3:31– Does faith nullify the Torah? What effect does faith have on the Torah?

3. Romans 7:12 – What three words does Paul use to describe the Torah?

4. Romans 7:14 – How does Paul describe the Torah?

5. Romans 7:22 – What did Paul joyfully concur with in his inner man?

6. 1 Corinthians 7:19 – What really matters as the important thing?

7. 1 Timothy 1:8 – What does Paul say about the Torah so long as it is used lawfully?

8. 1 Timothy 6:14 – The term "the commandment" is a synonym for the whole Torah. How does Paul instruct Timothy to keep "the commandment"?

# THE OFFENSE OF THE CROSS

ADDITIONAL NOTES, QUOTES, AND SOURCES

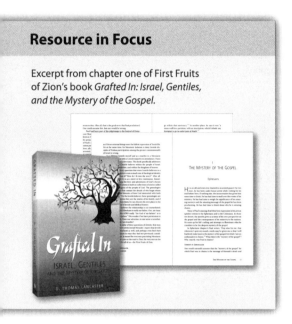

**Resource in Focus**

Excerpt from chapter one of First Fruits of Zion's book *Grafted In: Israel, Gentiles, and the Mystery of the Gospel.*

## Circumcision and the Offense of the Cross

*Brothers, if I am still preaching circumcision, why am I still being persecuted? In that case the offense of the cross has been abolished.* (Galatians 5:11, NIV)

The Gentile inclusion in Israel through the Messiah of Israel was the real offense of the gospel to Jewish ears. Paul understood this well. In Galatians 5:11 he made that plain enough by pointing out that if circumcision was a prerequisite to salvation, then "the offense of the cross has been abolished." What is the offense of the cross? From Paul's perspective in Galatians, the offense of the cross is Gentile inclusion in Israel.

Paul's mission to the Gentiles began to raise trouble for him even before he referred to himself as the apostle to the nations. As early as Acts 13, we learn that Paul's inclusive attitude toward Gentiles is going to cause problems. Acts 13 tells the story of Paul and Barnabas attending a synagogue service in the province of Galatia—in the city of Pisidian-Antioch. After the reading from the Torah and the Prophets, the synagogue officials invited Paul, the visiting rabbi from Jerusalem, to present a teaching. Paul stood up and delivered a stirring defense of the Messianic faith in Yeshua. The congregation received the sermon well. The book of Acts tells us, "The people invited them to speak further about these things on the next Sabbath. When the congregation was dismissed, many of the Jews and devout converts to Judaism followed Paul and Barnabas, who talked with them and urged them to continue in the grace of God."[1] Not what we would expect. Here was a synagogue full of Jewish people warmly accepting the message of the gospel and even inviting the speaker to return the next Sabbath and speak more on the topic.

However, others were in attendance as well. As Paul began his address he said, "Brothers, sons of Abraham, and you God-fearing Gentiles, it is to us that this message of salvation has been sent."[2] The threefold address refers to the three types of people one might find in any diaspora synagogue of the first century.

1. "Brothers" are Jews: In the context of the Pisidian-Antioch synagogue, Paul's brothers were his fellow Jews. He means to refer to those who are ethnically Jewish, born Jewish as physical descendants of Abraham, Isaac, and Jacob. In the first century, the word "Jew" did not specifically mean someone from the tribe of Judah. It was used as a broad designation to refer to any natural-born Israelite. Thus, Paul referred to himself as Jewish, though he was in actuality a Benjamite. The Jews, Paul's brothers, are the physical descendants of Israel.

2. "Sons of Abraham" are proselytes: The second type of congregant Paul found in the Pisidian-Antioch synagogue was the proselyte. They were Gentiles who had, for one reason or another, decided to make a formal, legal conversion to Judaism. According to the legal opinion of the rabbis, Gentiles who underwent ritual conversion were no longer regarded as Gentiles. Through the rituals

of circumcision and immersion (and sacrifice at the Temple when possible), they had been reborn as "sons of Abraham." Henceforth, they had legal Jewish status.

3. "God-fearing Gentiles" are non-Jews: The third type of congregant Paul addressed that day in the Pisidian-Antioch synagogue was the God-fearing Gentile. The term "God-fearing Gentiles" describes non-Jews who, for some reason or another, were attracted to Judaism. They worshipped in the synagogue with Jews and proselytes but chose not to undergo the ritual of conversion. They weren't exactly pagans anymore, but they were certainly not Jews. While they may have been tolerated in the synagogue, and even appreciated for their financial contributions to the community (as with the centurions in Luke 7 and Acts 10), they were not regarded as Jews. They did not enjoy the rights, privileges, and responsibilities of Judaism.

As Paul presented the good news of the gospel to the Pisidian-Antioch synagogue, he included all three types of people in his address. He declared, "Brothers, children of Abraham, and you God-fearing Gentiles, it is to us that this message of salvation has been sent."[3] His message was well received by the Jews and proselytes of the synagogue, and they invited him to speak again the subsequent Sabbath. As it turned out, however, the God-fearing Gentiles received the message even more enthusiastically. After all, Paul had included them in the good news. Salvation had been sent to them as well as to the Jews and converts.

Paul's gospel gave the God-fearing Gentiles status in the Jewish community without requiring them to become Jewish through legal conversion. According to Paul's gospel, the God-fearing Gentiles were sons of Abraham by merit of faith in Yeshua, and they could be regarded as brothers with the Jewish people. It was a provocative message. Word spread rapidly. By the time the next Sabbath arrived, "almost the whole city gathered to hear the word of the Lord."[4] The synagogue was packed out—standing-room only—filled with Gentiles.

A Gentile majority in the synagogue was a serious threat to the integrity of the Jewish community's identity. Jewish identity was precarious enough in the face of Hellenist society. The mainstream culture was always chipping away at the particulars of Jewish monotheism and Torah observance. A Gentile presence almost certainly would accelerate the tendency toward assimilation. Besides, it was annoying.

Jews were, after all, the chosen people. It was their synagogue. Crowding just about every Gentile in the city into the synagogue created both a practical nuisance ("Hey, that guy's sitting in my seat!") and a theological conundrum. (If everyone is God's chosen people, then being chosen loses its significance.)

Luke tells us, "When the Jews saw the crowds, they were filled with jealousy and talked abusively against what Paul was saying."[5] They were filled with jealousy. They were not jealous because they had never been able to raise such large crowds. (The synagogues were not about the business of trying to bring in big numbers. They were not "evangelical" as we would understand the term.) They were not jealous that Paul and Barnabas had such appeal or that their message seemed to be so popular. They were jealous that the message of the gospel was compromising the particularity of their theology. The message of the gospel was throwing the doors of Judaism wide open to the Gentile world. The religion that had previously been a members-only club was suddenly declared open to the public, no table reservations necessary. Paul and Barnabas shrugged off the Jewish objections and continued to teach and minister to the new Gentile believers. But eventually, pressure from the Jewish community forced them out of Pisidian-Antioch.

The message of the gospel itself raised no objections from the Galatian Jewish community. On the contrary, they listened eagerly and wanted to hear more. The message of Messiah's death, burial, and resurrection, and the justification and salvation available through Him, sounded good to their ears. They found no offense in the cross. There was really nothing "un-Jewish" or objectionable about the message of salvation in Yeshua.

Not until they saw the Gentiles crowding into the synagogue did they raise their objections. Not until they realized how this "good news" compromised the exclusive character of Judaism did they reject Paul's message. To the Jewish community of Galatia, the offense of the cross was the inclusion of the Gentiles.

This was a pattern Paul would see repeated over and over in city after city. In Thessalonica, the same problem emerged. Popular success at the synagogue was followed by the conversion of "a large number of God-fearing Greeks and not a few prominent women. But the Jews were jealous."[6] Everywhere Paul went, Gentiles flocked to the synagogue to hear him speak. All over Asia Minor Paul found Gentiles eager to hear the message of the gospel and Jews eager to be rid of that same message, not because of theological objections about Yeshua but because they objected to the inclusion of Gentiles in their faith, religion, and synagogue.

### Endnotes

1   Acts 13:42–43.
2   Acts 13:26.
3   Acts 13:26.
4   Acts 13:44.
5   Acts 13:45.
6   Acts 17:4–5.

# Lesson Six – Digging Deeper
# Paul's Nazirite Vow
### Further Study from this Week's HaYesod Lesson

## Paul the Nazirite

Paul took a Nazirite vow (see Acts 18:18). It has not always been recognized as a Nazirite vow because rather than saying, "He let his hair grow long," the text says, "He had his hair cut for he was keeping a vow." We would assume that if he were taking a Nazirite vow, he would not have his hair cut. This mistake may stem from a misunderstanding of the meaning of the Nazirite's hair.

The hair of the Nazirite, both symbolically and literally, represented the amount of time the Nazirite spent under the vow. When the term of the Nazirite's vow was completed, he cut his hair and burned it in the Temple. Burning the hair was a gesture symbolizing that the Nazirite was offering up to God the amount of time he had dedicated to the LORD as a Nazirite. If he had been a Nazirite for only a few months, the length of hair would represent only a few month's growth. If he had been a Nazirite for several years, it would have been several feet of hair. In order for the length of hair to accurately represent the term of the vow, the vow must begin with a shaved head. Acts 18:18 may be an indication that Paul had his hair cut in order to take a Nazirite vow.

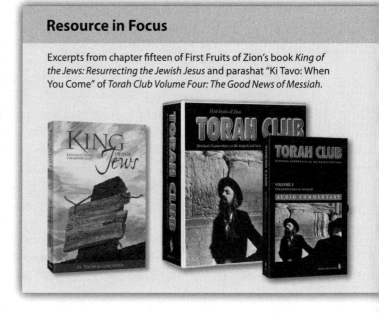

**Resource in Focus**

Excerpts from chapter fifteen of First Fruits of Zion's book *King of the Jews: Resurrecting the Jewish Jesus* and parashat "Ki Tavo: When You Come" of *Torah Club Volume Four: The Good News of Messiah*.

Another possibility is that Paul completed the term of his vow while in the Diaspora. Because a Nazirite vow can only be fulfilled at the Temple, the sages say that one who completes a Nazirite vow outside the land of Israel must repeat the vow within the land of Israel.

> One who made a Nazirite vow and completed his Nazirite term and afterwards came to the Land … must be a Nazirite all over again. It once happened that Queen Helene, whose son went to war, said, "If my son return safely from the war, I will be a Nazirite for seven years." And at the conclusion of the seven years she came up to the Land, and the School of Hillel instructed her that she had to be a Nazirite again for seven years more. (m.*Nazir* 3:6)

Perhaps in Acts 18 we see Paul completing a personal Nazirite vow before going on to Jerusalem, where he intends to formally undergo the vow again under the auspices of the priesthood.

A third possibility is that Paul became ritually unclean through corpse contamination during the course of the vow, so he shaved his head until he could return to Jerusalem for purification and to offer the sin offering and burnt offering that are required for such an instance. If the vow was inadvertently broken through contamination via a dead body, Numbers 6:9–12 mandates that the defiled Nazirite shave his head and start the vow over from the beginning of the term he had chosen.

Regardless of which situation Paul was in, the terms of the Nazirite vow required him to return to Jerusalem and the Temple to make the necessary sacrifices and to have his hair shaved in the Temple.

Once he arrived in Jerusalem (see Acts 21), he joined four more believers who had also taken Nazirite vows, and they all went to the Temple together for haircuts and sacrifices.[1]

## Nazirite among the Nazirites

Apparently it was a common problem for Nazirites to finish the term of their vows without the means to purchase the necessary sacrifices. James the Righteous had four Nazirite believers in the community who could not pay their own expenses to complete their vow. In the days when Alexander Yannai was king with his wife Salome Alexandra, Salome's brother Shimon ben Shetach had a similar problem.

> Three hundred Nazirites came up in the days of Shimon ben Shetach. [None of them could afford the sacrifices to fulfill their vows.] For one hundred and fifty he found legal grounds for dismissing their vow, but for the other hundred and fifty he could find no legal grounds. Therefore he went to King Yannai and said to him, "Three hundred Nazirites have come up to Jerusalem and they require nine hundred sacrifices in order to fulfill their vows. If you will provide for half of them, I will provide for half of them." Yannai did so, but a talebearer went and informed him that Shimon had not spent a single coin. When Shimon heard this he fled… [Sometime later King Yannai demanded,] "Why did you fool me?" "God forbid! I did not fool you. You gave from your wealth [money] while I gave from my wealth [Torah knowledge]. (Genesis Rabbah 91:3)

In an effort to prove his commitment to Torah obedience, Paul agreed to pay the expenses for the other four Nazirites who had finished their terms. Assuming that the vows were complete for the five of them,[2] the amount to be purchased and sacrificed would have been exorbitant.

**Expenses for Five Nazirites Completing Their Vows**
*Numbers 6:13–21*

| Item | Sacrifice |
| --- | --- |
| 5 unblemished yearling lambs | Burnt Offerings |
| 5 unblemished yearling ewe lambs | Sin Offerings |
| 5 unblemished rams | Fellowship Offerings |
| 33 liters (nearly 2 bushels) of fine flour mixed with oil | Supplementary Grain Offerings |
| 8 liters (2 gallons) of wine | Wine libations |
| 5 additional baskets of unleavened bread with oil | Grain Offerings |

In addition to the significant expense involved, we should also note that Paul was willingly participating in the sacrificial service of the Jerusalem Temple, offering no less than fifteen different animal sacrifices. If there was ever any truth to the idea that Yeshua's death abolished the sacrificial system, no one told Paul.

## Paul: All Things to All Men?

Had Paul wanted to make a theological statement about Grace vs. Torah, Acts 21 would have been the time to do it. Instead he consented to go through with the plan to prove himself Torah obedient.

Some have suggested that Paul agreed to the plan as part of ruse to convince the Jewish believers that he was still Torah observant, but in actuality, he was not. Such disingenuousness, it is claimed, is evidenced in his policy to "be all things to all men."

> To the Jews I became as a Jew, so that I might win Jews; to those who are under the Torah, as under the Torah though not being myself under the Torah, so that I might win those who are under the Torah; to those who are without Torah, as without Torah, though not being without the Torah of God but under the Torah of Messiah, so that I might win those who are without Torah. To the weak I became weak, that I might win the weak; I have become all things to all men, so that I may by all means save some. (1 Corinthians 9:20–22)

It is unfair to suppose that the Apostle Paul was such a poser and pretender that he put on a face of Torah observance when in Jerusalem, yet when in disaspora and among Gentiles he disregarded Torah. Is that really what he suggests we do? Does he mean that we should pretend to wield religious convictions we do not hold when it is convenient for us to do so? Of course not. In 1 Corinthians 9:20–22, Paul is simply pointing out that one needs to be aware of the context when communicating the gospel. Therefore when among Jewish people he can argue Torah to prove Messiah, but when among Greeks (as in Athens) he argues Messiah from a philosophical approach. It does no good to quote Bible verses at someone who does not know of or believe in the authority of the Bible.

In the above-quoted passage, Paul himself clearly states, "I am not free from God's Torah but am under Messiah's Torah." This is not to suggest that Messiah has some different Torah, but it is to understand the New Covenant is revealed in the Torah of Moses.

There is really no way around Acts 21. Paul meant to pay for the Nazirites to demonstrate that he lived in obedience to Torah and never taught contrary to Torah observance. Any seemingly contrary statements from his epistles must be weighed against Acts 21.

## Endnotes

1   Those who argue that his vow was not a Nazirite vow do so out of reluctance to see Paul bringing a lamb, a ewe, and a ram as a burnt offering, a sin offering, and a peace offering. New Testament commentators typically indicate that Paul is exercising his principle of "being all things to all men" (1 Corinthians 9:22) by participating in the vow. Those who propound that the apostle would make such a disingenuous and hypocritical pretense are ignoring the fact that Paul took the vow in Acts 18 long before coming under the pressure of James and the Jerusalem believers.

2   It is also possible that the five of them had all broken vows through corpse contamination, in which case, Paul would have been liable for a total of ten bird offerings for sin offerings and burnt offerings and five lambs for guilt offerings. This would explain the seven-day purification process.

**Notes:**

# HaYesod
## THE FOUNDATION

Lesson Seven
# OUR MAIL–
# HIS LETTERS

THE LAND, THE PEOPLE,
AND THE SCRIPTURES OF ISRAEL

# Lesson Seven
# OUR MAIL—HIS LETTERS

*Our beloved brother Paul, according to the wisdom given him, wrote to you, as also in all his letters, speaking in them of these things, in which are some things hard to understand, which the untaught and unstable distort, as they do also the rest of the Scriptures, to their own destruction.* (2 Peter 3:15–16)

## Lesson Overview

In last week's HaYesod lesson we learned that Paul of Tarsus was not an apostate from Judaism but lived a life of faithful adherence to the Torah even after becoming a believer. Many believers today might consider living in obedience to God's commandments if not for the writings of Paul. It is widely believed that Paul discouraged believers from practicing Torah and that he warned us from "going under the Law" and "falling from grace." But if that is really true, then Paul's writings hopelessly contradict what we know about Paul himself. This week we will examine a sampling of Pauline passages that have traditionally been interpreted as anti-Torah and anti-Jewish. We hope that we will be able to unravel these misunderstood passages to discover the true message of the Apostle Paul.

## Lesson Purpose

Here are the main points that you can expect to learn in this lesson:
- ❖ Learn key principles for reading the epistles of Paul.
- ❖ Dispel misunderstandings about several of Paul's teachings.
- ❖ Discover the true message of Paul's letters.
- ❖ Find encouragement from Paul's letters for your connection to the Land, the People, and the Scriptures of Israel.

## Field Trips to the Holy Land

- ❖ Tel Beersheva, Negev Region
- ❖ Southern Wall, Jerusalem Temple Mount
- ❖ Southern Steps, Jerusalem Temple Mount
- ❖ Caesarea Maritima, Mediterranean Coast

## Paul's Misunderstood Writings

A. Hard to Understand

B. Three Principles for Reading Paul

## Romans 7:1–14: The Law of Sin and Death

A. The Problem

B. The Context of Romans

C. The Context of the Passage

D. Dead to Sin

E. A Metaphor from Marriage

F. Is the Law Sin?

G. Holy, Righteous, and Good

H. Making Sense of the Analogy

I. Summary Romans 7:1–14

## Galatians 4:21–26: The Two Mothers

A. The Context of Galatians

B. Two Covenants in Galatians

C. Sons of Abraham

D. Paul's Midrash

E. Making Sense of the Midrash

F. Summary of Galatians 4:21–26

## Galatians 5: Circumcision and Uncircumcision

A. Galatians 5:1–6

B. 1 Corinthians 7:19

C. Romans 2:25–29

D. Galatians 5:1–6 Summary

## Ephesians 2:13–22: Dividing Wall of Partition

A. Ephesians 2:4–16

B. Ephesians 2:4–16 Summary

## Colossians 2:13–17: Canceling the Torah

A. Nailing the Torah to the Cross?

B. Summary Colossians 2:13–17

## Romans 14: Diet and Sabbath

A. The Strong and the Weak

B. The Sabbath Day

C. Akathartos vs. Koinos

D. Pagan Festival Days

E. Summary Romans 14

# Paul's Misunderstood Writings

Even the Apostle Peter admits that Paul's epistles contain some things which are difficult to understand.

*Our beloved brother Paul, according to the wisdom given him, wrote to you, as also in all his letters, speaking in them of these things, in which are some things hard to understand, which the untaught and unstable distort, as they do also the rest of the Scriptures, to their own destruction.*
(2 Peter 3:15–16)

## Ⓐ Hard to Understand

Several passages from the Pauline writings have been historically misunderstood as anti-Torah.

## Ⓑ Three Principles for Reading Paul ✎

1. Scripture does not contradict itself
2. Must be read in context
3. Paul was torah observant

# Romans 7:1–14: The Law of Sin and Death

Romans 7:1–14 is often misunderstood to mean that we have died to the Torah.

## Ⓐ The Problem

*You also were made to die to the Law through the body of Messiah.* (Romans 7:4)

*But now we have been released from the Law, having died to that by which we were bound, so that we serve in newness of the Spirit and not in oldness of the letter.* (Romans 7:6)

## Ⓑ The Context of Romans

Romans is written to a mixed community of Jewish and Gentile believers. The Gentile believers were "God-Fearers." A God-fearer was a Gentile who worshipped God but had not formally converted to Judaism.

## God-fearer (θεοσεβης) = a Gentile worshipper of God

**Key Verses**

Romans 5–8

**Key Words**

*Theosebes:* lit. "God-fearer." Greek word denoting a Gentile who had not gone through a formal conversion to become legally Jewish, but was nonetheless a worshipper of the God of Israel and participating in the local Jewish community.

*The Christians were not yet clearly distinguished from the wider Jewish community … they would meet presumably as a collegium or under the auspices of a synagogue.* (James Dunn, *Word Biblical Commentary*)[1]

## **C** The Context of the Passage

Romans 7 specifically falls into the larger context of Romans chapters 5–8, where Paul is making his argument about justification: salvation by grace through faith.

Freed from sin and enslaved to God:

*But now having been freed from sin and enslaved to God, you derive your benefit, resulting in sanctification, and the outcome, eternal life. For the wages of sin is death, but the free gift of God is eternal life in the Messiah Yeshua our Lord.* (Romans 6:22–23)

## **D** Dead to Sin

*Or do you not know, brethren (for I am speaking to those who know the [Torah]), that the [Torah] has <u>jurisdiction over a person as long as he lives</u>?* (Romans 7:1)

## Torah's "jurisdiction over a person" = the punishment for sin, i.e., death

Dead to sin

## E  A Metaphor from Marriage

*For the married woman is bound by law to her husband while he is living; but if her husband dies, she is released from the law concerning the husband. So then, if while her husband is living she is joined to another man, she shall be called an adulteress; but if her husband dies, she is free from the law, so that she is not an adulteress though she is joined to another man. Therefore, my brethren, you also were made to die to the Law through the body of Christ, so that you might be joined to another, to Him who was raised from the dead, in order that we might bear fruit for God.* (Romans 7:2–4)

When Paul says that we were "made to die to the Law through the body of Christ," he means that we are no longer under the Torah's condemnation of our sin.

## F  Is the Law Sin?

*For while we were in the flesh, the sinful passions, which were aroused by the Law, were at work in the members of our body to bear fruit for death. But now we have been released from the Law, having died to that by which we were bound, so that we serve in newness of the Spirit and not in oldness of the letter.* (Romans 7:5–6)

The problem is not the laws of the Torah. The problem is sin.

*What shall we say then? Is the Law sin? May it never be! On the contrary, I would not have come to know sin except through the Law; for I would not have known about coveting if the Law had not said, "You shall not covet." But sin, taking opportunity through the commandment, produced in me coveting of every kind; for apart from the Law sin is dead. I was once alive apart from the Law; but when the commandment came, sin became alive and I died; and this commandment, which was to result in life, proved to result in death for me; for sin, taking an opportunity through the commandment, deceived me and through it killed me.* (Romans 7:7–11; quoting Deuteronomy 5:21)

## G  Holy, Righteous, and Good  ✍

*So then, the Law [Torah] is holy, and the commandment is holy and righteous and good. Therefore did that which is good become a cause of death for me? May it never be! Rather it was sin, in order that it might be shown to be sin by effecting my death through that which is good, so that through the commandment sin would become utterly sinful. For we know that the Law [Torah] is spiritual, but I am of flesh, sold into bondage to sin.* (Romans 7:12–14)

The Torah is:

**Key Verses**

Romans 7:1–14

1. _holy_
2. _righteous_
3. _good_
4. _spiritual_

**H** **Making Sense of the Analogy** 🖋

1. Married Woman = _the unbeliever_
2. Widowed Woman = _the believer_
3. First Husband = _sin + it's punishment_
4. Adulteress = _a law breaker_
5. The Law = _the torah_
6. Second Husband = _righteousness + justification_

## 🔍 The Real Nature of the Torah

Paul proclaims in Romans 7:1–14:

*God's Torah is*
**HOLY**

*The Torah is*
**RIGHTEOUS**

*God's Torah is*
**GOOD**

*The Torah is*
**SPIRITUAL**

**Key Verses**

Romans 7:1–14

**Key Concepts**

*Bearing fruit:* A Hebrew idiom equated with keeping the commandments.

*For the <u>unbeliever</u> is bound by <u>Torah</u> to <u>sin and punishment</u> while sin is living; but if <u>sin and punishment</u> dies, the <u>unbeliever</u> is released from the <u>Torah's condemnation of sin</u>. So then, if while <u>sin and punishment</u> is alive the <u>unbeliever</u> is <u>declared righteous and justified</u>, the <u>unbeliever</u> shall be called <u>a lawbreaker</u>; but if <u>sin and punishment</u> dies, the <u>believer</u> is free from the <u>condemnation of the law</u>, so that the <u>believer</u> is not a <u>lawbreaker</u> though she is joined to <u>righteousness and justification</u>. Therefore, my brethren, you also were made to die to the <u>condemnation of</u> the Law through the body of Messiah, so that you might be joined <u>to righteousness and justification</u>, to Him who was raised from the dead, in order that we might bear fruit for God.* (Paraphrase of Romans 7:2–4)

## ❶ Summary Romans 7:1–14

Before faith in Messiah, the Torah condemned you for your sin. After faith in Messiah, the punishment for sin is paid and the Torah no longer condemns you.

*In order that we might bear fruit for God.* (Romans 7:4)

**bearing fruit = keeping Torah**

Bearing good fruit

# Galatians 4:21–26: The Two Mothers

*Tell me, you who want to be under law [Torah], do you not listen to the Law? For it is written that Abraham had two sons, one by the bondwoman and one by the free woman. But the son by the bondwoman was born according to the flesh, and the son by the free woman through the promise. This is allegorically speaking, for these women are two covenants: one proceeding from Mount Sinai bearing children who are to be slaves; she is Hagar. Now this Hagar is Mount Sinai in Arabia and corresponds to the present Jerusalem, for she is in slavery with her children. But the Jerusalem above is free; she is our mother.* (Galatians 4:21–26)

Hagar and Sarah

## Ⓐ The Context of Galatians

Paul wrote to the Gentile Galatians and scolded them for thinking that faith alone was insufficient for salvation and that they needed to go through the circumcision conversion to merit salvation.

## Ⓑ Two Covenants in Galatians

❖ Galatians 3–4 is NOT Old Covenant vs. New Covenant.
❖ Galatians 3–4 is Abrahamic Covenant vs. Sinai Covenant.

*What I am saying is this: the Law, which came four hundred and thirty years later, does not invalidate a covenant [i.e., the Abrahamic Covenant] previously ratified by God, so as to nullify the promise.* (Galatians 3:17)

**Key Verses**

Galatians 3:28–29

Genesis 21:14

Genesis 21:9–10

Genesis 21:12

Galatians 4:21–26

**Key Words**

*Ben Avraham:* Hebrew for "son of Abraham." Idiomatically, a title for a Gentile who has undergone ritual conversion to become legally Jewish.

*Midrash:* Hebrew word denoting a type of Bible study that employs rabbinic hermeneutics to explain the text incorporating word associations, creative retellings of the biblical story, fanciful accounts of biblical personages, parables, and moral teachings.

### C Sons of Abraham

A Gentile convert to Judaism who has undergone circumcision and ritual conversion is henceforth called a *ben Avraham*, that is a "son of Abraham."

> *ben Avraham* (בן אברהם) = "son of Abraham"

*There is neither Jew nor Greek, there is neither slave nor free man, there is neither male nor female; for you are all one in Christ Jesus. And if you belong to Christ, then you are Abraham's descendants, heirs according to promise.* (Galatians 3:28–29)

**Two Types of Gentile Sons of Abraham:**

1. Legal converts through circumcision
2. Spiritual converts through faith

### D Paul's Midrash

> *midrash* (מדרש) = a Bible study employing rabbinic hermeneutics

**Contrasts in the Galatians 4:21–26 Midrash**

| Hagar | Sarah |
| --- | --- |
| Slave | Free |
| Sinai Covenant | Abrahamic Covenant |
| Earthly Jerusalem | Heavenly Jerusalem |
| Ishmael (Son of Abraham) | Isaac (Son of Abraham) |
| Conceived by natural means | Conceived by promise and miracle |
| Flesh (physical) | Spiritual (by faith) |
| Ritual Circumcision and Conversion | Faith in Messiah |

**Your Israel Connection**

**Isaac and Ishmael**

*Tel Beersheva, Negev Region* – Beersheva is located in the biblical Negev, an arid and desert-like region of Israel situated on the edge of the great wilderness. Abraham and his family lived at Beersheva at the time of the expulsion of Hagar. "And she departed and wandered about in the wilderness of Beersheba" (Genesis 21:14).

## E Making Sense of the Midrash

The Symbolism of the Midrash

1. Legal conversion to become Jewish:

   *Under the law*

2. Gentile convert to Judaism through circumcision:

   *Ishmael*

3. Gentile convert through faith:

   *Isaac*

4. Sinai Covenant/Jerusalem:

   *Hagar*

5. Abrahamic Covenant/New Jerusalem:

   *Sarah*

*Tell me, you who want to <u>make a legal conversion to become Jewish</u>, do you not listen to the Torah? For it is written that Abraham had two sons, one by the <u>Sinai Covenant</u> and one by the <u>Abrahamic Covenant</u>. But the son by the <u>Sinai Covenant</u> was born according to the flesh, and the son by the <u>Abrahamic Covenant</u> through the promise. This is allegorically speaking, for these women are two covenants: one proceeding from Mount Sinai bearing children who are to be slaves; she is Hagar. Now this Hagar is Mount Sinai in Arabia and corresponds to the present Jerusalem, for she is in slavery with her children. But the Jerusalem above is free; she is our mother.* (Paraphrase of Galatians 4:21–26)

*And you brethren, like Isaac, are children of promise. But as at that time he who was born according to the flesh persecuted him who was born according to the Spirit, so it is now also. But what does the Scripture say? "Cast out the bondwoman and her son, for the son of the bondwoman shall not be an heir with the son of the free woman." So then, brethren, we are not children of a bondwoman, but of the free woman.* (Galatians 4:28–31; quoting Genesis 21:10)

## F Summary of Galatians 4:21–26

It's not about Old Covenant versus New Covenant, or Judaism versus Christianity.

It is about whether or not Gentiles need to become legally Jewish in order to merit salvation.

---

**Key Verses**

Galatians 4:21–26
Galatians 4:28–31
Genesis 21:10
Romans 11:6
Ephesians 2:8–9

**Key Words**

*Mikvah:* A ritual purification bath used by Jews on certain occasions, such as before the Sabbath or after menstruation. Ritual immersion in a mikvah is also one of the major components of the conversion process to Judaism.

**Your Israel Connection**

**Works of the Law**

*Southern Wall, Jerusalem Temple Mount* – Pictured is a ritual bath (*mikvah*) from the Temple Mount excavations. Immersing oneself in a ritual bath was an ordinary part of maintaining Levitical purity. In the days of the apostles, worshippers going to the Temple immersed in this *mikvah* and others like it. Immersion in a *mikvah* is the original form of baptism and was a prerequisite for Gentiles undergoing conversion to become Jewish.

**Refer to Resource**

*Torah Club Volume Five: Rejoicing of the Torah*
"Vayera: And He Appeared"
"Chayei Sarah: Life of Sarah"

# Galatians 5: Circumcision and Uncircumcision

A Gentile could go through a ritual conversion to become legally (halachically) Jewish.

Three "Works of the Law" to become legally Jewish:

1. Circumcision

2. Emersion

3. Sacrifice

**A** ## Galatians 5:1–6

In Galatians, Paul is not teaching against the Torah or keeping the Torah. He is not saying that a person who keeps the Torah has "fallen from grace." But he says that if you seek to be justified by keeping the Torah or think that you need to become Jewish before you will receive salvation, then you have given up on grace.

*It was for freedom that Messiah set us free; therefore keep standing firm and do not be subject again to a yoke of slavery. Behold I, Paul, say to you that if you receive circumcision, Messiah will be of no benefit to you. And I testify again to every man who receives circumcision, that he is under obligation to keep the whole [Torah]. You have been severed from the Messiah, you who are seeking to be justified by [Torah]; you have fallen from grace. For we through the Spirit, by faith, are waiting for the hope of righteousness. For in the Messiah Yeshua neither circumcision nor uncircumcision means anything, but faith working through love.* (Galatians 5:1–6)

Circumcision: legally Jewish

Uncircumcision: legally Gentile

**Refer to Resource**

*HaYesod Student Workbook*
"Some Other Gospel: Issues in Galatians"
Pages 7.23–7.25

Yoke of slavery

## Ⓑ 1 Corinthians 7:19

Being legally Jewish or not being legally Jewish is not important, the important thing is keeping the commandments of God.

*Circumcision is nothing, and uncircumcision is nothing, but what matters is the keeping of the commandments of God.*
(1 Corinthians 7:19)

## Ⓒ Romans 2:25–29

In Romans 2, Paul states that legal status in the eyes of man doesn't matter. What matters is the inward condition of your heart, your relationship to God, and obedience to the Torah.

*For indeed <u>being legally Jewish</u> is of value if you practice the Torah; but if you are a transgressor of the Torah, your <u>legal Jewish status</u> has become <u>the same as being legally Gentile</u>. So if the <u>legally Gentile</u> man keeps the requirements of the Torah, will not his <u>legally Gentile status</u> be regarded as <u>legal Jewish status</u>? And he who is <u>physically legally Gentile</u>, if he keeps the Torah, will he not judge you who though having the letter of the Torah and <u>being legally Jewish</u> are a transgressor of the Torah? For he is not a Jew who is one outwardly, nor is <u>Jewish status</u> that which is outward in the flesh. But he is a Jew who is one inwardly; and <u>Jewish status</u> is that which is of the heart, by the Spirit, not by the letter; and his praise is not from men, but from God.* (Paraphrase of Romans 2:25–29)

**Key Words**

Galatians 5:1–6
Psalm 122
Ephesians 2:13–22
Colossians 2:13–17

**Key Words**

*Aliyah:* lit. "going up." 1. Immigration to the land of Israel. 2. Being called to read from the Torah scroll as a part of a synagogue service. 3. In the days of the Temple, a pilgrimage to the Temple in Jerusalem.

📷 **Your Israel Connection**

**Dividing Wall of Hostility**

*Southern Steps, Jerusalem Temple Mount* – In the days of the apostles (70 AD/CE), the Temple of God in Jerusalem was destroyed by the Romans. Not one stone of the Temple remains upon another, but below the southern wall of the Temple Mount archaeologists discovered the remains of a monumental stairway pilgrims used to ascend on their way up to worship the God of Israel. The feet of Jesus and the apostles once climbed those stone stairs.

**Refer to Resource**

*Grafted In*
"The Eternal Purpose of God"
Pages 125–135

## Ⓓ Galatians 5:1–6 Summary

Gentile believers are already accepted into the kingdom by faith in Messiah. Therefore, to look toward conversion to become legally Jewish or any type of Torah observance as a means for earning salvation is taking on a yoke of slavery.

*[handwritten: We R almost done    That we are my completed]*

# Ephesians 2:13–22: Dividing Wall of Partition

In Ephesians 2, Paul uses the dividing wall of partition that stood between the court of the Gentiles and the Temple proper as a metaphor for the separation between Jews and Gentiles.

## Ⓐ Ephesians 2:14–16

*For He Himself is our peace, who made both groups into one and broke down the barrier of the dividing wall, by abolishing in His flesh the enmity, which is the Law of commandments contained in ordinances, so that in Himself He might make the two into one new man, thus establishing peace, and might reconcile them both in one body to God through the cross, by it having put to death the enmity.* (Ephesians 2:14–16)

## Ⓑ Ephesians 2:14–16 Summary

Messiah did not abolish the Torah; He abolished the enmity between Jew and Gentile engendered by Torah. Because of the inclusion of Gentile believers into the greater people of Israel, the Torah is no longer a wall of separation. In Messiah, Gentile believers have the prerogative to take hold of the covenant and take on the commandments. The enmity that kept Jews and Gentiles on opposite sides of the Torah wall has been removed.

# Colossians 2:13–17: Canceling the Torah

*When you were dead in your transgressions and the uncircumcision of your flesh, He made you alive together with Him, having forgiven us all our transgressions, having canceled out the certificate of debt consisting of decrees against us, which was hostile to us; and He has taken it out of the way, having nailed it to the cross.* (Colossians 2:13–14)

## Ⓐ Nailing the Torah to the Cross?

The "certificate of debt" is not the Torah, it is a record of sins.

Certificate of debt

**Key Verses**

Colossians 2:13–17

**Key Words**

*Cheirographon:* Greek word meaning "certificate of debt" or "a handwritten document."

**Key Concepts**

*Certificate of debt:* A document of our sin or violations of God's ordinances.

> **cheirographon** (χειρογραφον) = "certificate of debt, handwritten document"

*God has not only removed the debt; he has also destroyed the document on which it was recorded.* Cheirographon *denotes a "document," especially a "note of indebtedness" written in one's own hand as a proof of obligation. This meaning is well-attested in both the Jewish and Greco-Roman world. A common thought in Judaism was that of God keeping accounts of man's debt, calling in the debt through angels and imposing a just judgment based on the records kept in the ledger (cf. Rabbi Akiba's illustration of God as a shopkeeper, m.'Abot 3:20).* (Peter T. O'Brien, *Word Biblical Commentary*)[2]

*He used to say: "Everything is given on collateral and a net is spread over all the living. The shop is open; the Merchant extends credit; the ledger is open; the hand writes; and whoever wishes to borrow, let him come and borrow. The collectors make their rounds constantly, every day, and collect payment from the person whether he realizes it or not. They have what to rely upon; the judgment is a truthful judgment; and everything is prepared for the [final festive] banquet."* (m.*Avot* 3:17)

*Our preference is to understand the* [cheirographon] *as the signed acknowledgment of our indebtedness before God. Like an IOU it contained penalty clauses. The Jews had contracted to obey the law, and in their case the penalty for breach of this contract meant death. Paul assumes that the Gentiles were committed, through their consciences, to a similar obligation, to the moral law in as much as they understood it. Since the obligation had not been discharged by either group the "bond" remained against us.* (Peter T. O'Brien, *Word Biblical Commentary*)[3]

## ⓑ Summary Colossians 2:13–17

The certificate of debt nailed to the cross is a document of our sin, a document of our violations of God's ordinances, our violations of the Torah. It's like a guilty verdict written by a court of law, or a bill of indebtedness issued by a lender. Messiah canceled the document which recorded our sins and transgressions, nailing it to the cross, so to speak, when He Himself was nailed to the cross.

# Romans 14: Diet and Sabbath

*Now accept the one who is weak in faith, but not for the purpose of passing judgment on his opinions. One person has faith that he may eat all things, but he who is weak eats vegetables only. The one who eats is not to regard with contempt the one who does not eat, and the one who does not eat is not to judge the one who eats, for God has accepted him.* (Romans 14:1–3)

## ⓐ The Strong and the Weak

Romans 14 seems to say that someone who eats "kosher" is weak in faith, but the person who eats everything is strong in faith. Further on in the chapter, Paul even says that, in his opinion, no food is unclean.

**Refer to Resource**

*HaYesod Student Workbook*
"Doctrine of Demons"
Pages 7.26–7.27

Meat vs. only vegetables

*I know and am convinced in the Lord Jesus that nothing is unclean in itself; but to him who thinks anything to be unclean, to him it is unclean.* (Romans 14:14)

**Key Words**

Romans 14
Acts 10:28

## B The Sabbath Day

It sounds like Paul says that keeping the Sabbath day is simply a matter of opinion.

*One person regards one day above another, another regards every day alike. Each person must be fully convinced in his own mind. He who observes the day, observes it for the Lord, and he who eats, does so for the Lord, for he gives thanks to God; and he who eats not, for the Lord he does not eat, and gives thanks to God.* (Romans 14:5–6)

**Key Words**

*Koinos:* Greek word meaning "common." Used to refer to otherwise kosher food rendered unfit for consumption by contact with idolatry, non-Jews, or some other source of defilement.

*Akathartos:* Greek word meaning "unclean." Used in reference to Jewish dietary law, referring to meats which the Bible has declared unclean and forbidden.

## C Akathartos vs. Koinos

Paul's statement that "nothing is unclean in itself" is unrelated to the laws of clean and unclean animals. It is a question of whether or not food is permissible when it might potentially have been offered to an idol or prepared by a Gentile.

> *koinos* (κοινος) = **"common"**

When used in reference to Jewish dietary law, *koinos* refers to otherwise kosher food rendered unfit for consumption by contact with idolatry, non-Jews, or some other source of defilement.

> *akathartos* (ακαθαρτος) = **"unclean"**

When used in reference to Jewish dietary law, *akathartos* refers to the meats which the Bible has declared unclean and forbidden.

*I know and am convinced in the Lord Yeshua that nothing is ~~unclean~~* Common *in itself; but to him who thinks anything to be ~~unclean~~* COMMON *, to him it is ~~unclean~~* Common *.* (Romans 14:14)

**Your Israel Connection**

**Idol Food**

*Caesarea Maritima, Mediterranean Coast* – In the days of the apostles, Caesarea was the Roman capital of Judea. Like Rome itself, it was a thoroughly Hellenistic city where a small Jewish minority lived in uneasy tension in the midst of a pagan majority.

**Refer to Resource**

*Holy Cow!*
"Nothing is Unclean in Itself"
Pages 111–117

## D  Pagan Festival Days

*One person regards one day above another, another regards every day alike. Each person must be fully convinced in his own mind.*
(Romans 14:5)

Some Jewish people and even believers in Rome would not do business with Gentiles on or around their pagan days of worship.

*When an idolatrous [festival] takes place within a city it is permitted [to transact business with heathen] outside of it; if the idolatrous [festival] takes place outside of it, [business] is permitted within it. How about going there? If the road leads solely to that place, it is forbidden; but if one can go by it to any other place, it is permitted.* (b.Avodah Zarah 11b)

Some believers were concerned about doing business on pagan festival days: others considered every day alike. Paul says that each should be fully convinced in his own mind, and not judge one another for his conviction.

*He who observes the day, observes it for the Lord, and he who eats, does so for the Lord, for he gives thanks to God; and he who eats not, for the Lord he does not eat, and gives thanks to God.*
(Romans 14:6)

## E  Summary Romans 14

Romans 14 has nothing to say about whether or not we should keep the biblical dietary laws, and it has nothing at all to say about the Sabbath day. Paul was speaking about completely different issues.

### Endnotes

1  James Dunn, *Word Biblical Commentary: Volume 38a, Romans 1–8* (Nashville, TN: Thomas Nelson Publishers, 1988), liii.

2  Peter T. O'Brien, *Word Biblical Commentary: Volume 44, Colossians, Philemon* (Nashville, TN: Thomas Nelson Publishers, 1982), 124.

3  Ibid., 125.

# Lesson Seven
## LESSON SUMMARY

### First …

We noted that parts of Paul's epistles are easily misunderstood and that even in Peter's day Paul's epistles were hard to understand, so we adopted three rules for reading Paul:

- ❖ Remember that Scripture does not contradict.
- ❖ Remember that Paul's words must be understood in their context.
- ❖ Remember that Paul himself was Torah observant.

### Then …

We began studying some difficult Pauline passages, starting with Romans 7 where we learned that, in Messiah, we have died to the Torah's condemnation but not to Torah obedience.

### After that …

We saw that the contrast of Sarah and Hagar in Galatians 4:21–26 illustrates a contrast between:

- ❖ The Abrahamic Covenant and the Sinai Covenant
- ❖ Conversion through faith and conversion through circumcision
- ❖ The status of a Gentile believer and of a Gentile convert to Judaism

### Therefore …

The arguments about "circumcision and uncircumcision" and terminology about being "under the Law" are not against Torah itself but against requiring Gentiles to become legally (halachically) Jewish to earn salvation.

### Then …

We considered that Ephesians 2:15 says that Messiah abolished the enmity between Jew and Gentile, not the Torah. Likewise in Colossians 2:13–14, Messiah canceled our certificate of debt; he did not cancel the Torah.

### After that …

We learned that in Romans 14, Paul was not addressing whether a person should keep kosher or should keep the Sabbath but was dealing specifically with issues that pertained to living in the midst of an idolatrous city.

### Finally …

We realized that Paul's letters need to be read carefully from a Jewish and Torah perspective and that passages which at first appear to be anti-Torah often prove not to be.

# Lesson Seven
# LESSON REVIEW – Q&A

1.  What are the three principles to keep in mind when reading Paul's letters?

2.  In Romans 7, what is it that believers have died to and been set free from?

3.  What is a midrash? In Paul's Galatians 4 midrash regarding Sarah and Hagar, what do the two mothers represent? What do the two sons, Isaac and Ishmael, represent?

4.  What does Paul mean by the term "under the Law"? What does he mean by "circumcision"? According to Paul in 1 Corinthians 7:19, what is the important thing?

5.  In Ephesians 2:15, what is it that Messiah destroyed? What is the enmity engendered by the Torah?

6.  In Colossians 2:13–17, what is it that Messiah canceled and nailed to the cross?

7.  In Romans 14, why were some believers abstaining from eating anything but vegetables?

8.  What is the difference between "common" and "unclean"? In what way were some believers regarding one day over another, while others regarded every day alike?

# Lesson Seven
# EXTRA CREDIT
### SUPPLEMENTAL MATERIAL FOR THIS HAYESOD LESSON

---

**Extra Credit Instructions:**

1. This material is not mandatory, but it will serve as a helpful tool for further study.
2. Read the remaining English translations and underline the important discrepancies.

## Paul in Translation and Mistranslation

In this week's lesson, we learned that Paul's writings are often misunderstood when read outside of a Jewish context. Another factor that makes Paul seem anti-Torah is unintentional bias in translation.

### Colossians 2:16–17 in English

Bible translators rendering the Greek to English inadvertently translate according to their theological predisposition. A good example can be found in common English translations of Colossians 2:16–17. First read the Young's Literal Translation of the Greek, and then carefully read and compare the different versions, paying special attention to how they translate the second verse. Some versions translate the verb to a past-tense form to say that the things of Torah "were" shadows of things to come, thereby implying that they are no longer relevant. Some introduce a dismissive adjective and say that they are "mere" shadows, or "only" shadows. Some versions render the final phrase in such a way so as to avoid saying that the "body" of the things of Torah "is Christ." Underline the discrepancies in translation.

> Let no one, then, judge you in eating or in drinking, or in respect of a feast, or of a new moon, or of sabbaths, which are a shadow of the coming things, and the body *is* of the Christ. (Young's Literal Translation)

> So don't let anyone judge you because of what you eat or drink. Don't let anyone judge you about holy days. I'm talking about special feasts and New Moons and Sabbath days. They are only a shadow of the things that were going to come. But what is real is found in Christ. (New International Reader's Version)

> So don't put up with anyone pressuring you in details of diet, worship services, or holy days. All those things are mere shadows cast before what was to come; the substance is Christ. (The Message)

> Therefore do not let anyone judge you by what you eat or drink, or with regard to a religious festival, a New Moon celebration or a Sabbath day. These are a shadow of the things that were to come; the reality, however, is found in Christ. (New International Version)

> Therefore do not let anyone condemn you in matters of food and drink or of observing festivals, new moons, or sabbaths. These are only a shadow of what is to come, but the substance belongs to Christ. (New Revised Standard)

Therefore let no one pass judgment on you in questions of food and drink, or with regard to a festival or a new moon or a Sabbath. These are a shadow of the things to come, but the substance belongs to Christ. (English Standard Version)

Therefore no one is to act as your judge in regard to food or drink or in respect to a festival or a new moon or a Sabbath day— things which are a *mere* shadow of what is to come; but the substance belongs to Christ. (New American Standard Version)

Let no man therefore judge you in meat, or in drink, or in respect of an holyday, or of the new moon, or of the sabbath *days*: Which are a shadow of things to come; but the body *is* of Christ. (King James Version)

# Lesson Seven – Digging Deeper
# SOME OTHER GOSPEL: ISSUES IN GALATIANS
### ADDITIONAL NOTES, QUOTES, AND SOURCES

## Introduction to Galatians

The Galatians were new believers, converts out of paganism. They were the Gentiles of the city of Pisidian Antioch, Iconium, and Derbe. Faith in Yeshua was their only rite of conversion. But subsequent to their conversion out of the kingdom of darkness and into the kingdom of God, some brothers and sisters, perhaps from Jerusalem, paid them a visit. These visitors were Jewish brothers and sisters who still held fast to the conviction that only ethnic and legal Jews could have a place in God's covenant. Only Israel could be saved. Only Israel was in the kingdom.

The visitors taught that it was necessary, in addition to faith in Yeshua, for the Galatian Gentiles to also be circumcised—thereby signifying their formal and legal conversion to Judaism. According to these fellows, only after circumcision could the Gentiles be regarded as truly a part of the kingdom. Faith in Messiah alone was not adequate.

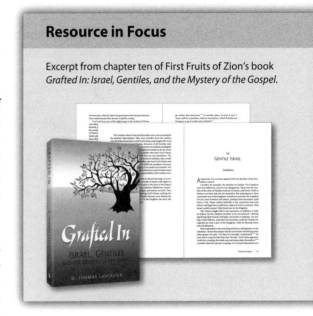

**Resource in Focus**

Excerpt from chapter ten of First Fruits of Zion's book *Grafted In: Israel, Gentiles, and the Mystery of the Gospel.*

Paul responded to this teaching with his scathing letter to the Galatians. He lost his temper and accused them of teaching "some other gospel." He said, "Let them be eternally condemned!" He even took it a step further than that. He said, "As for those agitators, I wish they would go the whole way and emasculate themselves!"[1] Consider what the apostle is saying: As if eternal damnation was not bad enough, Paul wanted them to be eternally damned with less than their whole apparatus.

Paul's rancor reveals his priorities. The gospel of salvation full and free, specifically salvation proclaimed to the Gentiles, salvation by faith through grace, was the very heartbeat of passion that fueled the old Pharisee's life. The Gentile inclusion through faith in Yeshua was the gospel to Paul. That was the good news. To him, anything that obscured that simple truth was some other gospel.

## The Apostle to the Uncircumcised

Subsequent to the Jerusalem Council of Acts 15, Paul referred to himself as the official "apostle to the Gentiles," as in Romans 11:13, for example. The Greek word he uses for Gentiles is *ethnos*, from which we derive the word "ethnicity." Paul identified himself as the apostle to the ethnic nationalities. His description of his apostleship is contrasted with Peter's apostleship to the Jews.

> *They saw that I had been entrusted with the task of preaching the gospel to the uncircumcised, just as Peter had been to the circumcised. For God, who was at work in the ministry of Peter as an apostle to the circumcised, was also at work in my ministry as an apostle to the Gentiles.* (Galatians 2:7–8, NIV)

In this passage, Paul uses the terms uncircumcised (*akrobustia*) synonymously with the term Gentiles (*ethnos*). From Paul's perspective, to be uncircumcised was to be a Gentile, one from the nations. The

Greek word *akrobustia*, which we are translating as uncircumcised, is perhaps more honestly rendered as "foreskinned."

Peter, on the other hand, is the apostle to the *peritome*, that is the circumcised.

But wait! Suppose you didn't have a foreskin. Take Paul's convert Lydia, for example: a weaver of purple cloth and, more to the point, a woman. Was she outside of Paul's purview because she was a woman and he was the apostle to the foreskinned? The point that needs to be understood is that the term "foreskinned" does not necessarily refer to the literal state of being circumcised or uncircumcised; it is used categorically to refer to those Gentile believers who had not made a conversion to legal Judaism. In a similar way, the term "circumcision" is used categorically to refer to Jews and to proselytes who have become Jewish through a legal conversion ritual. That's why Paul is able to say, "Circumcision is nothing and uncircumcision is nothing. Keeping God's commands is what counts."[2] Notice the apparent contradiction: Circumcision is one of God's commands. If keeping God's commands is what counts, then surely circumcision is something. The way Paul uses the term, circumcision refers specifically to the legal conversion ritual. Thus Paul is saying, "Regarding one's standing before God, legal conversion to Judaism is meaningless. Keeping God's commands is what counts."

Paul, then, is the apostle to the "foreskinned," by which he means Gentiles. Peter is the apostle to the "circumcised," by which Paul means Jews and proselytes to Judaism. If a foreskinned person (*akrobustia*) should choose to undergo a legal conversion ritual, which includes circumcision (*peritome*), he would no longer be regarded as a Gentile (*ethnos*). Indeed, such a person becomes legally Jewish.

Paul, the apostle to the foreskinned, was zealous to defend the Gentiles' right to retain their foreskins. If they were compelled to be circumcised before being admitted to the kingdom, that would have been the equivalent of declaring that Messiah's atonement was insufficient to save men with foreskins. If they were compelled to undergo a conversion to Judaism, the implication would be that Messiah was unable to save Gentiles.

## Paul Responds

Paul responded to the Galatians by saying, "Are you so foolish? After beginning with the Spirit, are you now trying to attain your goal by human effort?"[3] The specific human effort Paul was speaking of was a legal conversion to Judaism through the rite of circumcision. In the eyes of men, circumcision allowed for a conventional, physical, human position in Israel. It was a position attained through natural, physical, human methods. Paul asked the Galatians, "Are you now trying to attain your goal by human effort or by natural means? Are you trying to buy your way into the kingdom by converting to Judaism?"

## Misreading Paul

Paul goes on to develop this argument from several angles. Later readers of the epistle who were not aware of the contextual situation interpreted Galatians as an anti-Torah and anti-Jewish work. Based largely upon this misreading of Galatians, early Christianity jettisoned Torah and our connections to Judaism. We began to believe that anyone who attempted to keep a commandment of Torah was under the curse of the Torah. In retrospect, it was an absurd proposition, but to those who expounded the idea, it was consistent with their misreading of Galatians.

Paul was not preaching against Gentiles keeping the Torah. Technically, he was not even preaching against Gentiles becoming circumcised. He was preaching against Gentiles undergoing the conventional conversion into Judaism in order to achieve salvation and status in the Jewish community.

It would appear that the epistle to the Galatians was misunderstood even in Paul's own lifetime. When he arrived at Jerusalem in Acts 21, James warned him that there were false rumors going around to the effect that Paul was teaching "the Jews who live among the Gentiles to turn away from Moses, telling them not to circumcise their children" (NIV).[4] Acts 21 makes clear that the rumors were indeed false rumors, but it shows us how Paul's arguments concerning circumcision were already being misunderstood and misused.

Peter took note of people misunderstanding Paul. He said, Paul's "letters contain some things that are hard to understand, which ignorant and unstable people distort, as they do the other Scriptures, to their own destruction" (2 Peter 3:16, NIV). If sorting out Paul's arguments was difficult for the first-century believers, how much more so for later generations? When the epistle is removed from the argument about conversion, one can hardly wonder that we misunderstood.

Ironically, the epistle to the Galatians is the very scripture that Christians most often use to refute Gentile believers who are beginning to return to their Jewish roots and practice aspects of Messianic Judaism. As Christians begin to involve themselves in the various aspects of their heritage (such as Sabbath observance, kosher laws, daily prayer, etc.), they are often rebuked by other believers quoting from Galatians. That is turning it exactly backwards. Galatians was written to argue for Gentile inclusion in Israel, not Gentile exclusion from Israel.

## Endnotes

1   Galatians 5:12.
2   1 Corinthians 7:19.
3   Galatians 3:3.
4   Acts 21:21.

# Lesson Seven – Digging Deeper
## DOCTRINE OF DEMONS
### FURTHER STUDY FROM THIS WEEK'S HAYESOD LESSON

## 1 Timothy 4:1–5

In his first Epistle to Timothy, Paul warns him of the "doctrine of demons" which forbids marriage and commands abstinence from certain foods.

*But the Spirit explicitly says that in later times some will fall away from the faith, paying attention to deceitful spirits and doctrines of demons, by means of the hypocrisy of liars seared in their own conscience as with a branding iron, men who forbid marriage and advocate abstaining from foods which God has created to be gratefully shared in by those who believe and know the truth. For everything created by God is good, and nothing is to be rejected if it is received with gratitude; for it is sanctified by means of the word of God and prayer.* (1 Timothy 4:1–5)

Opponents of the Torah have used this passage to infer that Torah observance (i.e., the kosher food laws) is a "doctrine of demons." This is an impossible interpretation for a number of reasons. It is blasphemous to regard the commandments of God as a doctrine of demons. Paul himself kept kosher.[1] Furthermore, there is no prohibition on marriage in the Torah; rather, God commands us to be fruitful and multiply.

The early Gnostics, on the other hand, did teach abstinence from sex, marriage, and certain foods. Paul uses Genesis 1:31 to refute the teachings of the Gnostics. Whereas they taught that certain foods were intrinsically bad because they were part of the physical world, Paul points out that the Torah says, "Everything created by God is good." This goodness also applies to foods and to sexual relations, both of which were created to be enjoyed.

However, Paul does not mean to imply that we are free to indulge in every edible substance or every conceivable kind of sexual relationship. Rather, he says that sex and permissible foods are "sanctified by means of the word of God and prayer." Sanctified means set apart. That is to say, the Torah (God's Word) has sanctified permissible foods (Leviticus 11) and permissible sexual relationships (Leviticus 18) by defining them from those that are not permissible. Marriage and eating food share in common that they are both sanctified by God's commandments permitting and forbidding certain forms of them. They also share in common that, according to Jewish tradition, they are both instituted with blessings, i.e., prayer.

For us to reject as evil something that God has created as good and permissible is ungrateful. The Jerusalem Talmud expresses an almost identical sentiment.

*A man will have to give an account on the judgment day for every good and permissible thing which he might have enjoyed and did not.* (y.Kiddushin 4:12)

# Colossians 2:18–23

Colossae was not far from the province of Galatia, and the Colossian believers found themselves dealing with some of the same questions regarding Gentile circumcision (i.e., conversion) and Torah observance with which the Galatian communities struggled. In addition, the Colossians seem to have been incorporating Gnostic beliefs in their observances. Paul corrects this error in his Epistle to the Colossians.

> *Let no one keep defrauding you of your prize by delighting in self-abasement and the worship of the angels, taking his stand on visions he has seen, inflated without cause by his fleshly mind ... If you have died with Messiah to the elementary principles of the world, why, as if you were living in the world, do you submit yourself to decrees, such as, "Do not handle, do not taste, do not touch!" (which all refer to things destined to perish with use)—in accordance with the commandments and teachings of men? These are matters which have, to be sure, the appearance of wisdom in self-made religion and self-abasement and severe treatment of the body, but are of no value against fleshly indulgence.* (Colossians 2:18–23)

Opponents of the Torah often point to Colossians 2:20–21 as if Paul was referring to the commands and prohibitions of Torah as "the elementary principles of the world" and the "commandments and teachings of men." Because the beginning of the chapter speaks in reference to Torah observance (Sabbaths, festivals, new moons, kosher laws, [Colossians 2:16]) they assume that Paul is referring to those rites as "commands and teachings of men" all "destined to perish with use." This is wrong. "Elementary principles of the world" refers to paganism or Gnostic beliefs, not Torah. The prohibitions of Torah are the commands and teachings of God, not man. The larger context of the passage makes it clear that Paul is here referring to a Gnostic perversion of God's truth. It was apparently a secret knowledge, imparted by visions, which advocated a high level of asceticism.

The religious tendencies Paul here describes are "self-made" and based upon the "commandments and teachings of men." They are "of no value against fleshly indulgence." Torah, on the other hand, is God-given and based on the commandments and teachings of God. Regarding Torah, Paul says, "All scripture *is* given by inspiration of God, and *is* profitable for doctrine, for reproof, for correction, for instruction in righteousness" (2 Timothy 3:16).

Therefore, we may be certain that Paul is not speaking against the Torah, but against a perverse religious system of asceticism, which misapplies some observance of Torah. In Paul's view, the proto-Gnostic worldview that denigrated the physical world was at variance with the Torah. The Torah declares: "And God saw all that He had made, and behold, it was very good" (Genesis 1:32).

## Endnotes

1  See Acts 21:24, 23:1, 25:8, 28:17; 1 Corinthians 9:21.

# Notes:

Lesson Eight

# Our Calendar– His Appointments

THE LAND, THE PEOPLE,
AND THE SCRIPTURES OF ISRAEL

# Lesson Eight
# OUR CALENDAR—HIS APPOINTMENTS

*The LORD spoke again to Moses, saying, "Speak to the sons of Israel and say to them, 'The LORD'S appointed times which you shall proclaim as holy convocations—My appointed times are these … These are the appointed times of the LORD, holy convocations which you shall proclaim at the times appointed for them.'"* (Leviticus 23:1–4)

## Lesson Overview

The New Testament contains no specific commandments concerning the nature, place, or time that God desires for corporate worship. There is no commandment to assemble on Sunday morning or any other day of the week. The Torah, on the other hand, contains ample instruction about God's appointed times of worship. In the faith and practice of the apostolic community, believers followed the biblical calendar, kept the seventh-day Sabbath, and worshipped God at His appointed times. This lesson introduces the biblical calendar of Israel.

## Lesson Purpose

In this lesson we will outline the cycle of holy days described in Leviticus 23. We hope to demonstrate that:

- ❖ God has established appointed times for assembly and worship.
- ❖ The biblical Sabbath and holidays have not been abolished or replaced.
- ❖ The biblical Sabbath and holidays are relevant to believers today.
- ❖ The biblical Sabbath and holidays teach us about the work of Messiah.
- ❖ The biblical Sabbath and holidays create a cycle of sanctification.

## Field Trips to the Holy Land

- ❖ Tel Dan, Northern Israel
- ❖ Machaneh Yehudah, Jerusalem
- ❖ Jewish Quarter, Old City Jerusalem
- ❖ Qumran, Dead Sea Region

# Lesson Eight
## LESSON OUTLINE

### The Biblical Calendar

A. The Appointed Times
   1. The Lunar Calendar
   2. The Jewish Festivals
   3. Celebrating with God
   4. Perpetual Ordinances

### The Festival Cycle

A. Daily Times of Prayer
B. Weekly Sabbath
C. Monthly New Moons
D. Annual Festivals

### The Sabbath

### The Spring Festivals

A. Passover
B. Unleavened Bread
C. The Omer
   1. First Fruits of the Barley
   2. Counting the Days until Pentecost
D. Pentecost

### The Fall Festivals

A. The Feast of Trumpets
B. Day of Atonement
C. The Feast of Tabernacles
D. The Eighth Day

### Cycle of Sanctification

### Shadow of Things to Come

A. The Appointed Times Foreshadow Messiah and the Future
B. The Appointed Times Will Be Observed by Everyone in the Messianic Era
C. The Appointed Times Will Be Observed by all Nations in the Messianic Era

**Key Verses**

Leviticus 23:2

**Key Words**

*Mo'ed* (pl. *mo'adim*): Hebrew word meaning an "appointed time."

**Key Concepts**

*Biblical Calendar:* A combination of both the monthly lunar cycle and the annual solar cycle employed for determining time in the Bible and in Judaism today.

# The Biblical Calendar

The biblical festivals might not be familiar to most Christians, but these are the festivals that Yeshua and the apostles celebrated.

❖ The calendar is connected to the Land of Israel because it is an agricultural calendar.

❖ The calendar is connected to the People of Israel because it is the most defining element of their religious life.

❖ The calendar is connected to the Scriptures of Israel because it is derived directly from the Bible.

**Ⓐ The Appointed Times**

*Speak to the sons of Israel and say to them, "The LORD's appointed times which you shall proclaim as holy convocations—My appointed times are these."* (Leviticus 23:2)

The Biblical calendar

**Refer to Resource**

Free Monthly Biblical Calendar
www.ffoz.org/resources/erosh

*mo'ed* (מעד) = "appointed time,"
**plural form** *mo'adim* (מעדים)

God's daytimer

**Key Verses**

Leviticus 23:2
Romans 3:29

**Key Concepts**

*Lunar calendar*: Calendar based
on the phases of the moon. The
phases of the moon determine the
months, but the calendar is adjusted
periodically to keep it aligned with
the solar year.

## 1. The Lunar Calendar

The biblical calendar is a lunar calendar; it is based on the phases
of the moon. The waxing and waning of the moon determines the
day of the biblical month. The tiny sliver of the new moon always
appears on the first day of the month; the full moon indicates the
middle of the month; the disappearance of the moon indicates the
end of the month.

The first visible crescent of the new moon
marks the first day of the biblical month.

The full moon marks the middle
of the biblical month.

## 2. The Jewish Festivals

*The LORD's appointed times which you shall proclaim as holy
convocations—My appointed times are these.* (Leviticus 23:2)

*Is God the God of Jews only? Is He not the God of Gentiles also?
Yes, of Gentiles also.* (Romans 3:29)

To say that Gentile believers are not expected to keep God's appointed
times is the same as saying that Gentile believers are not supposed
to have any holy days or days of worship.

**Refer to Resource**

*Messiah Journal* 102
"Gentiles and the Festivals
of Israel"
Pages 31–38

**Key Verses**

Colossians 2:16–17
Leviticus 23
Numbers 28–29

**Key Words**

*Chukkat olam:* Hebrew for "eternal statute."

**Those Darn Pagans**

*Tel Dan, Northern Israel* – In an effort to stop the Israelites of the northern kingdom from keeping the festivals in Jerusalem, King Jeroboam built altars at Dan and Bethel and changed the dates of the festivals. Archaeology at Tel Dan has revealed the high place created by King Jeroboam.

3. **Celebrating with God**

The appointed times are:

a.

b.

c.

d.

e.

*Therefore no one is to act as your judge in regard to … a festival or a new moon or a Sabbath day—things which are a mere shadow of what is to come; but the substance belongs to Christ.* (Colossians 2:16–17)

4. **Perpetual Ordinances**

*A perpetual statute* [chukkat olam] *throughout your generations in all your dwelling places.* (Leviticus 23:14)

The appointed times will never be obsolete or done away with. Instead, they are to be celebrated and observed wherever we live.

How long is eternal?

*chukkat olam* (חקת עולם) = **"eternal statute"**

# The Festival Cycle

Leviticus 23 and Numbers 28–29 introduce the LORD's appointed times (*mo'adim*).

### Cycles in Time

| | Frequency | Appointment |
|---|---|---|
| 1 | | |
| 2 | | |
| 3 | | |
| 4 | | |

## A Daily Times of Prayer

Every single day contains special appointed times—the times of morning and afternoon sacrifice, that is, the daily times of prayer.

*You shall be careful to present My offering, My food for My offerings by fire, of a soothing aroma to Me, at their appointed time … two male lambs one year old without defect as a continual burnt offering every day. You shall offer the one lamb in the morning and the other lamb you shall offer at twilight.* (Numbers 28:2–4)

*Peter and John were going up to the temple at the ninth hour, the hour of prayer.* (Acts 3:1)

### Times of Prayer

| Morning Prayer (*Shacharit*, שחרית) | Afternoon Prayer (*Minchah*, מנחה) | Evening Prayer (*Ma'ariv*, מעריב) |
|---|---|---|
| The daily morning prayer service, corresponding with the daily morning burnt offering that was presented in the Temple. *Numbers 28:4; Acts 2:15* | The daily afternoon prayer service, corresponding with the daily afternoon burnt offering that was presented in the Temple. *Numbers 28:4; Acts 10:2–3* | The daily evening prayer services, comprised primarily of the *Shema* and the *Amidah*. The Talmud explains that it corresponds with the burning of the leftovers on the altar in the Temple and the night watches. *Leviticus 6:9* |
| Anytime between dawn and the third hour after sunrise. | Anytime between the early afternoon and sunset. | Anytime between sunset and midnight. |

## B Weekly Sabbath

Once a week, we are to set aside the Sabbath day for the LORD.

*Six days you shall labor and do all your work, but the seventh day is a sabbath of the LORD your God; in it you shall not do any work.* (Exodus 20:9–10)

> ### *Shabbat* (שבת) = "to cease" or "to rest"

*It is a sign between Me and the sons of Israel forever.* (Exodus 31:17)

**Key Verses**

Numbers 28:2–4
Acts 3:1
Acts 2:15
Acts 10:2–3
Leviticus 6:9
Exodus 20:9–10
Exodus 31:17

**Key Words**

*Shacharit:* 1. Morning. 2. The daily morning prayer service, corresponding with the daily morning burnt offering that was presented in the Temple.

*Minchah:* 1. A gift or offering. 2. Afternoon prayer.

*Ma'ariv:* 1. Evening or darkening. 2. The daily evening prayer service, comprised primarily of the *Shema* and the *Amidah*, and corresponding with the burning of the leftovers on the altar in the Temple and the night watches.

*Shabbat:* From the word *shavat*, meaning "to cease" or "to rest"; seventh day of the week.

**Refer to Resource**

FFOZ Video:
***Knocking on Heaven's Gates***

### Key Words

*Rosh Chodesh:* Hebrew for "head of the new month." *Rosh Chodesh* marks the beginning of the lunar month and is indicated by the new moon.

*Shevitah:* Hebrew word meaning "stopping work; going on strike." It derives from the same root word as Shabbat.

## ⓒ Monthly New Moons

The first visible and discernible new moon, which is just a tiny crescent sliver of moon in the sky, is the first day of the biblical month.

> *Rosh Chodesh* (ראש חדש) = "head of the new month"

*The new moons and the fixed festivals in the number set by the ordinance concerning them.* (1 Chronicles 23:31)

## ⓓ Annual Festivals

In addition to creating daily, weekly, and monthly cycles, God's appointed times also create an annual cycle.

| Spring Festivals | Fall Festivals |
| --- | --- |
| Passover, Unleavened Bread, First Fruits of the Barley, Pentecost | Feast of Trumpets, Day of Atonement, Feast of Tabernacles, The Eighth Day |

### 📷◀ Your Israel Connection

**Preparing for the Sabbath**

*Machaneh Yehudah, Jerusalem –* Preparing for the Sabbath is a regular part of life in Israel. Every Thursday and Friday the local market places fill with customers buying provisions for the Sabbath day meals. By mid-afternoon on Friday, the market is virtually empty as stores close for Sabbath.

# The Sabbath

The Sabbath candles

*For six days work may be done, but on the seventh day there is a sabbath of complete rest, a holy convocation. You shall not do any work; it is a sabbath to the LORD in all your dwellings.* (Leviticus 23:3)

| English Names of the Day | | | | | | |
|---|---|---|---|---|---|---|
| Sunday | Monday | Tuesday | Wednesday | Thursday | Friday | Saturday |

| Hebrew Names of the Day | | | | | | |
|---|---|---|---|---|---|---|
| 1st Day | 2nd Day | 3rd Day | 4th Day | 5th Day | 6th Day | Sabbath |

**Key Verses**

Leviticus 23:5
Leviticus 23:6–8
Leviticus 23:9–14
Leviticus 23:15–21
1 Corinthians 11:28

**Key Words**

*Pesach:* Hebrew for "Passover" (Leviticus 23:5).

# The Spring Festivals ✒

**The Spring Festivals**

| | Hebrew Name | English Name | Scripture |
|---|---|---|---|
| **1.** | *Pesach,* פסח | | Leviticus 23:5 |
| **2.** | *Chag HaMatzah,* חג המצה | | Leviticus 23:6–8 |
| **3.** | *Omer,* עומר | | Leviticus 23:9–14 |
| **4.** | *Shavu'ot,* שבועות | | Leviticus 23:15–21 |

## Ⓐ Passover

*In the first month, on the fourteenth day of the month at twilight is the LORD's Passover.* (Leviticus 23:5)

> *Pesach* (פסח) = **Passover**

Passover is the day on which the Passover lambs were slaughtered, the day before the week of Unleavened Bread begins.

*A man must examine himself, and in so doing he is to eat of the bread and drink of the cup.* (1 Corinthians 11:28)

**Key Words**

*Matzah:* Hebrew for "unleavened bread," which is bread made without yeast.

*Chag HaMatzah:* Festival of Unleavened Bread (Leviticus 23:6) which was given as a remembrance of the speed with which the Israelites were to leave Egypt.

*Chametz:* Leavened food items to be removed from homes during the Festival of Unleavened Bread.

**Key Concepts**

*Leaven as a symbol of sin:* A small amount of yeast, or leaven, permeates a whole lump of dough just as a small amount of sin can affect our whole lives. Yeshua is symbolized by unleavened bread because He was without sin.

## ⓑ Unleavened Bread

*Then on the fifteenth day of the same month there is the Feast of Unleavened Bread to the LORD; for seven days you shall eat unleavened bread.* (Leviticus 23:6)

| Nisan 14 | Nisan 15 | Nisan 16 | Nisan 17 | Nisan 18 | Nisan 19 | Nisan 20 | Nisan 21 |
|---|---|---|---|---|---|---|---|
| Passover Day | 1st Festival Day | 2nd Festival Day | 3rd Festival Day | 4th Festival Day | 5th Festival Day | 6th Festival Day | 7th Festival Day |
| | Seven Days of the Festival of Unleavened Bread | | | | | | |

*matzah* (מצה) = "unleavened bread"

*Chag HaMatzah* (חג המצה) = "Festival of Unleavened Bread"

*chametz* (חמץ) = "leavened items"

*Clean out the old leaven so that you may be a new lump, just as you are in fact unleavened. For Christ our Passover also has been sacrificed. Therefore let us celebrate the feast, not with old leaven, nor with the leaven of malice and wickedness, but with the unleavened bread of sincerity and truth.* (1 Corinthians 5:7–8)

*For as often as you eat this bread and drink the cup, you proclaim the Lord's death until He comes.* (1 Corinthians 11:26)

Passover Seder

## C The Omer

The Torah commanded the Israelites to bring the "sheaf of the first fruits" of the grain harvest to the Temple on the day after the Sabbath of Unleavened Bread.

*When you enter the land which I am going to give to you and reap its harvest, then you shall bring in the sheaf of the first fruits of your harvest to the priest.* (Leviticus 23:10)

### 1. First Fruits of the Barley

Barley harvest

The day of the First Fruits of the Barley (Omer) begins the forty-nine-day count-off to Pentecost (the fiftieth day).

> ### *omer* (עומר) = a measure of grain approximately two quarts in volume

The barley offering that was offered up on the day after the first Sabbath of Unleavened Bread was one omer of grain.

Messiah is the "first fruits of those who are asleep" (1 Corinthians 15:20).

### 2. Counting the Days Until Pentecost

*You shall count fifty days to the day after the seventh [week]; then you shall present a new grain offering to the LORD.* (Leviticus 23:16)

**Key Verses**

Leviticus 23:10
1 Corinthians 15:20
Leviticus 23:16

**Key Words**

*Omer:* A biblical measure of grain approximately two quarts in volume. The barley offering that was offered up on the day after the first Sabbath of Unleavened Bread was one omer of grain.

**Refer to Resource**

*Torah Club Volume Five: Rejoicing of the Torah*
"Emor: Say"

## Key Verses

Leviticus 23:21
Acts 2:1–4
Mark 14:23–24
1 Thessalonians 4:16
Exodus 35:3
Romans 3:1–2
Romans 11:17–18

## Key Words

*Pentecost:* Greek word meaning "fifty."

*Shavu'ot:* Hebrew word for "weeks" and the Hebrew name for the festival of Pentecost (Leviticus 23:16).

## Key Concepts

*The Counting of the Omer:* The forty-nine day period between the second day of Unleavened Bread and Pentecost, during which time each day is counted and marked with a special blessing.

> *Pentecost* (Πεντηκοστη) = "fifty"
>
> **Counting the Omer = the 49 days between the second day of Unleavened Bread and Pentecost**

## ❶ Pentecost

> *Shavu'ot* (שבועות) = "weeks"

The day of Pentecost is the anniversary of the day God spoke the Ten Commandments from Mount Sinai. In Judaism, the festival is also called "The Giving of the Torah."

Shavu'ot in Solomon's Portico (Acts 2)

*On this same [fiftieth] day you shall make a proclamation as well; you are to have a holy convocation. You shall do no laborious work. It is to be a perpetual statute in all your dwelling places throughout your generations.* (Leviticus 23:21)

*When the day of Pentecost had come, they were all together in one place. And suddenly there came from heaven a noise like a violent rushing wind, and it filled the whole house where they were sitting. And there appeared to them tongues as of fire distributing themselves, and they rested on each one of them. And they were all filled with the Holy Spirit and began to speak with other tongues, as the Spirit was giving them utterance.* (Acts 2:1–4)

# The Fall Festivals 

The fall festivals prophetically look forward to Messiah's second coming.

## The Fall Festivals

| | Hebrew Name | English Name | Scripture |
|---|---|---|---|
| **1.** | *Rosh HaShanah,* ראש השנה | | Leviticus 23:23–25 |
| **2.** | *Yom Kippur,* יום כפור | | Leviticus 23:26–32 |
| **3.** | *Sukkot,* סוכות | | Leviticus 23:33–44 |
| **4.** | *Shemini Atzeret,* שמיני עצרת | | Leviticus 23:36 |

### Key Verses

Leviticus 23:23–25
Leviticus 23:26–32
Leviticus 23:33–44
Matthew 24:31

### Key Words

*Rosh HaShanah:* Hebrew for "head of the year," or "New Year." This is the modern name for the Feast of Trumpets (Leviticus 23:23–25).

## Ⓐ The Feast of Trumpets

The first day of the seventh month is the Feast of Trumpets, a foreshadowing of the second coming of Messiah.

*Again the LORD spoke to Moses, saying, "Speak to the sons of Israel, saying, 'In the seventh month on the first of the month you shall have a rest, a reminder by blowing of trumpets, a holy convocation. You shall not do any laborious work, but you shall present an offering by fire to the LORD.'"* (Leviticus 23:23–25)

*He will send forth His angels with a great trumpet and they will gather together His elect from the four winds, from one end of the sky to the other.* (Matthew 24:31)

> *Rosh HaShanah* (ראש השנה) =
> "head of the year," i.e., "New Year"

### Refer to Resource

*HaYesod Student Workbook*
"A Closer Look at Rosh HaShanah"
Pages 8.24–8.27

## The Shofar WAS Sounded

- At the giving of the Torah to the people of Israel (Exodus 19:16–19)
- To announce the great sabbatical year of release (Leviticus 25:9)
- When Israel conquered Jericho (Joshua 6:20)
- To assemble Israel during war (Judges 3:27; 2 Samuel 20:1)
- To announce the ascension of a new king in Israel (1 Kings 34:39)
- To warn Israel of impending danger (Amos 3:6; Jeremiah 6:1; Ezekiel 33:6)

## The Shofar WILL BE Sounded

- At the final ingathering of the exiles of Israel (Isaiah 27:13)
- To announce God's miraculous end-time intervention to deliver the people of Israel (Zechariah 9:14)
- To herald the coming Messianic Age (Matthew 24:29–31)
- At the resurrection (1 Thessalonians 4:16, 17)
- At the coming of the King Messiah (Revelation 11:15–18)

| Civil Calendar Month No. | Israel's Calendar Month No. | Babylonian Month Name | Approx. English Equivalent | |
|---|---|---|---|---|
| 7th | 1st | Nisan | April | According to the Ancient Near Eastern reckoning (the civil calendar), the month of harvest in which Rosh HaShanah falls was the first month of the year. The month of springtime in which Passover falls was the seventh month of the year. God reordered the numbering of the months in Exodus 12:2 when He said, "This [springtime] month shall be the beginning of months for you; it is to be the first month of the year to you." Ever since then, the month of springtime has been referred to as "the first month." |
| 8th | 2nd | Iyar | May | |
| 9th | 3rd | Sivan | June | |
| 10th | 4th | Tammuz | July | |
| 11th | 5th | Av | August | |
| 12th | 6th | Elul | September | |
| 1st | 7th | Tishrei | October | |
| 2nd | 8th | Cheshvan | November | |
| 3rd | 9th | Kislev | December | |
| 4th | 10th | Tevet | January | |
| 5th | 11th | Shevat | February | |
| 6th | 12th | Adar | March | |

**Key Verses**

Exodus 12:2
Leviticus 23:27–28
Leviticus 16
Leviticus 23:42

**Key Words**

*Yom Kippur:* Hebrew for "Day of Atonement." This is a solemn biblical fast day (Leviticus 23:27–28).

*Days of Awe:* Ten days in between Rosh HaShanah and Yom Kippur.

*Sukkot:* Hebrew name for the festival of Tabernacles (Leviticus 23:42).

## B Day of Atonement

The tenth day of the seventh month is the biblically appointed time of Yom Kippur.

**_Yom Kippur_ (יום כפור) = "Day of Atonement"**

*On exactly the tenth day of this seventh month is the day of atonement; it shall be a holy convocation for you, and you shall humble your souls and present an offering by fire to the LORD. You shall not do any work on this same day, for it is a day of atonement, to make atonement on your behalf before the LORD your God.* (Leviticus 23:27–28)

Yom Kippur is a fast day, and the day the high priest entered the holy of holies (Leviticus 16).

## C The Feast of Tabernacles

**_Sukkot_ (סוכות) = "The Feast of Tabernacles"**

**Key Words**

*Sukkah* (pl. *sukkot*): Hebrew word meaning "booth" or "hut;" a temporary structure.

*Shemini Atzeret:* Hebrew for "Eighth-Day Assembly."

*Simchat Torah:* Hebrew for "The Rejoicing of the Torah" and the name for the eighth-day festival of Sukkot.

**⌖ Your Israel Connection**

**Which Calendar?**

*Qumran, Dead Sea Region* – The community that left behind the Dead Sea Scrolls observed an alternative reckoning of the biblical calendar. Their insistence on keeping the holy days according to their own calculations forced them into seclusion and isolation near the Dead Sea.

On the fifteenth day of the month, the Feast of Tabernacles begins, a seven-day festival during which the Jewish people are commanded to dwell in temporary shelters as a reminder of the post-exodus years when Israel lived in huts and booths, following God in the wilderness.

*You shall live in booths for seven days; all the native-born in Israel shall live in booths.* (Leviticus 23:42)

*sukkah* (סוכה) = "booth, hut"

Sukkah

### ❶ The Eighth Day

A special Sabbath called "the eighth day," immediately follows the seven days of Sukkot. It is the concluding Festival of Sukkot.

*Shemini Atzeret* (שמיני עצרת) = "Eighth-Day Assembly"

*On the eighth day you shall have a holy convocation.* (Leviticus 23:36)

In Israel, the eighth day of *Sukkot* is celebrated as "The Rejoicing of the Torah" (*Simchat Torah*, שמחת תורה), the day the Torah scroll is concluded and begun again in the synagogue.

*Simchat Torah* (שמחת תורה) = "The Rejoicing of the Torah"

# Cycle of Sanctification

The daily, weekly, monthly, and annual cycles of appointed times create opportunities for self-improvement in our spiritual walks.

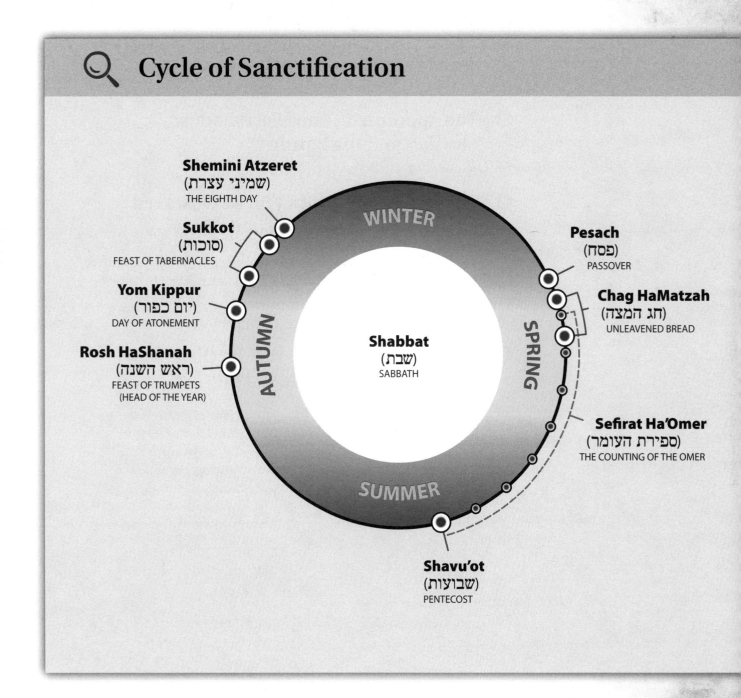

## Cycle of Sanctification

**Shemini Atzeret**
(שְׁמִינִי עֲצֶרֶת)
THE EIGHTH DAY

**Sukkot**
(סוכות)
FEAST OF TABERNACLES

**Yom Kippur**
(יום כפור)
DAY OF ATONEMENT

**Rosh HaShanah**
(ראש השנה)
FEAST OF TRUMPETS
(HEAD OF THE YEAR)

**Pesach**
(פסח)
PASSOVER

**Chag HaMatzah**
(חג המצה)
UNLEAVENED BREAD

**Sefirat Ha'Omer**
(ספירת העומר)
THE COUNTING OF THE OMER

**Shavu'ot**
(שבועות)
PENTECOST

**Shabbat**
(שבת)
SABBATH

WINTER

SPRING

SUMMER

AUTUMN

# Shadow of Things to Come

Gentile believers have a divine invitation to participate in the cycle of sanctification. If God is throwing a party, and He has invited all of His children, all of His children should come.

*Therefore no one is to act as your judge in regard to … a festival or a new moon or a Sabbath day—things which are a mere shadow of what is to come; but the substance belongs to Christ.* (Colossians 2:16–17)

**A** **The Appointed Times Foreshadow Messiah and the Future**

**B** **The Appointed Times Will Be Observed by Everyone in the Messianic Era**

*"And it shall be from new moon to new moon and from sabbath to sabbath, all mankind will come to bow down before Me," says the LORD.* (Isaiah 66:23)

**C** **The Appointed Times Will Be Observed by all Nations in the Messianic Era**

*All the nations … will go up from year to year to worship the King, the LORD of hosts, and to celebrate the Feast of Booths. And it will be that whichever of the families of the earth does not go up to Jerusalem to worship the King, the LORD of hosts, there will be no rain on them.* (Zechariah 14:16–17)

# Lesson Eight
# LESSON SUMMARY

## First …

We learned about the biblical, lunar calendar.

❖ We saw that God has made daily, weekly, monthly, and annual appointments in time on His calendar.

❖ In Hebrew, appointed times are called *mo'adim*.

❖ We learned that these appointments are perpetual ordinances.

## Then …

We began to go through the appointed times and learn a little bit about each one of them:

❖ The Sabbath day allows us to slow down enough to spend quality time in God's presence, learning the things of His Word and plugging into extended periods of prayer, study, and worship.

The Spring Festivals include:

❖ Passover and the Feast of Unleavened Bread—the anniversaries of the redemption from Egypt.

❖ The Counting of the Omer and Pentecost—a remembrance of the journey to Sinai and the giving of the Torah.

The Fall Festivals include:

❖ The Feast of Trumpets—a day of blowing the shofar that anticipates Messiah's return.

❖ The Day of Atonement—a fast day, the day the high priest went into the holy of holies.

❖ The Feast of Tabernacles and the Eighth Day—a remembrance of when God had the Israelites live in booths after leaving Egypt.

## After that …

We saw how all of the festivals form a "cycle of sanctification," and are daily, weekly, monthly, and annual opportunities for self-improvement in our spiritual walks.

## Finally …

We discovered that the appointed times foreshadow things to come, and that the Sabbath and festivals will be observed by all nations in the Messianic Age to come.

# Lesson Eight
## LESSON REVIEW – Q&A

1. What does the Hebrew word *mo'adim* mean?

2. In what passages do we find the cycle of the appointed times in the Bible?

3. Beginning with Sabbath, list the appointed times in order as they appear in the year.

4. What are some of the functions of the appointed times?

5. When does an "eternal statute" or "perpetual ordinance" expire?

6. What are the daily times of prayer?

7. What are the names of the spring festivals? How do they foreshadow Messiah?

8. What are the names of the fall festivals? How do they foreshadow Messiah?

# Lesson Eight
## EXTRA CREDIT
### SUPPLEMENTAL MATERIAL FOR THIS HAYESOD LESSON

---

**Extra Credit Instructions:**

1. This material is not mandatory, but it will serve as a helpful tool for further study.
2. We have assigned five categories to each festival: Key Concept, Atmosphere, Ancient Observances, Modern Observances, and Festival Accessories. Read the designated passages and do your best to provide an answer for each category.

## Worship Calendar

For this lesson's Extra Credit exercise, fill out the festival chart. It will help you establish the biblical festivals in your mind and get you thinking about how you might incorporate God's appointed times into your spiritual walk.

1. **Key Concept:** The special theological emphasis for the holy day. Does it memorialize something? Is it meant to accomplish some purpose?

2. **Atmosphere:** What kind of spiritual/emotional atmosphere is associated with this day?

3. **Ancient Observances:** How was the day celebrated in ancient Israel?

4. **Modern Observances:** How can the day be celebrated in our modern homes and congregations without a Temple?

5. **Festival Accessories:** What sorts of objects, if any, does the festival require?

## Shabbat

1. **Key Concept:** Exodus 20:9–11

2. **Atmosphere:** Isaiah 58:13–14

3. **Ancient Observances:** Exodus 35:2–3; Numbers 28:9–10

4. **Modern Observances:** Exodus 31:15–16

5. **Festival Accessories:** Exodus 16:23–29

## Passover and Unleavened Bread

1. **Key Concept:** Exodus 12:14–20, 26–27; Deuteronomy 16:3


2. **Atmosphere:** *Joy and Gratitude*


3. **Ancient Observances:** Deuteronomy 16:1–8


4. **Modern Observances:** Exodus 12:14–19


5. **Festival Accessories:** Exodus 12:8


## The Omer and Pentecost

1. **Key Concept:** Exodus 19–20; Deuteronomy 16:9–10


2. **Atmosphere:** Deuteronomy 16:11–12


3. **Ancient Observances:** Leviticus 23:10–22


4. **Modern Observances:** Leviticus 23:15


5. **Festival Accessories:** *A reading of the Ten Commandments from the Torah is traditional.*


## The Feast of Trumpets

1. **Key Concept:** Leviticus 23:23–25; 1 Thessalonians 4:16


2. **Atmosphere:** Nehemiah 8:1–12


3. **Ancient Observances:** Numbers 29:1–6


4. **Modern Observances:** Numbers 29:1


5. **Festival Accessories:** Numbers 29:1

## The Day of Atonement 🖎

1. **Key Concept:** Leviticus 16:3, 30–34


2. **Atmosphere:** Leviticus 16:29–31


3. **Ancient Observances:** Leviticus 16


4. **Modern Observances:** Leviticus 16:29–31


5. **Festival Accessories:** *Not Applicable*


## Tabernacles and the Eighth Day 🖎

1. **Key Concept:** Leviticus 23:39, 41–43


2. **Atmosphere:** Deuteronomy 16:13–15


3. **Ancient Observances:** Numbers 29:12–40


4. **Modern Observances:** Leviticus 23:39–43


5. **Festival Accessories:** Leviticus 23:39–43

# Lesson Eight – Digging Deeper
## A CLOSER LOOK AT ROSH HASHANAH
### FURTHER STUDY FROM THIS WEEK'S HAYESOD LESSON

**Resource in Focus**

Excerpt from parashat "Emor: Say" of First Fruits of Zion's *Torah Club Volume Two: Shadows of the Messiah.*

*In the seventh month on the first of the month you shall have a rest, a reminder by blowing of trumpets, a holy convocation. (Leviticus 23:24)*

On the first day of the seventh month is this festival the Torah simply calls a "reminder by blowing of trumpets." This is the festival we call the "Feast of Trumpets," the day of trumpet-blowing. The Torah tells us to celebrate the Feast of Trumpets by blowing a ram's horn (*shofar*, שׁופר). The Feast of Trumpets is a festival that is meant to prepare us for the holy Day of Atonement that comes ten days later.

The Torah commands us to blow the shofar on the Feast of Trumpets as a memorial, but it does not tell us what the blowing of the shofar memorializes. The sages offered various attempts to explain the festival. They searched through the Scriptures for references to shofars and trumpet blasts and derived a plethora of different remembrances. Other meanings attached to the festival were handed down from generation to generation through the oral tradition. The early medieval sage, Rav Saadiah Gaon, codified these various explanations of the Feast of Trumpets and listed them. According to Rav Saadiah Gaon, there are ten primary remembrances for which the shofar is blown on the Festival of Trumpets.[1] Each of these remembrances highlights a unique aspect of the festival. Each remembrance is a key facet to the holiday and its accompanying prayer service.

1. **Coronation:** In the Scriptures, the shofar is sounded at the coronation of a king.[2] The blast of the shofar announces the newly crowned king and proclaims his ascent to sovereignty. Thus the shofar blast of the Feast of Trumpets might be construed to be a proclamation of coronation of the King of the Universe.

   According to ancient Jewish tradition, the first day of the seventh month is the yearly anniversary of God's completion of creation. As such, it is also the New Year's Day of the biblical calendar. That is why the festival is usually called *Rosh HaShanah* (the head of the year). This is the Hebrew way of saying New Year's Day. The Feast of Trumpets marks the anniversary of the completion of creation as well as the day that God became king over that new creation. Therefore, the sound of the shofar on the Feast of Trumpets symbolizes our acceptance of God as king.

2. **Repentance:** The Festival of Trumpets marks the beginning of a ten-day countdown to the Day of Atonement. Because the Day of Atonement is judgment day, the shofar is sounded as a reminder that judgment is near and the time for repentance is short.

   In Temple times, the priesthood sounded three trumpet blasts every morning to announce the opening of the Temple gates.[3] So too Jewish tradition teaches that the shofar blasts of the Feast of Trumpets announce the opening of the gates of heaven.[4] In this tradition, the gates of heaven are opened to receive our prayers of repentance and remain open until the conclusion of the Day of Atonement. The Day of Atonement service is concluded with one long shofar blast that announces that the gates of heaven have closed and judgment is complete. Therefore, the sound of the shofar on the Feast of Trumpets is a remembrance of the need to repent before judgment is made.

3. **Sinai:** When God descended onto Mount Sinai in Exodus 19, a heavenly shofar sounded loud and long. The sound of the shofar at Sinai was one of the miraculous signs that accompanied the giving of the Torah and the invitation to covenant. Therefore, the sound of the shofar on the Feast of Trumpets is a remembrance of the day at Mount Sinai when Israel accepted the Torah.

4. **Warning:** In ancient Israel, a watchman blew a shofar to sound an alarm when danger was approaching, much the way civil defense sirens are used in our modern world. Ezekiel compares the words of the prophets to the sound of the shofar warning: "Then he who hears the sound of the trumpet and does not take warning, and a sword comes and takes him away, his blood will be on his own head" (Ezekiel 33:4).[5] If a person hears the words of the prophet but does not take warning from them, it will be his own fault when the trouble comes. Therefore, the sound of the shofar on the Feast of Trumpets is a remembrance of the need to take warning from the words of the prophets.

5. **Temple:** In the ancient Near East, the shofar was blown as a battle cry during sieges and assaults. The prophets invoked the battle cry of the shofar as they repeatedly warned of the impending destruction of Jerusalem and the Temple.[6] Therefore, the sound of the shofar on the Feast of Trumpets is a remembrance of the destruction of the Temple and a reminder to pray for its rebuilding.

6. **The Binding of Isaac:** A shofar trumpet is made from a ram's horn. The most famous ram in the Torah is the ram of Genesis 22, which was sacrificed in Isaac's stead. The Torah reading for the second day of the Feast of Trumpets is Genesis 22. The binding of Isaac is a central theme of the festival liturgies. Therefore, the sound of the shofar on the Feast of Trumpets is a remembrance of the binding of Isaac and a prayer for mercy on the merit of a sacrificed son.

7. **Fear:** As stated above, the ancient Israelite watchman blew a shofar to sound an alarm when danger was approaching a city. Amos employs this image of the fear inspired by the shofar blast when he says, "If a trumpet is blown in a city will not the people tremble?" (Amos 3:6). The danger that approaches on the Feast of Trumpets is God Himself as He readies the heavenly court for judgment. In Jewish observance, the intervening days between the Feast of Trumpets and the Day of Atonement are called the "days of awe." They are to be days of intense soul-searching and repentance and even fear as we prepare to enter the presence of the Judge of all creation. Amos reminds us to fear the judgment of God as we would tremble at the sound of the watchman's shofar. Therefore, the sound of the shofar on the Feast of Trumpets is a remembrance to fear God.

8. **Judgment:** The prophet Zephaniah reminds us that the "day of the shofar" is a day of wrath, darkness, gloom, and alarm. Indeed, it is the Day of the LORD.[7] According to the Feast of Trumpets traditions, the heavenly court is convened on the Feast of Trumpets. Because the Feast of Trumpets is the Torah New Year's Day (that is, the anniversary of the completion of creation), it is also the end of the heavenly fiscal year. As at the end of our calendar year, New Year's Day is the day when the ledgers must be settled. Tradition says that on the Feast of Trumpets the books of judgment are opened, and all the deeds of each person are reviewed by the heavenly court for judgment.[8] On the Day of Atonement, the righteous are written in the Book of Life but the wicked are written in the Book of Death. The intervening days between the Feast of Trumpets and the Day of Atonement are traditionally regarded as prime time to

sway the heavenly court's decision through serious prayer, repentance, and acts of charity. Therefore, the sound of the shofar on the Feast of Trumpets is a remembrance of judgment at the hands of Heaven.

9. **Ingathering:** Perhaps the most famous shofar reference out of all the prophets is Isaiah 27:13: "It will come about also in that day that a great trumpet will be blown, and those who were perishing in the land of Assyria and who were scattered in the land of Egypt will come and worship the Lord in the holy mountain at Jerusalem." This verse is a prophecy of the great ingathering of all Israel. The ingathering is to commence with the return of Messiah.[9] Therefore, the sound of the shofar on the Feast of Trumpets is a remembrance of the ultimate ingathering of Israel.

10. **Resurrection:** The tenth and final reason Rav Saadiah Gaon gives for the blowing of the shofar on the Feast of Trumpets is a remembrance of the resurrection of the dead. The sages understood the words of Isaiah 18:3 to be a prophecy directed to the dead. "As soon as the trumpet is blown, you will hear it," the prophet said. The sages interpreted this to mean that when the final shofar is blown, the dead will hear it and rise. The Jewish legends of the coming of Messiah include a great shofar blast that wakes up those sleeping in the dust. Therefore, the sound of the shofar on the Feast of Trumpets is a remembrance of the future resurrection of the dead.[10]

How does the Feast of Trumpets foreshadow Messiah? In the biblical year, there has been a long period without festivals or appointed times. Ever since the feast of *Shavu'ot* (Pentecost) in the third month, there has not been a festival. In the same way, there is a long absence of Messiah. Ever since the bestowing of the Spirit at Pentecost we have been awaiting His return. The years have passed and turned into centuries.

Then suddenly the silence is interrupted by a trumpet blast, a signal that things are in motion once again. Even as we wait to hear the trumpet blast of the king, the great shofar of our returning Redeemer, we celebrate the appointed time of the Feast of Trumpets. The annual blast of the shofar during the Feast of Trumpets foreshadows that day when the heavens will be rent by the blast of Messiah's trumpet. For disciples of the Messiah, the Feast of Trumpets is a reminder of that appointed time yet to come when the Master "will send forth His angels with a great trumpet and they will gather together His elect from the four winds, from one end of the sky to the other" (Matthew 24:31). It is a day on which we anticipate the coming judgment, the trumpets of the book of Revelation, and the beginning of the end. It is a glimpse of the future, a shadow cast through time. As such, the Feast of Trumpets is relevant for everyone who believes in Messiah's return. It is an important festival for the disciples of Yeshua.

## Endnotes

1   Phillip Goodman, *The Shavuot Anthology* (Philadelphia, PA: Jewish Publication Society, 1992).

2   See 1 Kings 1:39 for an example of this rite. The shofar blast as a coronation acclamation is also illustrated in Psalms 47:5 and 98:6.

3   Alfred Edersheim, *The Temple, Its Ministry and Services* (Grand Rapids, MI: Eerdmans Publishing, 1992).

4   The imagery of the trumpet announcing the opening of the gates is borrowed in Revelation 4:1.

5   See also Jeremiah 4:19–21.

6   Ibid.

7   Zephaniah 1:14–16.

8   This imagery is reflected in Revelation 20:12–15, where John sees the ultimate and final Day of Judgment.

9   See Matthew 24:30–31.

10   See 1 Corinthians 15:52 for Paul's association of the shofar blast and the resurrection of the dead.

# Notes:

**Notes:**

## Lesson Nine
# OUR BOUNDARIES– HIS COMMANDMENTS

THE LAND, THE PEOPLE,
AND THE SCRIPTURES OF ISRAEL

# Lesson Nine
# OUR BOUNDARIES— HIS COMMANDMENTS

*As obedient children, do not be conformed to the former lusts which were yours in your ignorance, but like the Holy One who called you, be holy yourselves also in all your behavior; because it is written, "You shall be holy, for I am holy."* (1 Peter 1:14–16)

## Lesson Overview

According to tradition, there are 613 commandments in the Torah. That seems like a lot. We need to take some time to examine specific commandments in the Torah and their function for the people of God. God's commandments sanctify Israel by setting God's people apart. The laws of holiness define what the people of God should look like. The dietary laws provide a menu for the people of God. The commands to love God and love one's neighbor summarize all the commandments in the Torah.

## Lesson Purpose

In this lesson we will:

- ❖ Discuss the difference between applicable and non-applicable commandments.
- ❖ Explain how the commandments sanctify God's people by setting them apart.
- ❖ Examine the biblical dietary laws.
- ❖ Consider how the Torah teaches us to love God and love our neighbor.

## Field Trips to the Holy Land

- ❖ Southern Wall, Jerusalem Temple Mount
- ❖ Ben Yehudah Street, Jerusalem
- ❖ Korazin Synagogue, Northern Galilee
- ❖ Yemin Moshe, Jerusalem

# Lesson Nine
# LESSON OUTLINE

## 613 Commandments

A. Positive and Negative Commandments

B. Applicable Commandments

C. It's Not Impossible

D. Torah for Christians

## Sanctified by the Commandments

A. The Blessing for a Mitzvah
1. Grateful Obedience
2. Set Apart by His Commandments

B. Be Holy for I am Holy
1. What is Holiness?
2. The Holy Nation

C. Things Pertaining to Holiness
1. Fear Your Parents
2. Working for Success
3. Honesty
4. Equal Weights
5. Giving the Benefit of the Doubt
6. The Slanderer
7. Storing Bitterness
8. Gray Hair

## A Kosher Diet

A. Fit and Unfit Animals
1. Land Animals
2. Fish and Sea Creatures
3. Fowl
4. Insects

B. Holy Food

C. You Are What You Eat
1. Food for the Stomach
2. Unclean Animals as Metaphor

D. The Kosher Gentile

E. Respect for Others

F. Rabbinically Kosher vs. Biblically Kosher

## The Greatest Commandment

A. Light and Weighty Matters

B. The Least of the Commandments
1. The Bird's Nest
2. The Same Reward

C. The Greatest Commandment
1. The Shema
2. Loving God
3. Talmud Torah
4. Tefillin
5. Mezuzah

## Loving our Neighbor

A. Do Unto Others

B. 613 Opportunities

# 613 Commandments

Our Master says, "The mouth speaks out of that which fills the heart" (Matthew 12:34). In that case, the commandments are directly from the heart of God. Each one is an expression of godliness, descended from heaven.

Traditional Judaism has counted and codified a total of 613 commandments within the Torah.

> # 613 = commandments in the Torah

*The emptiest among you is filled with commandments as a pomegranate is filled with seeds. (Song of Songs Rabbah 4:7)*

Pomegranates with seeds

## Ⓐ Postive and Negative Commandments

❖ Positive Commandments: "Thou Shalt"

❖ Negative Commandments: "Thou Shalt Not"

*Rabbi Simlai once said while preaching, "God spoke six hundred and thirteen commandments to Moses, three hundred and sixty-five negative commandments, corresponding to the number of days in a year, and two hundred and forty-eight positive commandments, corresponding to the number of the inner-parts of a man's body." (b.Makkot 23b)*

| 365 | Negative Commandments |
|-----|----------------------|
| 248 | Positive Commandments |
| 613 | Total Commandments |

The 365 negative commandments are _____.

The 248 positive commandments are _____.

## B Applicable Commandments

Not every commandment is applicable in our current situation.

*For there are many commandments that are in force in the Land of Israel but not in countries outside the Land; and there are [commandments] in force only at the time the Sanctuary exists. There are those which are related to ritual holiness and purity; there are those in force only at a* beth din *(court of law) of ordained and authorized judges [i.e., the Sanhedrin].* (Chofetz Chaim, *The Concise Book of Mitzvoth*)[1]

| | |
|---|---|
| 77 | Applicable Positive Commandments |
| 194 | Applicable Negative Commandments |
| 26 | Commandments Applicable Only in the Land of Israel |

## C It's Not Impossible

Torah is never all or nothing. With God, something is always better than nothing.

*For this commandment which I command you today is not too difficult for you, nor is it out of reach. It is not in heaven, that you should say, "Who will go up to heaven for us to get it for us and make us hear it, that we may observe it?" Nor is it beyond the sea, that you should say, "Who will cross the sea for us to get it for us and make us hear it, that we may observe it?" But the word is very near you, in your mouth and in your heart, that you may observe it.* (Deuteronomy 30:11–14)

## D Torah for Christians

Just by living the Christian life, the average Christian is already keeping most of the Torah.

**Your Israel Connection**

**Ceremonial Law**

*Southern Wall, Jerusalem Temple Mount* – Massive stones from the upper courses of the Temple Mount's retaining walls pushed down by the Roman armies still lie piled on the Herodian-era street which ran below the Temple Mount. Our Master once walked that street as He went in and out of the Temple district. Today the stones testify to the truth of His words and the tragedy of the Temple's destruction.

**Key Verses**

Deuteronomy 6:9
Leviticus 23:15–16
Deuteronomy 22:8
Leviticus 23:42
Hebrews 10:10

# Sanctified by the Commandments

In Jewish liturgy, it is common to offer a blessing to God before performing a specific commandment.

## Ⓐ The Blessing for a Mitzvah

Here are some examples of blessings offered before performing specific commandments:

❖ For putting up a mezuzah (Deuteronomy 6:9)

*Blessed are you LORD our God, king of the universe, who has sanctified us with his commandments and commanded us to affix the mezuzah. Amen.*

❖ For counting the days until Pentecost (Leviticus 23:15–16)

*Blessed are you LORD our God, king of the universe, who has sanctified us with his commandments and commanded us concerning the counting of the omer. Amen.*

❖ For building a parapet around one's roof (Deuteronomy 22:8)

*Blessed are you LORD our God, king of the universe, who has sanctified us with his commandments and commanded us to build a parapet. Amen.*

❖ For dwelling in the sukkah ("booth") at the Feast of Tabernacles (Leviticus 23:42)

*Blessed are you LORD our God, king of the universe, who has sanctified us with his commandments and commanded us to dwell in the sukkah. Amen.*

### 1. Grateful Obedience

We thank God for giving us an opportunity to serve Him. The commandment is not looked at as some sort of unpleasant chore and painful mandate; it is seen as a special privilege, an opportunity to serve God.

### 2. Set Apart by His Commandments

In what way has God sanctified (set apart) His people Israel with His commandments?

*We have been sanctified through the offering of the body of Jesus Christ once for all.* (Hebrews 10:10)

## B  Be Holy for I am Holy

**Key Verses**

Leviticus 19:2
1 Peter 2:9
Exodus 19:6
1 Peter 1:14–16

*Speak to all the congregation of the sons of Israel and say to them,
"You shall be holy, for I the LORD your God am holy."* (Leviticus 19:2)

### 1.  What is Holiness?

**Key Words**

*Kadosh:* From the word *kadash*, meaning "holy" or "set apart."

Holiness means "set apart" or "set apart for God." God "sanctifies us by His commandments," which is to say, "He separates us from the world by His commandments."

> *kadosh* (קדוש) = "set apart, holy"

*Kadash* (קדש) = ........................................................................................

### 2.  The Holy Nation

Israel is the holy nation. But holy living is not only for the Jewish people. The Apostle Peter refers to the Gentile believers in the same language.

*But you are a chosen race, a royal priesthood, a holy nation, a people for God's own possession, so that you may proclaim the excellencies of Him who has called you out of darkness into His marvelous light.* (1 Peter 2:9; quoting Exodus 19:6)

*As obedient children, do not be conformed to the former lusts which were yours in your ignorance, but like the Holy One who called you, be holy yourselves also in all your behavior; because it is written, "You shall be holy, for I am holy."*
(1 Peter 1:14–16; quoting Leviticus 19:2)

## C  Things Pertaining to Holiness

*Seeing then that we are the special portion of a Holy God, let us do all things that pertain unto holiness.* (1 Clement 30:1 [Lightfoot])

## 🔍 Clement

According to church tradition, Clement of Rome was a disciple of Peter. In some papal lists he is regarded as the second or fourth pope over the Roman Church, but this is an anachronism. Pseudepigraphical church literature has left several works that were allegedly written by Clement, but scholars agree that only the *First Epistle of Clement to the Corinthians* should be regarded as authentic. The rest of the works credited to him are later forgeries.

**Key Verses**

Leviticus 19:3
Exodus 20:12
Mark 7
Leviticus 19:9

**Key Words**

*Yare:* Hebrew word meaning "to fear" or "revere."

## 1. Fear Your Parents

Holiness is reflected in the way we treat our parents.

*Every one of you shall <u>reverence</u> [yare] his mother and his father.* (Leviticus 19:3)

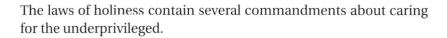

*yare* (ירא) = **"fear, revere"**

<u>Honor</u> *your father and your mother.* (Exodus 20:12)

You shall honor:

*"Honor" means that [at a minimum] he must give him food and drink, clothe and cover him, lead him in and out.* (b.*Kiddushin* 31b)

You shall reverence:

*[The son] must neither stand in [the father's] place nor sit in his place, nor contradict his words, nor tip the scales against him.* (b.*Kiddushin* 31b)

Holiness means ........................................................................................................... .

## 2. Working for Success

The laws of holiness contain several commandments about caring for the underprivileged.

*Now when you reap the harvest of your land, you shall not reap to the very corners of your field, nor shall you gather the gleanings of your harvest.* (Leviticus 19:9)

Harvesting the corners

*Pure and undefiled religion in the sight of our God and Father is this: to visit orphans and widows in their distress.* (James 1:27)

Holiness means ........................................................................... .

3. **Honesty**

*You shall not steal, nor deal falsely, nor lie to one another.* (Leviticus 19:11)

When a religious person conducts himself no differently than the common, ordinary people around him, he makes God look common and ordinary too. A believer who steals, deceives, lies, or perjures damages God's reputation.

The opposite of "holy" is "profane."

> ## holy = "set apart"
>
> ## profane = "common and ordinary"

*You shall not oppress your neighbor, nor rob him.* (Leviticus 19:13)

Holiness means ........................................................................... .

4. **Equal Weights**

Holiness requires honesty and ethics in business.

Equal weights

*You shall do no wrong in judgment, in measurement of weight, or capacity. You shall have just balances, just weights, a just ephah, and a just hin; I am the LORD your God, who brought you out from the land of Egypt.* (Leviticus 19:35–36)

**Key Verses**

James 1:27
Leviticus 19:11
Leviticus 19:13
Leviticus 19:35–36

**Key Concepts**

*Holy vs. profane:* The opposite of "holy" is "profane." Holy means "set apart" and profane means "common and ordinary."

**Refer to Resource**

*Hallowed Be Your Name*
"How Do We Sanctify God's Name?"
Pages 39–44

**Key Verses**

Deuteronomy 25:13–14
Leviticus 19:15–17
Leviticus 19:32

**Key Words**

*Lashon hara:* lit. the "evil tongue," referring to gossip and slander.

**Refer to Resource**

*Torah Club Volume Five:
The Rejoicing of the Torah*
"Kedoshim: Holy"

---

*You shall not have in your bag differing weights, a large and a small. You shall not have in your house differing measures, a large and a small.* (Deuteronomy 25:13–14)

Holiness means _____.

5. **Giving the Benefit of the Doubt**

*You are to judge your neighbor fairly.* (Leviticus 19:15)

The commandment to judge one's neighbor fairly means giving the benefit of the doubt.

Holiness means _____.

6. **The Slanderer**

*You shall not go about as a slanderer among your people, and you are not to act against the life of your neighbor; I am the LORD.* (Leviticus 19:16)

> *lashon hara* (לשון הרע) =
> "evil tongue, gossip, slander"

To spread negative information about someone—even if it is true—harms the person's character and degrades the image in which he was created.

Holiness means _____.

7. **Storing Bitterness**

The Torah forbids the carrying of a grudge.

*You shall not hate your fellow countryman in your heart; you may surely reprove your neighbor, but shall not incur sin because of him.* (Leviticus 19:17)

Holiness means _____.

8. **Gray Hair**

Torah culture honors gray hair and the wisdom earned through years.

*You shall rise up before the grayheaded and honor the aged, and you shall revere your God; I am the LORD.* (Leviticus 19:32)

Holiness means _____.

# A Kosher Diet

Food permissible to eat is described as *kosher*, a word that means "fit" or "proper." Leviticus 11 and Deuteronomy 14 describes which animals the Torah deems fit and proper to eat, and which it does not.

> *kosher* (כשר) = "fit, proper"

Kosher means appropriate or acceptable; meeting the standards of biblical and Jewish law, especially as it relates to food.

## Ⓐ Fit and Unfit Animals

Animals that are permissible for food are described as clean. Animals that are forbidden are described as unclean.

Sources for biblical dietary laws: Leviticus 11; Deuteronomy 14

*Speak to the sons of Israel, saying, "These are the creatures which you may eat from all the animals that are on the earth."* (Leviticus 11:2)

| "Kosher" Animals "Fit" for consumption | |
| --- | --- |
| | Must have divided (cloven) hooves and must ruminate (chew its cud). |
| | Must have both fins and scales. |
| | No common criteria, but must not be a bird of prey. |
| | Must have jointed legs above the other legs. Must not creep on the ground. |

### 1. Land Animals

A "clean" animal must have divided (cloven) hooves and must ruminate (chew its cud).

*Whatever divides a hoof, thus making split hoofs, and chews the cud, among the animals, that you may eat.* (Leviticus 11:3)

**Key Verses**

Leviticus 11
Acts 15
Deuteronomy 14

**Key Words**

*Kosher*: Hebrew word meaning "fit, proper, appropriate, or acceptable;" meeting the standards of biblical and Jewish law, especially as it relates to food.

**◉ Your Israel Connection**

**What Makes Burger King Kosher?**

*Ben Yehudah, Jerusalem* – Ben Yehudah Street is a busy street in downtown Jerusalem, connecting Zion Square with the intersection of Jaffa Road and King George Street. Lined with shops and restaurants, the street is a center for Jerusalem night-life and a popular tourist attraction. The street is named after the founder of modern Hebrew, Eliezer Ben-Yehudah.

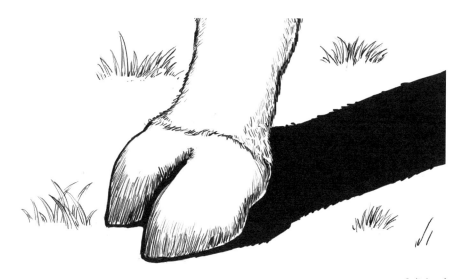

Split hoof

2. **Fish and Sea Creatures**

Must have both fins and scales.

*These you may eat, whatever is in the water: all that have fins and scales, those in the water, in the seas or in the rivers, you may eat.* (Leviticus 11:9)

3. **Fowl**

No common criteria, but must not be a bird of prey.

*These, moreover, you shall detest among the birds; they are abhorrent, not to be eaten: the eagle and the vulture and the buzzard.* (Leviticus 11:13)

4. **Insects**

Must have jointed legs above the other legs. Must not creep on the ground.

*Yet these you may eat among all the winged insects which walk on all fours: those which have above their feet jointed legs with which to jump on the earth.* (Leviticus 11:21)

**Refer to Resource**

*HaYesod Student Workbook*
"More About the Biblical Dietary Laws"
Pages 9.27–9.29

## **B** Holy Food

The Torah dispels the idea that the kosher laws are some sort of health-food diet by informing us that they are really about holiness.

*For I am the LORD your God. Consecrate yourselves therefore, and be holy, for I am holy. And you shall not make yourselves unclean with any of the swarming things that swarm on the earth. For I am the LORD who brought you up from the land of Egypt to be your God; thus you shall be holy, for I am holy.* (Leviticus 11:44–45)

*You shall be holy men to Me, therefore you shall not eat any*
*flesh torn to pieces in the field; you shall throw it to the dogs.*
(Exodus 22:31)

**Key Verses**

Exodus 22:31
Genesis 2–3
Genesis 25
Leviticus 11
Matthew 15:11
1 Corinthians 6:13
Matthew 13:47–48

The biblical dietary laws are (choose the answer that best completes the sentence):

a. ............... the way to make healthier food choices

b. ............... canceled by the New Testement

c. ............... laws of holiness to set us apart

d. ............... a means to avoid refrigeration

## C  You Are What You Eat

Major problems in the Bible center on food. Food is one of the strongest desires of man.

### 1. Food for the Stomach

*It is not what enters into the mouth that defiles the man,*
*but what proceeds out of the mouth, this defiles the man.*
(Matthew 15:11)

*Food is for the stomach and the stomach is for food, but*
*God will do away with both of them. Yet the body is not for*
*immorality, but for the Lord, and the Lord is for the body.*
(1 Corinthians 6:13)

### 2. Unclean Animals as Metaphor

Clean and unclean animals are sometimes used metaphorically to represent moral and immoral behaviors respectively.

*Again, the kingdom of heaven is like a dragnet cast into*
*the sea, and gathering fish of every kind; and when*
*it was filled, they drew it up on the beach; and they*
*sat down and gathered the good fish into containers,*
*but the bad they threw away.* (Matthew 13:47–48)

**Refer to Resource**

*Holy Cow: Does God Care About*
*What We Eat?*

*What the Bible Says About Healthy*
*Living Cookbook*

Rome and the swine

*For this reason: when the swine is lying down it puts out its hooves, as if to say, "I am clean;" so does this wicked state rob and oppress, yet pretend to be executing justice.* (*Genesis Rabbah* 65:1)

## D The Kosher Gentile

*And concerning food [regulations], bear what you are able; but against that which is sacrificed to idols be exceedingly on thy guard; for it is the service of dead gods.* (Didache 6:3)

If Gentile believers see the importance of keeping a biblical diet in order to maintain their identity as a participant in the holy nation, why should they be discouraged? After all, Yeshua kept kosher.

## 🔍 Didache

The *Didache* is a brief treatise of moral and community instruction for Gentile believers in Yeshua which may have been written as early as the end of the first century. The full title of the work is *The Teaching of the Lord through the Twelve Apostles to the Gentiles*, sometimes referred to as *The Teaching of the Twelve Apostles*. Scholars disagree about the possibility of apostolic origin, but all agree that it is an ancient piece of Christian literature preserving early Christian tradition.

## E  Respect for Others

A person who decides to adopt the dietary laws should not quarrel with those who hold a different opinion on the matter.

*Food will not commend us to God; we are neither the worse if we do not eat, nor the better if we do eat.* (1 Corinthians 8:8)

*The one who eats is not to regard with contempt the one who does not eat, and the one who does not eat is not to judge the one who eats, for God has accepted him … [After all] the kingdom of God is not eating and drinking, but righteousness and peace and joy in the Holy Spirit.* (Romans 14:3, 17)

## F  Rabbinically Kosher vs. Biblically Kosher

A careful study of the biblical kosher laws reveals that there is a biblical basis for many of the stringencies of rabbinical dietary laws.

❖ Biblical dietary laws: Regulations on food that can be derived directly from the Bible.

❖ Rabbinical dietary laws: Additional regulations on food based upon biblical exegesis and Jewish tradition.

# The Greatest Commandment

The commandments of God sanctify us by setting us apart, but the commandments are also expressions of love.

## A  Light and Weighty Matters 🖎

*You tithe mint and dill and cummin, and have neglected the weightier provisions of the law: justice and mercy and faithfulness; but these are the things you should have done without neglecting the others.* (Matthew 23:23)

The weighty matters of the Torah are:

............................................................................................

## B  The Least of the Commandments

Yeshua teaches that we should not neglect even the smallest of the commandments.

*Whoever then annuls one of the least of these commandments, and teaches others to do the same, shall be called least in the kingdom of heaven.* (Matthew 5:19)

**Key Verses**

1 Corinthians 8:8
Romans 14:3, 17
Matthew 23:2–4
Exodus 18:14
Matthew 16:19
Matthew 23:23
Matthew 5:19

📹◀ **Your Israel Connection**

**Seat of Moses**

*Korazin Synagogue, Northern Galilee* – In the archaeological remains of the synagogue at Korazin, an ornate stone chair was discovered. Scholars speculate that it may have been a seat of honor stationed next to the ark and Torah scrolls. Some have suggested that the teacher's chair in the synagogue may been called "the seat of Moses," as in Matthew 23:2.

## 1. The Bird's Nest

*If you happen to come upon a bird's nest along the way, in any tree or on the ground, with young ones or eggs, and the mother sitting on the young or on the eggs, you shall not take the mother with the young; you shall certainly let the mother go, but the young you may take for yourself, in order that it may be well with you and that you may prolong your days.*
(Deuteronomy 22:6–7)

Driving away the mother bird

## 2. The Same Reward

*God did not reveal the reward for keeping His commandments, except for two of them: the weightiest and least weighty. The requirement to honor one's father and mother is the very weightiest commandment, and its reward is long life, as it is written [in Exodus 20:12], "Honor your father and mother, that your days may be long ..." The requirement to send away the mother bird is the least weighty commandment, and what is its reward? "said, "Honor ..." And the sending away of the mother bird is the least weighty, and what is its reward? As it is written [in Deuteronomy 22:7], "... that you may prolong your days." (Deuteronomy Rabbah 6:2)*

*Be as scrupulous observing a small commandment as you are observing a great commandment for you do not know what the reward of each is. (m.Avot 2:1)*

| Weight of Command | Commandment | Reward |
|---|---|---|
| **Weightiest** | Honor Parents (Exodus 20:12) | "That your days may be long." |
| **Lightest** | Driving Away Mother Bird (Deuteronomy 22:7) | "That you may prolong your days." |

**Key Verses**

Exodus 20:12
Deuteronomy 22:7
Matthew 22:35–40
Deuteronomy 6:4–9
Leviticus 19:18

**Key Words**

*Shema:* From the word *shama*, meaning "listen, hear, obey."

## ⓒ The Greatest Commandment

Yeshua taught that the greatest commandment is the commandment to love God.

*And one of them, a lawyer, asked Him a question, testing Him, "Teacher, which is the great commandment in the Law?" And He said to him, "'You shall love the LORD your God with all your heart, and with all your soul, and with all your mind.' This is the great and foremost commandment. The second is like it, 'You shall love your neighbor as yourself.' On these two commandments depend the whole Law and the Prophets."* (Matthew 22:35–40; quoting Deuteronomy 6:5 and Leviticus 19:18)

### 1. The Shema

> *shema* (שמע) = "listen, hear, obey"

*Hear, O Israel! The LORD is our God, the LORD is one! You shall love the LORD your God with all your heart and with all your soul and with all your might. These words, which I am commanding you today, shall be on your heart. You shall teach them diligently to your sons and shall talk of them when you sit in your house and when you walk by the way and when you lie down and when you rise up. You shall bind them as a sign on your hand and they shall be as frontals on your forehead. You shall write them on the doorposts of your house and on your gates.* (Deuteronomy 6:4–9)

### 2. Loving God ✍

Loving God is divided up into three categories: with all one's heart, soul, and mind.

#### a. *With all your heart …*

*"With all your heart" means, with your two impulses, the evil impulse as well as the good impulse; "with all your soul" means, even though he takes your soul [life]; "with all your might" means, with all your money.* (m.Berachot 9:5)

**Key Verses**

Romans 7:21
Matthew 6:24
Matthew 4:1–11
Deuteronomy 6:5
1 John 5:3
Deuteronomy 6:7

**Key Words**

*Nefesh:* Hebrew word meaning "life" or "soul."

*Me'od:* Hebrew word meaning: 1. Additional. 2. In Deuteronomy 6:4, "strength, property, wealth."

*Talmud Torah:* The study of Torah.

---

*I find then the principle that evil is present in me, the one who wants to do good.* (Romans 7:21)

Loving God with all your heart means loving Him with

...........................................................................................................................................  .

**b.   With all your soul …**

> *nefesh* (נפש) = "life, soul"

Loving God with all your soul means loving Him with

...........................................................................................................................................  .

**c.   With all your strength (might) …**

> *me'od* (מאד) = "strength, property, wealth"

*You cannot serve God and wealth.* (Matthew 6:24)

Loving God with all your strength means loving Him with

...........................................................................................................................................  .

**3.   Talmud Torah**

Deuteronomy 6:5 says that we are to show our love for God by keeping His commandments on our hearts. To love God means keeping His commandments.

*For this is the love of God, that we keep His commandments; and His commandments are not burdensome.* (1 John 5:3)

Loving God .......................................... Keeping His Commandments

> *talmud Torah* (תלמוד תורה) = "the study of Torah"

*You shall teach them diligently to your sons and shall talk of them when you sit in your house and when you walk by the way and when you lie down and when you rise up.* (Deuteronomy 6:7)

*Our Rabbis taught: "And thou shall teach them diligently" [means] that the words of the Torah shall be clear-cut in your mouth, so that if anyone asks you something, you should not show doubt and then answer him, but [be able to] answer him immediately.* (b.Kiddushin 30a)

*This book of the law shall not depart from your mouth, but you shall meditate on it day and night, so that you may be careful to do according to all that is written in it; for then you will make your way prosperous, and then you will have success.* (Joshua 1:8)

*Say not: "When I shall have leisure I shall study;" perhaps you will never have leisure.* (m.Avot 2:4)

**Key Verses**

Joshua 1:8
Deuteronomy 6:8–9
Matthew 23:5

**Key Words**

*Tefillin:* Black boxes containing scrolls on which passages of scripture are written, bound to a man's arm and forehead using leather straps.

## 4. Tefillin

Tefillin, commonly called phylacteries, are small, black leather boxes with parchments of hand-written scripture folded inside them. Observant Jewish men attach these boxes to their foreheads and arms with leather straps, thereby literally fulfilling the commandment of binding God's word to the forehead and hand.

> *tefillin* (תפילין) = leather boxes containing passages of Scripture

*You shall bind them as a sign on your hand and they shall be as frontals on your forehead. You shall write them on the doorposts of your house and on your gates.* (Deuteronomy 6:8–9)

*But they do all their deeds to be noticed by men; for they broaden their phylacteries and lengthen the tassels of their garments.* (Matthew 23:5)

*Just as Jesus faulted the ostentatious wearing of* tzitziyot *(tassels), which he himself wore, he was probably wearing* tefillin *while he criticized those who wore them hypocritically. Had he not worn* tefillin, *it is unlikely that his criticism would have been directed only at the excess. Criticizing the way they were worn implies Jesus' acceptance of the practice and the sages' literal interpretation of the biblical commandment.*
(David Bivin, *New Light on the Difficult Words of Jesus*)[2]

**Refer to Resource**

*Mayim Chayim: You Shall Bind*

Tefillin, mezuzah with scroll

**Key Verses**

Deuteronomy 6:9

Luke 24:53

Acts 2:42

Deuteronomy 11:13

Matthew 22:39–40

Leviticus 19:18

Matthew 7:12

**Key Words**

*Mezuzah:* 1. Doorpost. 2. A small parchment scroll placed in a case affixed to the doorpost of a home.

*Avodah:* Hebrew word that can mean worship, service, sacrifice, and/or prayer.

## Your Israel Connection

**Prayer = Relationship**

*Yemin Moshe, Jerusalem* – City of Prayer/Overlook from Yemin Moshe neighborhood, the first settlement built outside the city walls in the modern era. Jerusalem is revered by religious Jews as the most important place of prayer in the world because it contains the Temple Mount. Hundreds of thousands of people from all over the world congregate each year at the Western Wall in Jerusalem to pray to the God of Israel. All over the world, people turn toward Jerusalem to pray.

**Refer to Resource**

*Mayim Chayim: Mezuzah*

### 5. Mezuzah

*You shall write them on the doorposts [mezuzah] of your house and on your gates.* (Deuteronomy 6:9)

> ### *mezuzah* (מזוזה) = "doorpost" or small case containing a parchment scroll

A *mezuzah* is a small case with a hand written scroll of scripture in it, attached to the doorframe of one's home.

The Hebrew letter *shin* (ש) on a *mezuzah* stands for God's name *Shaddai* (שדי), "Almighty."

# Loving our Neighbor

Yeshua taught that the second greatest commandment is the commandment to love one's neighbor.

*The second is like it, "You shall love your neighbor as yourself." On these two commandments depend the whole Law and the Prophets.* (Matthew 22:39–40; quoting Leviticus 19:18)

## Ⓐ Do Unto Others

The "golden rule" is the Master's paraphrase of Leviticus 19:18.

*You shall love your neighbor as yourself; I am the LORD.* (Leviticus 19:18)

*In everything, therefore, treat people the same way you want them to treat you, for this is the [Torah] and the Prophets.* (Matthew 7:12)

*If there is any other commandment, it is summed up in this saying, "You shall love your neighbor as yourself."* (Romans 13:9; quoting Leviticus 19:18)

*The whole [Torah] is fulfilled in one word, in the statement, "You shall love your neighbor as yourself."* (Galatians 5:14; quoting Leviticus 19:18)

*If, however, you are fulfilling the <u>royal law</u> according to the Scripture, "You shall love your neighbor as yourself," you are doing well.* (James 2:8; quoting Leviticus 19:18)

**Key Verses**

Romans 13:9
Leviticus 19:18
Galatians 5:14
James 2:8

## Ⓑ 613 Opportunities

The Torah gives us 613 opportunities to show our love for our Father in heaven, and our love for our fellow man.

### Endnotes

[1] Chofetz Chaim, *The Concise Book of Mitzvoth* (trans. Charles Wengrov; New York: Feldheim Publishers, 1990), 11.

[2] David Bivin, *New Light on the Difficult Words of Jesus: Insights from His Jewish Context* (Holland, MI: En Gedi Resource Center, 2005), 53.

# Lesson Nine
## LESSON SUMMARY

### First …

We distinguished between the positive and negative commandments in the Torah, and realized that not all 613 commandments are applicable today. Most Christians are already keeping most of the Torah.

### Then …

We talked about what it means to be sanctified, and we learned that God's commandments set us apart. We took a look at the commandments of Leviticus 19—the laws of holiness.

### After that …

We examined the biblical dietary laws to learn about what is on the menu for God's people. We saw that

- ❖ Land Animals: Must have divided (cloven) hooves and must ruminate (chew its cud).
- ❖ Fish and Sea Creatures: Must have both fins and scales.
- ❖ Fowl: Must not be a bird of prey.
- ❖ Insects: Must have jointed legs above the other legs, must not creep on the ground.

### After that …

We considered the difference between light and heavy commandments. Yeshua taught us that the greatest two commandments are:

- ❖ To love God
- ❖ To love one's neighbor

This gave us the opportunity to learn about the commandments in the *Shema*.

- ❖ Loving God
- ❖ The study of Torah
- ❖ Tefillin
- ❖ Mezuzah

It also gave us the opportunity to see how the "golden rule" is a paraphrase of the commandment to love our neighbor, a summary of the whole Torah.

### Finally …

We learned that the Torah gives us 613 opportunities to show our love for our Father in heaven, and our love for our fellow man.

# Lesson Nine
## LESSON REVIEW – Q&A

1. How many commandments are traditionally ascribed to the Torah? How many are positive? How many are negative? How many are applicable today outside of Israel?

2. What does it mean to be sanctified by the commandments? What is holiness? How do the commandments make Israel holy?

3. What are some of the things pertaining to holiness? What does a holy person look like? How does he behave differently?

4. What are the four categories into which the Torah divides the animal kingdom? What makes each category clean or unclean?

5. How does the Bible sometimes use unclean animals as metaphors? Can you think of any examples?

6. According to the rabbis, which is the weightiest commandment? Which is the least weighty? What is the reward for the weightiest commandment? What is the reward for the least weighty?

7. According to our Master, what is the first, foremost, and greatest commandment? What does it mean to love God with heart, soul, and might?

8. According to our Master, what is the second greatest commandment? How is the "golden rule" a paraphrase of Leviticus 19:18? How is it a summary of the Torah and prophets?

# Lesson Nine
# EXTRA CREDIT
### SUPPLEMENTAL MATERIAL FOR THIS HAYESOD LESSON

---

**Extra Credit Instructions:**

1. This material is not mandatory, but it will serve as a helpful tool for further study.
2. Read Acts 10:1–11:18 and Ezekiel 4:9–17.
3. Provide answers to each question based upon the passages indicated.

## Peter and the Sheet from Heaven

Bible readers often misunderstand the story of Peter and the animals on the sheet lowered from heaven in Acts 10. Teachers sometimes claim that God abolished the dietary laws when He showed Peter the vision. By telling Peter to, "Get up, kill and eat," was the LORD indicating that Levitical dietary standards had all been cancelled? Were Jewish believers now free to eat the meat of unclean animals?

This is a puzzling interpretation because, if true, it would mean that God changed the Torah. For this week's Extra Credit work, we will revisit that story and take a closer look. By comparing a similar story from Ezekiel 4:9–17 and carefully reading Acts 10:1–11:18, we will try to find a better interpretation to the vision.

1. Read Ezekiel 4:9–17. With what was Ezekiel supposed to bake his bread?

2. Compare Ezekiel 4:14 and Acts 10:14. What did Ezekiel say? What did Peter say?

3. Was God using this prophetic sign to teach Ezekiel that it was now proper to eat food cooked with human dung? If not, what was the meaning of the prophetic sign? (Ezekiel 4:16–17)

4. Did Ezekiel actually eat food cooked with human dung? (Ezekiel 4:15)

5. Did Peter actually eat an unclean animal in the sheet? (Acts 10:16–17)

6. What instructions did God give Peter after the vision? (Acts 10:19–20)

7. According to Peter, what was the meaning of the vision? (Acts 10:28–29)


8. What does Peter conclude from the vision and Cornelius' story? (Acts 10:34–35)


9. When Peter reports the vision to the rest of the Apostles in Acts 11, what conclusion do they draw? (Acts 11:17–18)


10. What do you think? Did God intend to vision of the sheet to overturn the dietary laws of Leviticus 11 and Deuteronomy 14?

# Lesson Nine – Digging Deeper
# MORE ABOUT THE BIBLICAL DIETARY LAWS
## FURTHER STUDY FROM THIS WEEK'S HAYESOD LESSON

## Reasons for the Dietary Laws

Why does God say that some animals are clean (ritually fit) while others are unclean (ritually unfit)? Many books have been written discussing this subject, and various commentators have struggled to find a common rationale. One popular theory is that the permitted types of animals are better for our bodies. The unfit animals tend to be scavengers, and perhaps their meats carry more toxins and other harmful elements. A growing body of scientific evidence seems to lend support to that notion.[1] Surely God, in His wisdom, knew what foods would be good for His people and what foods would be harmful for them. But there is more to it than simply good health. The kosher laws are not God's version of holistic health food.

Previously we have learned that someone ritually fit is allowed to enter the Tabernacle and eat of the sacrifices, while a ritually unfit person is not. The laws of what is fit and what is unfit have to do with being able to participate in the Tabernacle worship system. Things that make a person unfit include death, leprosy, mildew, and human mortality. Some of the animals designated as "unfit" are predators or scavengers that feed on carrion. Some of them carry associations with ritual contamination. Perhaps the Almighty designated some animals as unfit because of their associations with ritual uncleanness. God desires His people to be a kingdom of priests, and that requires implementing ritual concern in daily life.

**Resource in Focus**

Excerpt from parashat "Sh'mini: Eighth" of First Fruits of Zion's *Torah Club Volume One: Unrolling the Scroll.*

These are just guesses, though. We really do not know the reason some animals are called fit and others are not. The rabbis explain that the kosher laws belong to a category of commandment that has no rational explanation (*chukkim*, חקים). Asking why a buffalo is kosher while a giant sloth is not is like asking why the Sabbath is on the seventh day of the week and not the first day of the week or why the sun rises in the east instead of the west. Some things we have to accept simply because God says so. Who are we to question God? He decided that certain creatures are not food for His people Israel. That is completely within His prerogative.

Though we may not be able to deduce why God designated some animals as fit and others as unfit, we do know why He imposed the dietary laws on His people. The Torah tells us that it is a matter of holiness:

> *You shall not make yourselves unclean with them so that you become unclean. For I am the LORD your God. Consecrate yourselves therefore, and be holy, for I am holy. And you shall not make yourselves unclean with any of the swarming things that swarm on the earth. For I am the LORD who brought you up from the land of Egypt to be your God; thus you shall be holy, for I am holy.* (Leviticus 11:43–45)

God gave His people the dietary laws to make them holy. Remember, the word *holy* does not refer to a moral/ethical quality. It means to be set apart. Israel is supposed to demonstrate to the world that it is a nation set apart for the LORD. One of the ways that the people of Israel are to do that is by maintaining a distinctive diet that, on some levels, keeps them separate from others. The distinctive requirements of the kosher diet have forced the Jewish people to cluster together in communities while limiting their potential interactions with other communities.

Some people regard the thought of eating an unclean animal as revolting. Personal taste preferences and appetites are the wrong reasons for avoiding unfit foods. Likewise, health reasons alone are not a good motivation for keeping kosher. A famous rabbi from the days just after the time of the apostles taught that a person should not say, "I think pork is disgusting." Instead he should say, "I would certainly eat it, but My Father in heaven has forbidden me to eat of it, so I will not."[2]

If we obey God only when it makes good sense to us or when we happen to have a similar inclination, that is not really obedience. This can be compared to a child whose father insisted on an eight o'clock bedtime. On the first night, the child felt drowsy around seven thirty, so he obeyed his father. "How wise my father is to send me to bed at eight," the child thought. The next night, though, he did not feel tired. He could think of no rational reason for going to bed so early. The eight o'clock bedtime mandate seemed arbitrary and unnecessary, so he chose to ignore it. It is not obedience if we only obey when it suits us to do so.

## Who Should Eat Kosher?

*For I am the LORD your God. Consecrate yourselves therefore, and be holy, for I am holy. And you shall not make yourselves unclean with any of the swarming things that swarm on the earth.* (Leviticus 11:44)

To whom do the biblical dietary laws apply? The Torah clearly indicates that God intended the dietary laws to set Israel apart from the pagan nations, so at a minimum, these laws apply to the Jewish people. But do they also apply to Gentile believers? After all, Gentile believers have been grafted into the people of Israel and have become honorary members of the greater commonwealth of Israel, spiritual sons and daughters of Abraham. Should Gentiles be required to eat according to the biblical dietary laws too?

It is not worthwhile for us to speak in terms of "should" or "must" or "have to" when discussing these laws or any of the ritual laws of Torah. As we have noted, the apostles laid out the minimum "should," "must" and "have to" for the Gentile believers in Acts 15, where they commanded them to abstain from blood, meat sacrificed to idols, and the meat of strangled animals. It is not useful to try to impose higher standards on the Gentile believers than the apostles themselves imposed. However, the apostles offered those standards as a minimum threshold of dietary law, not a maximum. They pointed the Gentiles in the direction of the Torah's higher standards by encouraging them to remain in the synagogues and learn Torah from the weekly readings:

*For Moses from ancient generations has in every city those who preach him, since he is read in the synagogues every Sabbath.* (Acts 15:21)

With these words, the apostles invited the Gentile believers to take hold of their spiritual heritage by learning more of the ways of Torah. This attitude of Gentile inclusion and invitation to Torah is consistent with some of the earliest church writings on the subject. The *Didache*, a late first-century manual of instructions for Gentile believers that scholars believe originated with the Jewish believers, encourages the Gentiles to take on as much of the dietary laws as they are able:

*And concerning food [regulations], bear what you are able; but against that which is sacrificed to idols be exceedingly on thy guard; for it is the service of dead gods.* (Didache 6:3)

If someone who is not Jewish wants to eat a biblically kosher diet, how can anyone object? How could it possibly hurt to do so? How could it be wrong to obey the Bible?

Of course, keeping the commandments in order to merit, earn, or maintain salvation is a dead end. This warning applies to Jewish and Gentile believers both. Salvation is a gift bestowed upon us by grace, not on the basis of what we had for breakfast!

## Obsolete Laws

> *This is the law regarding the animal and the bird, and every living thing that moves in the waters and everything that swarms on the earth.* (Leviticus 11:46)

There are several passages in the Apostolic Writings (New Testament) that could be interpreted in antithesis to the dietary laws of Leviticus 11. Based on their understanding of these passages, many brothers and sisters in the faith believe that the biblical dietary laws are obsolete and that observing them would be a step toward legalism and bondage to the Law. A person who decides to adopt the dietary laws should not quarrel with those who hold a different opinion on the matter. The person who decides to keep kosher needs to vigilantly guard his heart from looking down on other believers who do not share his conviction. It is all too easy to fall into the trap of spiritual pride. Paul says, "Food will not commend us to God; we are neither the worse if we do not eat, nor the better if we do eat" (1 Corinthians 8:8). If we want other people to respect our convictions, we need to respect theirs as well.

Nevertheless, we certainly can argue against the idea that keeping the biblical dietary laws places us under legalistic bondage. Legalism is the idea that one must keep the commandments to earn salvation. Obeying the commandments of God out of a heart of willing submission is not legalism. If it were, one could argue against keeping any of the commandments of the Torah.

A person engaged in such an argument could rhetorically ask, "Is it permissible for a Gentile believer to keep the Torah at all?" If our fellow Christians agree that it is permissible for a Gentile believer to keep a ritual commandment like the Sabbath day or the commandment of eating unleavened bread at Passover, they have no basis for forbidding Gentile believers from keeping kosher.

I would argue that keeping the dietary laws and other ceremonial laws of Torah is completely natural for believers. After all, if we are under the new covenant, God has written His Torah on our hearts:

> *"But this is the covenant which I will make with the house of Israel after those days," declares the LORD, "I will put My Torah within them and on their heart I will write it; and I will be their God, and they shall be My people."* (Jeremiah 31:33)

Keeping the dietary laws is a natural expression of who we are in Messiah. It is part of our identity in the new covenant. If believers see the importance of keeping a biblical diet in order to maintain their identity as a participant in the holy nation, why should they be discouraged? After all, Yeshua kept kosher.

### Endnotes

1   For example, Hope Egan, *Holy Cow! Does God Care About What We Eat?* (Marshfield, MO: First Fruits of Zion, 2005).

2   Rabbi Elezar ben Azaryah in *Yalkut Shimoni, Kedoshim,* 626.

# Notes:

## THE FOUNDATION

Lesson Ten

# OUR WALK–
# HIS PATH

THE LAND, THE PEOPLE,
AND THE SCRIPTURES OF ISRAEL

# Lesson Ten
# OUR WALK—HIS PATH

*Do not urge me to leave you or turn back from following*
*you; for where you go, I will go, and where you lodge,*
*I will lodge. Your people shall be my people, and your*
*God, my God. Where you die, I will die, and there I will*
*be buried. Thus may the LORD do to me, and worse, if*
*anything but death parts you and me.* (Ruth 1:16–17)

## Lesson Overview

After reviewing the nine foundations we have learned in previous HaYesod lessons, we are ready to take a look into the prophetic future of the people of God. The People of Israel are destined to return to the Scriptures of Israel and to be gathered back together the Land of Israel. The Gentile believers have a share in this destiny because they have been grafted into Israel and become fellow-heirs with Israel. The work of preparing for the Final Redemption requires the restoration of a Jewish Messiah, a Jewish gospel, a Jewish concept of discipleship, and a Jewish understanding of Torah.

## Lesson Purpose

In this lesson we will review the previous nine lessons and then:

❖ Examine the prophetic destiny of the Jewish people.

❖ Examine the prophetic destiny of the Gentile believers.

❖ Discuss the concept of being "grafted in" to Israel.

❖ Sort through the implications for both Jewish and Gentile believers.

## Field Trips to the Holy Land

❖ Castel, Mevaseret Zion

❖ Old City Walls, Jerusalem

❖ Talpiot, Haas Promenade

❖ Jaffa Gate, Old City Jerusalem

# Lesson Ten
# LESSON OUTLINE

## The Foundations

A. Lesson One: The Torah

B. Lesson Two: Born Again

C. Lesson Three: Covenants of Promise

D. Lesson Four: Rabbi Yeshua

E. Lesson Five: Discipleship

F. Lesson Six: Paul vs. Saul

G. Lesson Seven: Paul's Writings

H. Lesson Eight: The Appointed Times

I. Lesson Nine: The Commandments

## Jewish Destiny

A. An Ancient Prophecy (Deuteronomy 30)

B. The Three Returns
   1. Return to the LORD
   2. Return to Torah
   3. Return to the Land
      a. Repent, Restore, Return
      b. The Final Redemption

C. Zionism and Messianic Zionism

D. Is This the Final Redemption?

## Gentile Destiny

A. Take Hold (Zechariah 8:23)
   1. Ten Men
   2. Tzitzit
   3. Tzitzit of One Jew

B. Isaiah 56

C. Gentiles in Israel

## Fellow-Heirs

A. Grafted In

B. Fellow-Heirs and Fellow Members

C. One in the Messiah

D. What's the Difference?
   1. Divine Mandate
   2. Divine Invitation

E. The Yoke of the Lord

## Four Restorations

A. Messiah

B. Gospel

C. Discipleship

D. Torah

# The Foundations

*HaYesod* means "the foundation," and we want to make sure the foundation is securely laid in place before concluding.

### Ⓐ Lesson One: The Torah

The Torah is God's _____ for His people Israel, and

the _____ for the whole Bible.

### Ⓑ Lesson Two: Born Again

Salvation is by _____ alone, but it results in a

_____ living out the _____ of God.

### Ⓒ Lesson Three: Covenants of Promise

*"Behold, days are coming," declares the LORD, "when I will make a new covenant with the house of Israel and with the house of Judah ... this is the covenant which I will make with the house of Israel after those days," declares the LORD, "I will put My [Torah] within them and on their heart I will write it; and I will be their God, and they shall be My people."* (Jeremiah 31:31–33)

The _____ does not _____ the

_____ ; the _____ is part of the

_____ .

Moses at Mount Sinai

## D  Lesson Four: Rabbi Yeshua 🖊

Yeshua was a ........................................., ........................................., fully

........................................., the ............................. made ............................. .

## E  Lesson Five: Discipleship 🖊

......................................... is the ......................... of ......................................... .

## F  Lesson Six: Paul vs. Saul 🖊

The Apostle Paul ...............................................................................................

to the ............................. until the end of his life.

Saul vs. Paul

## G  Lesson Seven: Paul's Writings 🖊

Paul's writings do not teach ........................................................; they

........................................ about the ........................................

proper ........................................................ to the Land, the People,

and the Scriptures of Israel in Messiah.

## Ⓗ Lesson Eight: The Appointed Times ✍

The ............................, biblical ............................, and

............................ are not ............................ ;

they teach us about ............................ and ............................ .

Blowing the shofar

## Ⓘ Lesson Nine: The Commandments ✍

Proper application of the Torah comes from a ............................ for God,

............................ out of a ............................ .

The Torah gives us — ............................ !

# Jewish Destiny

The same prophecies that predicted the suffering and exile of Israel also predict that the Jewish people have an amazing destiny ahead of them—a full, Messianic restoration called the Final Redemption.

## Ⓐ An Ancient Prophecy (Deuteronomy 30)

Deuteronomy 30 is referred to as the "Portion of Repentance" because it lays out the pattern for repentance and the restoration of Israel.

*So it shall be when all of these things have come upon you, the blessing and the curse which I have set before you, and you call them to mind in all nations where the LORD your God has banished you, and you <u>return</u> to the LORD your God and obey Him with all your heart and soul according to all that I command you*

**Your Israel Connection**

**Anti-Semitism**

*Castel, Mevaseret Zion* – Ten kilometers outside of Jerusalem on a hill that straddles the Jerusalem/Tel Aviv highway stands the ruins of a Crusader era castle which was built upon the remains of a Roman fortress. The hill was a theater of intense battles in the 1948 War of Independence.

*today, you and your sons, then the LORD your God will <u>restore</u> you from captivity, and have compassion on you, and will gather you again from all the peoples where the LORD your God has scattered you. If your outcasts are at the ends of the earth, from there the LORD your God will gather you, and from there <u>He will bring you back</u>. The LORD your God will bring you into the land which your fathers possessed, and you shall possess it; and He will prosper you and multiply you more than your fathers.* (Deuteronomy 30:1–5)

**Key Verses**

Deuteronomy 30:1–5
Romans 11:26
Deuteronomy 30:8

**Key Words**

*Shuv*: Hebrew word meaning "to turn" or "to return."

*Teshuvah*: Hebrew word meaning "repentance" or "turning around," derived from the root *shuv*.

## B The Three Returns

> *teshuvah* (תשובה) = "repentance, turning around"
>
> *shuv* (שוב) = "to turn" or "to return"

Deuteronomy 30 foretells of a return to the ............................, a return to the ............................, and a return to the ............................ .

### 1. Return to the LORD

The first "return" is a return to the LORD.

*All Israel will be saved.* (Romans 11:26)

*It shall be when … you return [shuv] to the LORD your God and obey Him with all your heart and soul according to all that I command you today.* (Deuteronomy 30:1–2)

### 2. Return to Torah

The second "return" is a return to the Torah.

*You shall again obey the LORD, and observe all His commandments which I command you today.* (Deuteronomy 30:8)

**Refer to Resource**

*Torah Club Volume Two: Shadows of the Messiah*
"Nitzavim: You Are Standing"

### 3. Return to the Land

The third "return" is a return to the Land.

*Then the LORD your God will restore* [shuv] *you from captivity.* (Deuteronomy 30:3)

Map of Israel

#### a. Repent, Restore, Return

*It shall be when ... you* _____ *to the LORD your God and obey Him with all your heart and soul according to all that I command you today ... then the LORD your God will* _____ *you from captivity, and have compassion on you, and will gather you again from all the peoples where the LORD your God has scattered you.* (Deuteronomy 30:1–3)

#### b. The Final Redemption

According to the Scriptures of Israel, there will be an end-times ingathering of the people of Israel into the land of Israel. In Judaism, these three returns—the return to the LORD, the return to Torah, and the return to the Land—are called the Final Redemption.

**The Final Redemption**

| The Messiah will: |
| --- |
| Return Israel to the LORD. |
| Return Israel to the Torah. |
| Return Israel to the Land. |

## ⓒ Zionism and Messianic Zionism

Zionism was the international, secular, political movement that called for a homeland for the Jewish people.

Theodore Herzl

| Hebrew Year | Civil Year |
|---|---|
| 5708 | 1948 |
| Verse Number 5708 in Masoretic text of Torah: | The LORD your God will bring you into the land which your fathers possessed, and you shall possess it; and He will prosper you and multiply you more than your fathers. (Deuteronomy 30:5)[1] |

## ⓓ Is This the Final Redemption?

The current state of Israel is not the Final Redemption. Zionism and the State of Israel are only the beginning of the promised return to the land.

*Our Father who is in heaven, Rock of Israel and its Redeemer, bless the State of Israel, the first flowering of our redemption.*
(Prayer for the State of Israel, *Siddur*)

# Gentile Destiny

In the Final Redemption, God will make good on all of His covenant promises to the people of Israel: The Messiah will come and fight for them, return them to their Land, and establish them above all peoples. He will reign over them as the Davidic King in their midst. But where does this prophetic destiny leave Gentiles?

**▶️ Your Israel Connection**

**Heaven and Earth**

*Old City Walls, Jerusalem* – Jerusalem's Old City walls are lit by night. The walls date back to the Turkish period, and in many places, they follow the lines of ancient Jerusalem. Jerusalem is the common ground between heaven and earth, the place where God has placed His Name forever.

# Prayer for the State of Israel

Our Father who is in heaven, Rock of Israel and its Redeemer, bless the State of Israel, the first flowering of our redemption. Defend her with the pinion of Your devotion, spread over her the shelter of Your peace, and send Your light and truth to her leaders, officials, and advisors, affirming them with good counsel from You. Strengthen the hands of the defenders of our holy land, grant them salvation, and crown them with a crown of triumph. May You give peace in the land and eternal gladness to its inhabitants.

Please take note of our brothers, the entire house of Israel, in all the lands to which they have been dispersed, and quickly lead them upright to Zion, Your city, and to Jerusalem, the dwelling place of Your Name. As it is written in the Torah of Moses Your servant: "If Your dispersed ones will be at the ends of the heavens, from there the LORD, your God, will gather you, and from there He will take you. And the LORD, your God, will bring you to the land that your fathers possessed, and cause you to possess it, and He will grant more goodness and abundance than your fathers" (Deuteronomy 30:4–5).

Unite our hearts to love and fear Your Name, and to keep all of the words of Your Torah. Quickly send us the son of David, Your righteous Messiah, to ransom those who wait for Your final salvation.

Appear in the beauty of the brilliance of Your strength over all the inhabitants of Your world, and let all who have breath say, "The LORD, God of Israel is king, and His kingdom rules over all." Amen, selah.

A common synagogue prayer for the State of Israel, composed after the formation of the modern state in 1948.

## Ⓐ Take Hold (Zechariah 8:23)

*It will yet be that peoples will come, even the inhabitants of many cities. The inhabitants of one will go to another, saying, "Let us go at once to entreat the favor of the LORD, and to seek the LORD of hosts; I will also go." So many peoples and mighty nations will come to seek the LORD of hosts in Jerusalem and to entreat the favor of the LORD. Thus says the LORD of hosts, "In those days ten men from all the nations will grasp the garment of a Jew, saying, 'Let us go with you, for we have heard that God is with you.'"* (Zechariah 8:20–23)

### 1. Ten Men

In the Torah, ten men is a quorum, a *minyan*, the minimum number to form a congregation.

*In those days <u>ten men from all the nations</u> will grasp the garment of a Jew, saying, "Let us go with you, for we have heard that God is with you."* (Zechariah 8:23)

*Men from every tribe and tongue and people and nation.* (Revelation 5:9)

> *minyan* (מנין) = a quorum of ten men that qualifies as a formal congregation

Ten men = ..................................................................................................

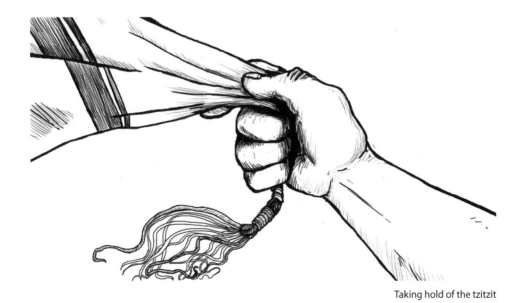

Taking hold of the tzitzit

**Key Verses**

Zechariah 8:20–23
Revelation 5:9

**Key Words**

*Minyan*: A quorum of ten men that qualifies as a formal congregation by Jewish law. The Torah alludes to this concept in Genesis 18:32 and Exodus 18:21.

**Key Words**

*Tzitzit:* Hebrew word meaning a ritual tassel that the Torah instructs must be attached to each of the four corners of a garment.

*Canaf:* Hebrew word meaning "corner" or "wing."

*Tallit:* 1. A prayer shawl. This four-cornered garment, to which *tzitziyot* have been attached, is usually worn during prayer. 2. In ancient times, an outer garment or cloak.

*Tallit katan:* A poncho-like, four-cornered garment worn under the shirt with *tzitziyot* attached to each corner. The *tallit katan* is typically worn all day (not just during prayer), with the *tzitziyot* either tucked in or pulled out. This garment makes it easier to fulfill the commandment of *tzitziyot* during daily activity.

**Refer to Resource**

*Mayim Chayim: Tzitzit*

## 2. Tzitzit

*They shall make for themselves tassels [tzitzit] on the corners [canaf] of their garments … It shall be a tassel [tzitzit] for you to look at and remember all the commandments of the LORD.* (Numbers 15:38–39)

*The sun of righteousness will rise with healing in [his corners (canaf)].* (Malachi 4:2)

*In those days ten men from all the nations will grasp the [corner of the garment (canaf)] of a Jew, saying, "Let us go with you, for we have heard that God is with you."* (Zechariah 8:23)

> ### *tzitzit* (ציצית) = tassels attached to the four corners of a garment

This commandment is traditionally interpreted to be obligatory for men, who observe the commandment by wearing a *tallit* and/or *tallit katan.*

> ### *canaf* (כנף) = "corner" or "wing"

This is the corner of a garment where the ritual tassel is attached.

*Ten men will _____ of the _____ of a Jew.* (Zechariah 8:23)

## 3. Tzitzit of One Jew

Tzitzit = _____

The one Jew that the ten men of Zechariah 8:23 take hold of is the Messiah. The Gentile believers attach themselves to the Messiah, and take hold of the commandments by attaching themselves to Him.

One Jew = _____

*And many peoples will come and say, "Come, let us go up … that He may teach us concerning His ways … for the Torah will go forth from Zion."* (Isaiah 2:3)

**B** Isaiah 56

Who is the Gentile that takes hold of the covenant and the Sabbath in Isaiah 56?

*How blessed is the man who does this, and the son of man who takes hold of it; who keeps from profaning the sabbath, and keeps his hand from doing any evil. Let not the foreigner who has joined himself to the LORD say, "The LORD will surely separate me from His people." Nor let the eunuch say, "Behold, I am a dry tree."* (Isaiah 56:2–3)

*No one who is emasculated or has his male organ cut off shall enter the assembly of the LORD.* (Deuteronomy 23:1)

*For thus says the LORD, "To the eunuchs who keep My sabbaths, and choose what pleases Me, and hold fast My covenant, to them I will give in My house and within My walls a memorial, and a name better than that of sons and daughters; I will give them an everlasting name which will not be cut off. Also the foreigners who join themselves to the LORD, to minister to Him, and to love the name of the LORD, to be His servants, every one who keeps from profaning the sabbath and holds fast My covenant; even those I will bring to My holy mountain and make them joyful in My house of prayer. Their burnt offerings and their sacrifices will be acceptable on My altar; for My house will be called a house of prayer for all the peoples."* (Isaiah 56:4–7)

All nations will go up to Jerusalem

# Once You Were Not a People ...

## Now You Are the People of God

Peter refers to the Gentile believers as "a chosen race, a royal priesthood, a holy nation, a people for God's own possession" (1 Peter 2:9)—terms that the *TaNaK* uses exclusively to describe Israel.

- The LORD has chosen you to be a people for His own possession. (Deuteronomy 14:2)
- The people which You have chosen (1 Kings 3:8)
- Israel, My servant, Jacob whom I have chosen (Isaiah 41:8)
- Israel My chosen one (Isaiah 45:4)

**Chosen Race**

- And you shall be to Me a kingdom of priests. (Exodus 19:6)

**Royal Priesthood**

- For you are a holy people to the LORD your God. (Deuteronomy 7:6)
- The LORD will establish you as a holy people. (Deuteronomy 28:9)
- And you shall be to Me a kingdom of priests and a holy nation. (Exodus 19:6)

**Holy Nation**

- You shall be My own possession among all the peoples. (Exodus 19:5)
- The people whom He has chosen for His own inheritance (Psalm 33:12)
- For you are a holy people to the LORD your God; the LORD your God has chosen you to be a people for His own possession out of all the peoples who are on the face of the earth. (Deuteronomy 7:6)
- For the LORD has chosen Jacob for Himself, Israel for His own possession. (Psalm 135:4)

**God's Own Possession**

Who is the Gentile of Isaiah 56? Two answers:

1. ........................................................................................................

2. ........................................................................................................

*What matters is that they <u>keep my Sabbaths, choose that in which I delight, and lay hold of my covenant</u>. These people are on God's side. They love what he loves, hate what he hates, want what he wants. They do not keep the Sabbaths because they must or [else] they will be destroyed. They keep them because they are the Lord's Sabbaths. Their behavior is an expression of a relationship. This is what God longs for in his people, and if anyone will do this, their parentage or their body has nothing to do with their acceptability.*
(John Oswalt, *The New International Commentary on the Old Testament*)[2]

## C  Gentiles in Israel

Even though they did not force the Gentiles to convert or to become Torah observant, the apostles gave the Gentile believers an honorary and spiritual status in the people of Israel.

*But you are a chosen race, a royal priesthood, a holy nation, a people for God's own possession, so that you may proclaim the excellencies of Him who has called you out of darkness into His marvelous light; for you once were not a people, but now you are the people of God; you had not received mercy, but now you have received mercy.* (1 Peter 2:9–10; quoting Exodus 19:6)

*Therefore remember that formerly you, the Gentiles in the flesh, who are called "Uncircumcision" by the so-called "Circumcision," which is performed in the flesh by human hands—remember that you were at that time separate from Messiah, excluded from the commonwealth of Israel … But now in the Messiah Yeshua you who formerly were far off have been brought near by the blood of Messiah.* (Ephesians 2:11–13)

**Key Verses**

Isaiah 56
1 Peter 2:9–10
Exodus 19:6
Ephesians 2:11–13
Romans 11:24
Romans 11:17–18
Exodus 35:1

📷◀ **Your Israel Connection**

**Grafted In**

*Talpiot, Haas Promenade* – The Haas Promenade provides a magnificent overlook of Old City Jerusalem and the Mount of Olives from the south. These hills were once terraced with rich olive groves. The olive industry is still an important part of Israel's agriculture today.

**Key Verses**

Romans 11:17
Romans 11:18
Ephesians 3:6
Ephesians 2:15

**Key Worlds**

*Kahal:* Hebrew word meaning "assembly."

*Ekklesia:* Greek word meaning "assembly."

# Fellow-Heirs

When a Gentile believer is grafted into the nation of Israel, he doesn't become Jewish, but he is attached to Israel.

*You, being a wild olive, were grafted in among them and became partaker with them of the rich root of the olive tree.* (Romans 11:17)

Grafted in

## Ⓐ Grafted In

It's not about Israel becoming part of the church. Instead, the church is part of Israel.

*Do not be arrogant toward the branches; but if you are arrogant, remember that it is not you who supports the root, but the root supports you.* (Romans 11:18)

> ***ekklesia* (εκκλησια) = *kahal* (קהל) = "assembly"**

**Refer to Resource**

*Grafted In: Israel, Gentiles, and the Mystery of the Gospel*
"The Eternal Purpose of God"
Pages 125–135

## Ⓑ Fellow-Heirs and Fellow Members

Gentile believers are grafted in to the olive tree of Israel, and they have been made "fellow-heirs" along with Israel.

*The Gentiles are fellow heirs and fellow members of the body, and fellow partakers of the promise in the Messiah Yeshua through the gospel.* (Ephesians 3:6)

*The two into one new man, thus establishing peace.* (Ephesians 2:15)

Oneness ............................ Sameness

## C  One in the Messiah

*For all of you who were baptized into Messiah have clothed yourselves with Messiah. There is neither Jew nor Greek, there is neither slave nor free man, there is neither male nor female; for you are all one in the Messiah Yeshua.* (Galatians 3:27–28)

Jewish and Gentile believers, slave and free, males and females are all one in the Messiah because we have all been "clothed with Messiah." But this does not erase distinction.

In reality, there is still a difference between men and women, even after salvation. There is also a difference between Jew and Gentile, even after salvation.

## D  What's the Difference?

What distinction remains between Jewish and Gentile believers after salvation?

1.  **Divine Mandate**

    Jewish believers have a unique relationship to the Land, the People, and the Scriptures of Israel.

    a.  The Jewish people are the People of Israel.

    b.  The Land is unambiguously promised to the Jewish people—the descendants of Abraham, Isaac, and Jacob.

    c.  The Jewish people are the people of Israel, and the Bible is the Scriptures that have been entrusted to us.

    *Who are Israelites, to whom belongs the adoption as sons, and the glory and the covenants and the giving of the [Torah] and the temple service and the promises, whose are the fathers, and from whom is the Messiah according to the flesh.* (Romans 9:4–5)

    Jewish believers have an ongoing _____ to keep the Torah.

Key words

*Didache:* Greek word meaning "teaching;" a document containing moral and community instruction for Gentile believers in Yeshua, written as early as the end of the first century.

## 2. Divine Invitation

The Gentile believer's relationship to Israel and the Torah comes through the Messiah. He is not required to keep the specific signs of Torah that were given to Israel.

*No one is to act as your judge in regard to food or drink or in respect to a festival or a new moon or a Sabbath day.*
(Colossians 2:16)

Naomi and Ruth

*Do not urge me to leave you or turn back from following you; for where you go, I will go, and where you lodge, I will lodge. Your people shall be my people, and your God, my God. Where you die, I will die, and there I will be buried. Thus may the LORD do to me, and worse, if anything but death parts you and me.* (Ruth 1:16–17)

Gentile believers have a biblical ................................

to ................................ along with Israel in keeping the Torah.

## Ⓔ The Yoke of the Lord

Just like the apostolic decision in Acts 15, the *Didache* does not bind Gentile believers to the Torah. Instead, it encourages them to take on as much as they are able.

> ### *Didache* (Διδαχη) = "teaching"

*For if you are able to bear all the yoke of the Lord, you will be perfect; but if you are not able, do what you are able to do.*
(*Didache* 6:2)

Yoke of the Lord = .......................................................

Ancient yoke

**Key Verses**

Psalm 122:1–2
Isaiah 2:3
Isaiah 51:4
Isaiah 56
Isaiah 60:3–4
Isaiah 62:10

# Four Restorations

We live in a prophetic time of restoration, and we are committed to seeing the whole body of Messiah, Jews and Gentiles, restoring four essential elements of apostolic faith.

## (A) Messiah

Yeshua is Jewish. When He comes again, He will still be Jewish. Yeshua's life was rooted in the land and in the Judaism of His day.

Restoration One: .........................................................

## (B) Gospel

The gospel is Jewish. The rich fullness of the good news, the gospel preached by Yeshua and His disciples must be restored to its original message.

Restoration Two: .........................................................

## (C) Discipleship

Real discipleship, in a Jewish sense, requires us to be careful students of Yeshua, learning His words and seeking to do all things as He did.

Restoration Three: .........................................................

**Your Israel Connection**

**Welcome to Jerusalem**

*Jaffa Gate, Old City Jerusalem* – In the Messianic Era all mankind will make pilgrimage to the holy city of Jerusalem. Our destination is Messianic Jerusalem. "I was glad when they said to me, 'Let us go to the house of the LORD.' Our feet are standing within your gates, O Jerusalem" (Psalm 122:1–2).

## ⓓ Torah ✍

The Torah is God's eternal standard of righteousness and must return to its place of prominence and authority in the community of faith.

Restoration Four: ........................................................................................

### Endnotes

1    Benjamin Blech, *Understanding Judaism: The Basics of Deed and Creed* (Northvale, NJ: Jason Aronson, 1991), 327–328.

2    John Oswalt, *The New International Commentary on the Old Testament: The Book of Isaiah Chapters 40–66* (Grand Rapids, MI: Eerdmans Publishing Company), 458.

# Lesson Ten
# LESSON SUMMARY

## First ...

We reviewed the first nine foundational teachings of the HaYesod program.

## Then ...

We took a look into the prophetic destiny of the Jewish people as described in Deuteronomy 30, and we saw that the future will bring three returns:

1. Return to the LORD
2. Return to Torah
3. Return to the Land

We also discussed how the Zionist movement and the modern State of Israel may be the first flowering of the Final Redemption.

## After that ...

We shared the prophetic destiny of the Gentile believers and saw Gentiles taking hold of the commandments of Torah in Zechariah 8 and Isaiah 56.

## Then ...

We looked at how the Gentile believers have become:

- ❖ Fellow-heirs with the Jewish believers
- ❖ Grafted in to the olive tree of Israel
- ❖ Fellow members of the common wealth of Israel
- ❖ One in the Messiah with Israel

This led us to conclude:

1. Jewish believers have an ongoing mandate to keep the Torah.
2. Gentile believers have a biblical invitation to participate along with Israel in keeping the Torah.

## Finally ...

We considered four things that we need restored to our faith:

A. The Jewishness of Messiah
B. The Torah context of the gospel
C. The Jewish tradition of discipleship
D. The prominence of Torah in the body of Messiah

# Lesson Ten
## LESSON REVIEW – Q&A

1. What are the three "returns" predicted in Deuteronomy 30?

2. What is Zionism? Is the modern State of Israel the Final Redemption?

3. Who are the "ten men" of Zechariah 8:23? Who is the "one Jew"? What do the tzitzit ("tassels") represent?

4. In Isaiah 56, what do Gentiles and eunuchs have in common? Who is the Gentile of Isaiah 56? Give two answers.

5. What does it mean to be "grafted in"? What is the difference between Jewish and Gentile obligation to the Torah?

6. In the quotation from the *Didache*, what is the "yoke of the Lord"? What does the *Didache* recommend regarding Gentiles and Torah?

7. What are the four restorations?

8. What is the most memorable and significant thing you have learned in the HaYesod program?

# Lesson Ten – Extra Credit/Digging Deeper
# AN INTRODUCTION TO TORAH CLUB
## FURTHER STUDY FROM THIS WEEK'S HAYESOD LESSON

*Mazel Tov!* (Congratulations!) You have completed HaYesod. For this week's Extra Credit and Digging Deeper material, we want to introduce you to a way to further your exploration of the Land, the People, and the Scriptures of Israel.

**Resource in Focus**

Now that you've completed the HaYesod program, you're ready to continue your study of the Scriptures with Torah Club. Start with *Torah Club Volume One: Unrolling the Scroll*, a friendly introduction to the five books of Moses and the Jewish roots of Christianity. From here you can proceed through all other volumes sequentially. A free introductory sample of the first *parashah* (weekly portion) is available for download in PDF format from **www.torahclub.org**. Learn more about all the Torah Clubs, download free samples, and listen to online samples of the audio CD online!

**Notes:**

**Notes:**

**Notes:**

_____

_____

_____

_____

_____

_____

_____

_____

_____

_____

_____

_____

_____

_____

_____

_____

_____

_____

_____

**Notes:**

# Notes:

# APPENDICES

THE LAND, THE PEOPLE,
AND THE SCRIPTURES OF ISRAEL

# Appendix A
# GLOSSARY

For more definitions, see www.ffoz.org/torahclub/dictionary.html.

*Adon.* אדון (HEBREW) Lord, Master, or Sir. See *Kurios* and *Mar*.

*akathartos.* ακαθαρτος (GREEK) Unclean; when used in reference to Jewish dietary law, *akathartos* refers to the meats which the Bible has declared unclean and forbidden.

*aliyah.* עליה (HEBREW) lit. "going up." 1. Immigration to the land of Israel. 2. Being called to read from the Torah scroll as a part of a synagogue service. 3. In the days of the Temple, a pilgrimage to the Temple in Jerusalem.

*Amidah* עמידה (HEBREW) lit. "standing." The core prayer in each of the daily prayer services, consisting of nineteen blessings on the weekdays and seven on the Sabbath. The *Amidah* is believed to have originated during the reforms of Ezra and Nehemiah.

*anomia.* ανομια (GREEK) Lawlessness, iniquity, or specifically, Torahlessness.

*avodah.* עבודה (HEBREW) Worship, service, sacrifice, or prayer.

*batel.* בטל (HEBREW) Abolish.

*bati.* באתי (HEBREW) lit. "I came to," indicating purpose and intention.

*beit midrash.* בית מדרש (HEBREW) A study hall; a school that is usually part of a synagogue; the third stage of Jewish education in the Second-Temple period and beyond. Students in the *beit midrash* learned the Torah, both oral and written, in greater detail.

*ben Avraham.* בן אברהם (HEBREW) Son of Abraham. Idiomatically, this is a title for a Gentile who has undergone ritual conversion to become legally Jewish. Such a person adopts "Abraham" as a patronym.

*berit.* ברית (HEBREW) Covenant.

*Berit Chadashah.* ברית חדשה (HEBREW) The New Covenant.

*CE.* Common Era. This abbreviation replaces the previously used AD (*anno Domini*, Latin for "in the year of the Lord"). The Common Era covers the time from Christ's birth to the present day.

*chadash.* חדש (HEBREW) New or renewed.

*chata.* חטא (HEBREW) 1. To miss a mark. 2. To sin or commit an error, either intentionally or unintentionally.

*charis.* χαρις (GREEK) Grace; God's favor; unmerited favor. See *chen*.

*Chag HaMatzah.* חג המצה (HEBREW) Feast of Unleavened Bread.

*chametz.* חמץ (HEBREW) Leavened items; a grain product that has come in contact with moisture for a duration of time before being fully cooked, allowing fermentation to take place. Fermentation was the primary type of leavening in the biblical era.

*cheirographon.* χειρογραφον (GREEK) Handwritten document; a "note of indebtedness" written in one's own hand as a proof of obligation; an "IOU."

*chen.* חן (HEBREW) Grace or favor. See *charis*.

*Christos.* Χριστός (GREEK) Christ, also Anointed One; the Messiah. See *Mashiach*.

*chukkat olam.* חקת עולם (HEBREW) A perpetual, eternal statute.

*Chumash.* חומש (HEBREW) 1. The books of Moses, which are the first five books of the Bible: Genesis, Exodus, Leviticus, Numbers, and Deuteronomy. 2. A bound volume containing the five books of

Moses, also commonly containing the *haftarot* (selections from the Prophets) arranged according to the reading schedule for use in the synagogue and weekly study.

**davak.** דבק (Hebrew) To cling, cleave, or keep close.

**devekut.** דבקות (Hebrew) Attachment.

**Didache.** Διδαχη (Greek) 1. Teaching or instruction. 2. The title of a brief treatise of moral and community instruction for Gentile believers in Yeshua, which may have been written as early as the end of the first century. The full title of the work is "The Teaching of the Lord through the Twelve Apostles to the Gentiles," sometimes referred to as "The Teaching of the Twelve Apostles."

**didaskalia.** διδασκαλια (Greek) Teaching. This term is used in Apostolic Writings to indicate sound doctrinal teaching.

**didaskalos.** διδασκαλος (Greek) This word is usually translated as "teacher." In the Gospels, the Hebrew term "rabbi" probably lies behind this Greek word.

**ekklesia.** εκκλησια (Greek) An assembly or congregation, Typically translated into English as "church." See *kahal*.

**elegmos.** ελεγμος (Greek) Reproof, rebuke, or conviction.

**emunah.** אמונה (Hebrew) 1. Belief or faith. 2. Faithfulness.

**epanorthosis.** επανορθωσις (Greek) Correcting; restoring to an upright position or to a right state; setting straight that which had become bent or twisted.

**erga.** εργα (Greek) Works, deeds, or observances of Torah. See *ma'asim*.

**eved.** עבד (Hebrew) Servant or slave.

**Gamaliel.** גמליאל (Hebrew) Gamaliel was a first-century sage, president of the Sanhedrin, grandson of Hillel the elder, and Paul's teacher. Gamaliel means "Bestowed of God."

**gezerah shavah.** גזרה שוה (Hebrew) Equivalent decrees; verbal analogy. This is also a method of interpretation where similar words used in different contexts are connected to expound upon one another.

**Haggadah.** הגדה (Hebrew) 1. Telling. 2. A book used during a Passover Seder as a guide to each of its steps.

**halachah.** הלכה (Hebrew) The legal judgments of Judaism that define the way in which the Torah is applied. Biblical examples of this practice include Deuteronomy (Second Law), which clarified previous laws in the Torah, and the reforms of Ezra after the return from Babylonian exile. The development of *halachah* continued in the days of Talmud and subsequent Jewish legal codes.

**haya yoshev vedoresh.** היה יושב ודורש (Hebrew) This expression, appearing in rabbinic literature, means "he sat down and interpreted" and implies giving instruction in an authoritative manner.

**hayesod.** היסוד (Hebrew) The foundation.

**Hillel.** הלל (Hebrew) A rabbi of the late first century BCE and early first century CE—perhaps the most influential rabbi—whose Torah academy was known as Beit Hillel ("The House of Hillel"). Jewish tradition records that he was the head of the Sanhedrin, along with his contemporary, Shammai. Although both were Pharisees, they disagreed on almost every issue of *halachah*, with Hillel often taking the more lenient view.

**Iesous.** Ιησους (Greek) The Greek transliteration for the names Yeshua and Yehoshua. The familiar form, Jesus, is the result of transliteration from Hebrew to Greek to Latin to German to English.

**kabbalah.** קבלה (Hebrew) Received; what has been received by tradition.

**kadosh.** קדוש (Hebrew) From the root word *kadash*, meaning "holy."

**kadash.** קדש (Hebrew) Holy, sanctified, sacred, or set apart.

**kahal.** קהל (Hebrew) Assembly. See *ekklesia*.

**kanaf.** כנף (Hebrew) 1. A wing. 2. A corner. 3. The corner of a garment where the ritual tassel (*tzitzit*) is attached. See *tzitzit*.

***karat.*** כרת (HEBREW) To cut; used in connection with covenant-making.

***kaval.*** קבל (HEBREW) 1. To receive or accept. 2. To take obligation upon one's self.

***ketubah.*** כתבה (HEBREW) A legal Jewish marriage contract given by a husband to his bride.

***Ketuvim.*** כתובים (HEBREW) 1. Writings. 2. The third division of the Hebrew Scriptures, containing poetry, wisdom literature, and historical narrative.

***kiyem.*** קיים (HEBREW) Fulfill.

***koinos.*** κοινος (GREEK) Common. When used in reference to Jewish dietary law, it refers to otherwise kosher food rendered unfit for consumption by contact with idolatry, non-Jews, or some other source of defilement.

***kosher.*** כשר (HEBREW) Proper; appropriate or acceptable; meeting the standards of biblical and Jewish law, especially as it relates to food.

***Kurios.*** Κυριος (GREEK) Lord, Master, or Sir. See ***Mar*** and ***Adon***.

***lashon hara.*** לשון הרע (HEBREW) The "evil tongue;" gossip or slander.

***Logos.*** λογος (GREEK) Something said, a word, message, saying, teaching, talk, or conversation. 1. In the Greek philosophical world, *logos* was first used by Heraclitus in 600 BCE to describe the impersonal divine reason or plan that coordinates the universe. 2. In the Jewish world, *logos* was used to translate the Hebrew *davar* in the Septuagint, and was frequently used by Philo. It corresponds to the Aramaic *dibberah* and *memra*, which were used to describe the manifested projections of God, such as His presence seated on the ark and in the burning bush. It was also used in Jewish literature as synonymous with the Torah.

***ma'ariv.*** מעריב (HEBREW) 1. Evening or darkening 2. The daily evening prayer services, comprised primarily of the *Shema* and the *Amidah*. The Talmud explains that it corresponds with the burning of the leftovers on the altar in the Temple and the night watches.

***ma'asim.*** מעשים (HEBREW) Works, deeds, or observances of Torah. See ***erga***.

***malchut.*** מלכות (HEBREW) Kingdom.

***malchut hashamayim.*** מלכות השמים (HEBREW) The kingdom of heaven.

***Mar.*** מר (ARAMAIC) Lord; Master; Sir. See ***Kurios*** and ***Adon***.

***Mashiach.*** משיח (HEBREW) Messiah. Also Anointed One; the king. See ***Christos***.

***masorah.*** מסורה (HEBREW) Transmitted; what has been transmitted by tradition.

***matzah.*** מצה (HEBREW) Unleavened bread; bread consisting usually of only flour and water, baked fully before fermentation or natural leavening is able to occur. In ancient times, *matzah* may have been a somewhat soft flatbread; today, it is usually crispy like a cracker. *Matzah* must be eaten during the Passover Seder and the Feast of Unleavened Bread.

***melachah.*** מלאכה (HEBREW) Creative work, which is prohibited on the Sabbath. The term is used in the Bible in two contexts: the creation narrative and the construction of the Tabernacle, such as sewing or building. Jewish law identifies thirty-nine general categories of prohibited labor.

***me'od.*** מאד (HEBREW) 1. Additional 2. In Deuteronomy 6:4, "strength, property, wealth."

***mezuzah.*** מזוזה (HEBREW) 1. lit. "doorpost." 2. A small parchment scroll placed in a case affixed to the doorpost of a home. On the scroll are the words of Deuteronomy 6:4–9 and 11:13–21, which include the instruction to perform this commandment.

***mikvah.*** מקוה (HEBREW) A ritual purification bath used by Jews on certain occasions, such as before the Sabbath or after menstruation. Ritual immersion in a mikvah is also one of the major components of the conversion process to Judaism. Pl. *mikvot*.

***midrash.*** מדרש (HEBREW) A type of Bible study that employs rabbinic hermeneutics to explain the text. This method created a large body of interpretation that includes word associations, creative re-tellings of the biblical story, fanciful accounts of biblical personages, parables, and moral teachings. The body of *midrash* was orally transmitted among the sages from generation to generation. Eventually the interpretations were written down in various collections.

**minchah.** מנחה (HEBREW) A gift or offering.

**minyan.** מנין (HEBREW) A quorum of ten men that qualifies as a formal congregation by Jewish law.

**Mishnah.** משנה (HEBREW) 1. Repetition. 2. Also referred to as the Oral Torah, a collection of legislation containing the traditional rulings, applications and legal disputes of the sages that were passed along orally until being redacted at the beginning of the third century CE by Rabbi Yehudah HaNasi. The Mishnah is considered to be the explanations of how to keep the commandments found in the Torah.

**mistorin.** מסתורין (HEBREW) Mysteries. Used at times in rabbinic literature to refer to the Oral Law.

**mo'ed.** מעד/מעדים (HEBREW) 1. An appointment, meeting, or appointed time. 2. Biblical festivals and holy days. Pl. *mo'adim.*

**nefesh.** נפש (HEBREW) Person, life force, living being, or soul.

**ne'emar.** נאמר (HEBREW) It is written (said). This is a technical term employed when citing a verse from the *TaNaK.*

**Nevi'im.** נביאים (HEBREW) 1. Prophets. 2. The second division of the *TaNaK,* so called because it contains books compiled by the prophetic community. Some of the books are prophecy, while others are historical narrative.

**nomos.** νομος (GREEK) Law. This is the word used throughout the Bible to translate the Hebrew word "Torah."

**ol.** על (HEBREW) Yoke.

**omer.** עמר (HEBREW) A measure of grain approximately two quarts in volume. The barley offering that was offered up on the day after the first Sabbath of Unleavened Bread was one *omer* of grain.

**paidagogos.** παιδαγωγος (GREEK) Pedagogue. A child-conductor, which is a type of caretaker entrusted with supervising and directing a child's conduct and moral behavior. This term is used figuratively of the Torah in the book of Galatians.

**paideia.** παιδεια (GREEK) Training.

**Paulos.** Παυλος (GREEK/LATIN) Paul.

**Pentecost.** Πεντηκοστή (GREEK) 1. Fifty. 2. The Greek name for the feast of *Shavu'ot.*

**Pesach.** פסח (HEBREW) Passover.

**pikkuach nefesh.** פקוח נפש (HEBREW) Saving a life.

**pistis.** πιστις (GREEK) Belief and faithfulness.

**pleroo.** πληροω (GREEK) To make full; to fill; to fill up.

**rabbi.** רבי (HEBREW) An honorific title meaning "my great one." Idiomatically, a title for a teacher. See **didaskalos.**

**Rosh Chodesh.** ראש חדש (HEBREW) 1. Head of the new month. 2. New moon.

**Rosh HaShanah.** ראש השנה (HEBREW) 1. Head of the year, i.e., "New Year." 2. The first day of the seventh month.

**Seder.** סדר (HEBREW) 1. An arrangement, agenda, or order. 2. A meal or event that follows a set order, especially a Passover meal.

**Shabbat.** שבת (HEBREW) 1. From the root word *shavat,* meaning "to cease or to rest." 2. The Sabbath day.

**shacharit.** שחרית (HEBREW) 1. Morning. 2. The daily morning prayer service, corresponding with the daily morning burnt offering that was presented in the Temple.

**Shaddai.** שדי (HEBREW) Almighty.

**shaliach.** שליח (Hebrew) An emmisary: someone sent on a mission to represent the interests of someone else. Pl. *shelichim*.

**Shammai.** שמאי (Hebrew) An important rabbi of the late first century BCE and early first century CE whose Torah academy was known as Beit Shammai ("The House of Shammai"). Jewish tradition records that he was the president of the Sanhedrin, along with his contemporary Hillel. Although both were Pharisees, they disagreed on almost every issue of *halachah*, with Shammai often taking the stricter view.

**shamayim.** שמים (Hebrew) 1. Heaven, or sky. 2. A circumlocution for God's Name.

**Shaul.** שאול (Hebrew) Saul, meaning "asked."

**Shavu'ot.** שבועות (Hebrew) 1. Weeks. 2. The Feast of Pentecost.

**Shema.** שמע (Hebrew) 1. From the root word *shama*, meaning "listen, hear, obey." 2. A sequence of scriptural passages that are recited twice daily, in the morning and evening prayer services, beginning with the line, "Hear, O Israel, the LORD is our God, the LORD is One." The *Shema* is often considered a primary declaration of faith.

**Shemini Atzeret.** שמיני עצרת (Hebrew) Eighth-Day Assembly.

**shevitah.** שביתה (Hebrew) Hebrew word meaning "stopping work; going on strike." It derives from the same root word as Shabbat.

**Simchat Torah.** שמחת תורה (Hebrew) "The Rejoicing of the Torah." It is the name for the eighth-day festival of *Sukkot*.

**sukkah.** סכה; סוכה (Hebrew) A makeshift hut, originally intended to provide shade during harvest seasons. The Torah instructs that they be built to celebrate the festival of *Sukkot*. Jewish law instructs that the roof of the structure be made of loose plant material through which stars can be seen.

**shuv.** שוב (Hebrew) To turn, or to return.

**Sukkot.** סוכות (Hebrew) 1. Booths, shacks, or huts. 2. The Feast of Booths, i.e., "Feast of Tabernacles."

**suzerain.** A feudal lord to whom fealty was due.

**talmid.** תלמיד (Hebrew) A student.

**tallit.** טלית (Hebrew) 1. A prayer shawl. This four-cornered garment to which *tzitziyot* have been attached is usually worn during prayer. 2. In ancient times, an outer garment or cloak. See *tzizit*.

**tallit katan.** טלית קטן (Hebrew) A poncho-like, four-cornered garment worn under the shirt with *tzitziyot* attached to each corner. The *tallit katan* is typically worn all day (not just during prayer), with the *tzitziyot* either tucked in or pulled out. This garment makes it easier to fulfill the commandment of *tzitziyot* during daily activity. See *tzizit*.

**Talmud.** תלמוד (Hebrew) A voluminous record of rabbinic discussions about the Oral Law. The text of the *Talmud* contains both the *Mishnah* and later argumentation about the *Mishnah*. The later argumentation is called the *Gemara*. It contains legal disputes, ethical instruction, *midrash*, stories about the sages, Jewish customs, and historical anecdotes. Two different compendiums of *Talmud* exist. The *Jerusalem Talmud* contains the discussions of the sages in the land of Israel, and the *Babylonian Talmud* contains the discussions of the sages in Babylon. The *Talmuds* were completed in the fifth and sixth centuries CE but also contain material dating back to Ezra's time.

**talmud Torah.** תלמוד תורה (Hebrew) The study of Torah.

**TaNaK.** תנ״ך (Hebrew) The Hebrew Bible; Old Testament. The acronym for the Hebrew Scriptures: Torah ("Law"), *Nevi'im* ("Prophets"), and *Ketuvim* ("Writings"). The *TaNaK* is essentially the same as the Christian Old Testament, although the books are arranged in a different order; there are some discrepancies in verse numbering, and it is based entirely on the Hebrew Masoretic text, without influence from the Septuagint.

**tefillin.** תפילין (Hebrew) Black boxes containing scrolls on which passages of scripture are written, bound to a man's arm and forehead using leather straps.

***teshuvah.*** תשובה (Hᴇʙʀᴇᴡ) Repentance; turning around.

***theosebes.*** θεοσεβής (Gʀᴇᴇᴋ) God-fearer. In the apostolic era this referred to a Gentile who had not gone through a formal conversion to become legally Jewish, but who was nonetheless a worshipper of the God of Israel and who participated in the local Jewish community.

***Torah.*** תורה (Hᴇʙʀᴇᴡ) 1. Teaching, instruction, or guidance. 2. The Torah of Moses; i.e., the first five books of the Bible. 3. The entire *TaNaK*, as well as commentaries and related material. 4. All of God's instruction.

***tzaddik gamur.*** צדיק גמור (Hᴇʙʀᴇᴡ) Perfectly righteous.

***tzitzit.*** ציצית (Hᴇʙʀᴇᴡ) Ritual tassels that the Torah instructs must be attached to each of the four corners of a garment. This commandment is traditionally interpreted to be obligatory for men, who observe the commandment by wearing a *tallit* and/or a *tallit katan*. Pl. *tsitsiyot*.

***vassal.*** A person, nation, or state dominated by another.

***ve'ahavta.*** ואהבת (Hᴇʙʀᴇᴡ) And you shall love.

***Yamim Nora'im.*** ימים נוראים (Hᴇʙʀᴇᴡ) Days of Awe, which are the ten days in between Rosh HaShanah and Yom Kippur.

***yarah.*** ירה (Hᴇʙʀᴇᴡ) 1. Aim, cast, throw, or shoot. 2. The root of Hebrew words relating to shooting arrows, sending rain, and teaching.

***yare.*** ירא (Hᴇʙʀᴇᴡ) To fear or revere.

***Yeshua.*** ישוע (Hᴇʙʀᴇᴡ/Aʀᴀᴍᴀɪᴄ) An Aramaic given name, most notably the original form of the name Jesus. Masculine form of the word *yeshu'ah*, which means "salvation." Yeshua is a diminutive form of the name Yehoshua, meaning "the LORD saves," often rendered "Joshua." The two are sometimes used interchangeably, both being transliterated into Greek the same way. The familiar form, Jesus, is the result of transliteration from Hebrew to Greek to Latin to German to English.

***yesod.*** יסוד (Hᴇʙʀᴇᴡ) Foundation.

***yoshia.*** יושיע (Hᴇʙʀᴇᴡ) He will save.

***Yom Kippur.*** יום כפור (Hᴇʙʀᴇᴡ) Day of Atonement.

# Appendix B
# BIBLIOGRAPHY

*The Apostolic Fathers*. Translated by J. B. Lightfoot. Lawrence, KS: Digireads.com Publishing, 2007.

Arndt, William F., and F. Wilbur Gingrich. *Bauer's Greek-English Lexicon of the New Testament and Other Early Christian Literature*. Chicago, IL: The University of Chicago Press, 1957.

*Babylonian Talmud*. Translated by Isidore Epstein et al. 30 vols. London: The Soncino Press, 1990.

Bacchiocchi, Samuele. *From Sabbath to Sunday: A Historical Investigation of the Rise of Sunday Observance in Early Christianity*. Rome: The Pontifical Gregorian University Press, 1977.

Basser, Herbert W. *Studies in Exegesis: Christian Critiques of Jewish Law and Rabbinic Responses*. Boston, MA: Brill, 2002.

Bauckham, Richard. *James: Wisdom of James, Disciple of Jesus the Sage*. London: Routledge, 2006.

Berkowitz, Ariel and D'vorah. *Torah Rediscovered*. Jerusalem, Israel: First Fruits of Zion, 1998.

Berkowitz, Ariel and D'vorah. *Take Hold*. Jerusalem, Israel: First Fruits of Zion, 1998.

Bivin, David and Roy Blizzard Jr. *Understanding the Difficult Words of Jesus*. Austin, TX: Center for Judaic-Christian Studies, 1984.

Bivin, David. *New Light on the Difficult Words of Jesus: Insights from His Jewish Context*. Holland, MI: En-Gedi Resource Center, 2005.

Blech, Benjamin. *Understanding Judaism: The Basics of Deed and Creed*. Northvale, NJ: Jason Aronson, 1991.

Bloch, Abraham P. *The Biblical and Historical Background of the Jewish Holy Days*. New York, NY: KTAV Publishing House, 1978.

Bonchek, Avigdor. *Studying the Torah: A Guide to In-Depth Interpretation*. Northvale, NJ: Jason Aronson, 1997.

Bromiley, Geoffrey W., ed. *The International Standard Bible Encyclopedia*. 4 vols. Grand Rapids, MI: Eerdmans, 1979.

Brown, Colin, ed. *The New International Dictionary of New Testament Theology*. 3 vols. Grand Rapids, MI: Zondervan, 1979.

Brown, Francis, S.R. Driver, and Charles A. Briggs. *The Brown-Driver-Briggs Hebrew and English Lexicon*. Peabody, MA: Hendrickson Publishers, 1999.

Bruce, F. F. *The Book of Acts: The New International Commentary of the New Testament*. Grand Rapids, MI: Eerdmans, 1988.

Bruce, F. F. *The Epistle of Paul to the Romans*. Tyndale New Testament Commentaries. Grand Rapids, MI: Eerdmans, 1963, 1977.

Chavel, Charles B. *Maimonides the Commandments Volume One: Positive*. New York, NY: Soncino Press, 1967.

Chofetz Chaim, *The Concise Book of Mitzvoth*. Translated by Charles Wengrov. New York: Feldheim Publishers, 1990.

Cohen, A. *Everyman's Talmud*. New York: Shocken Books, 1975.

Coxe, A. Cleveland. *Ante-Nicene Fathers*. Edited by Alexander Roberts and James Donaldson. 10 vols. Peabody, MA: Hendrickson, 2004.

Cranfield, C. E. B. *Romans: International Critical Commentaries*. 2 vols. Edinburgh, Scotland: T & T Clark, 1979.

Culpepper, R. Alan. *John, the Son of Zebedee.* Columbia, SC: University of South Carolina Press, 1994.

*Daily Prayer Book.* Translated by Philip Birnbaum. New York: Hebrew Publishing Co., 1977.

Dalman, Gustaf. *Jesus–Jeshua: Studies in the Gospels.* Translated by Paul P. Levertoff. Whitefish, MT: Kessinger Publishing, 2008.

Danielou, Jean. *The Theology of Jewish Christianity.* Translated by John A. Baker. Philadelphia, PA: The Westminster Press, 1978.

Daube, David. *The New Testament and Rabbinic Judasim.* Peabody, MA: Hendrickson Publishers, 1956.

Dunn, James D. G. *Jesus, Paul, and the Law.* Louisville, KY: Westminster/John Knox Press, 1990.

Dunn, James D. G. *The Parting of the Ways.* London, England: SCM Press and Philadelphia, PA: Trinity Press International, 1991.

Dunn, James D. G. *Word Biblical Commentary: Romans 1–8, Volume 38a.* Dallas, TX: Word Books, Publisher, 1988.

Eby, Aaron and Toby Janicki. *Hallowed be Your Name: Sanctifying God's Sacred Name.* Marshfield, MO: First Fruits of Zion, 2008.

Eby, Aaron. *Boundary Stones.* Marshfield, MO: First Fruits of Zion, 2009.

Edersheim, Alfred. *The Life and Times of Jesus the Messiah.* Grand Rapids, MI: Eerdmans, 1991.

Edersheim, Alfred. *Sketches of Jewish Social Life.* Peabody, MA: Hendrickson, 1994.

Egan, Hope. *Holy Cow: Does God Care About What We Eat?* Marshfield, MO: First Fruits of Zion, 2007.

*Encyclopedia Judaica Second Edition.* Edited by Fred Skolnik. 22 vols. Farmington Hills, MI: Macmillan Reference USA, 2007.

Falk, Harvey. *Jesus the Pharisee.* Eugene, OR: Wipf and Stock Publishers, 2002.

Flusser, David. *Jewish Sources in Early Christianity.* Tel Aviv, Israel: MOD Books, 1989.

Flusser, David. *Judaism and the Origins of Christianity.* Jerusalem, Israel: The Magnes Press, 1988.

Flusser, David. *The Sage from Galilee: Rediscovering Jesus' Jewish Genius.* Grand Rapids, MI: Eerdmans Publishing Company, 2007.

Frustenberg, Yair. "Defilement Penetrating the Body: A New Understanding of Contamination in Mark 7:15." *New Testament Studies* 54 (2008): 182.

Gleason, Archer, R. Laird Harris, and Bruce Waltke. *Moody Press Theological Wordbook of the Old Testament.* Chicago, IL: Moody Publishers, 2003.

Goodman, Philip. *The JPS Holiday Anthologies: Purim, Passover, Shavuot, Rosh Hashana, Yom Kippur, Sukkot/Simhat Torah, and Hanukkah.* Philadelphia, PA: The Jewish Publication Society, 1988.

Hertz, J. H. *Pentateuch and Haftarahs.* London, England: Soncino Press, 1987.

Heschel, Abraham Joshua. *The Sabbath.* New York: Noonday Press, 1975.

Howard, Kevin and Marvin Rosenthal. *The Feasts of the Lord.* Nashville, TN: Thomas Nelson, 1997.

Instone-Brewer, David. *Traditions of the Rabbis from the Era of the New Testament: Volume 1.* Grand Rapids, MI: Eerdmans, 2004.

Jacobs, Louis. *The Book of Jewish Belief.* West Orange, NJ: Behrman House, 1984.

Janicki, Toby. *Mezuzah: You Shall Write Them Upon the Doorposts of Your House and Upon Your Gates.* Marshfield, MO: First Fruits of Zion, 2007.

Jastrow, Marcus. *A Dictionary of the Targumim, the Talmud Babli and Yerushalmi, and the Midrashic Literature.* 2 vols. New York: Pardes Publishing House, 1950.

*The Jerusalem Talmud on CD-ROM.* Translated by Jacob Neusner. Peabody, MA: Hendrickson Publishers, 2009.

*Josephus: The Essential Works.* Translated by Paul L. Maier. Grand Rapids, MI: Kregal, 1998, 1994.

Juster, Daniel. *Jewish Roots*. Rockville, MD: DAVAR, 1986.

Kaiser, Walter C., Jr. *Toward an Old Testament Theology*. Grand Rapids, MI: Zondervan, 1978.

Kaiser, Walter C., Jr. *Toward Old Testament Ethics*. Grand Rapids, MI: Zondervan, 1983.

Kaiser, Walter C., Jr. *Toward Rediscovering the Old Testament*. Grand Rapids, MI: Zondervan, 1987.

Kasden, Barney. *God's Appointed times*. Baltimore, MD: Lederer, 1993.

Kehati, Pinhas. *The Mishnah*. 21 vols. New York: Feldheim, 2005.

Kinzer, Mark. *Post-Missionary Messianic Judaism*. Grand Rapids, MI: Brazos Press, 2005.

Kister, Menahem. "Law, Morality, and Rhetoric in Some Sayings of Jesus." Pages 145–154 in *Studies in Ancient Midrash*. Edited by James L. Kugel. Harvard University Press, 2001.

Klausner, Joseph. *Jesus of Nazareth: His Life, Times, and Teaching*. New York: Bloch Publishing Company, 1989.

Lachs, Samuel Tobias. *A Rabbinic Commentary on the New Testament: The Gospels of Matthew, Mark, and Luke*. Hoboken, New Jersey: KTAV Publishing House, 1987.

Lancaster, D. Thomas. *Grafted In*. Marshfield, MO: First Fruits of Zion, 2009.

Lancaster, D. Thomas. *King of the Jews*. Marshfield, MO: First Fruits of Zion, 2006.

Lancaster, D. Thomas. *Restoration*. Marshfield, MO: First Fruits of Zion, 2009.

Levertoff, Paul P. *Love and the Messianic Age*. Marshfield, MO: Vine of David, 2009.

Levertoff, Paul P. *St. Matthew*. London: Thomas Murby & Co., 1940.

Levine, Baruch A. *The JPS Torah Commentary: Leviticus*. Philadelphia, PA: Jewish Publication Society, 1989.

Lewis, C.S. *Mere Christianity*. San Francisco, CA: Harper Collins, 2001.

Lichtenstein, R. Yehiel Zvi. *Commentary on the Books of the New Testament: John*. Translated by Robert Morris. Marshfield, MO: Vine of David, forthcoming.

Liddell, Henry George and Robert Scott. *A Greek-English Lexicon*. Oxford, England: The Clarendon Press, 1893, 1985.

Lightfoot, John. *A Commentary on the New Testament from Talmud and Hebraica*. 4 vols. Grand Rapids, MI: Baker Book House, 1979.

Lindsey, Robert A. *Jesus Rabbi and Lord*. Oak Creek, WI: Cornerstone Publishing, 1990.

Majeski, Rabbi Shloma. *Yechudis: The Essence of Chosid-Rebbe Relationship*. Audiotape lectures. Brooklyn, NY: Sichos in English. 4 cassettes.

Marshall, I. Howard. *The Acts of the Apostles: Tyndale New Testament Commentaries Volume 5*. Grand Rapids, MI: Eerdmans, 1980.

*Mekhilta De-Rabbi Ishmael*. 2 vols. Translated by Jacob Z. Lauterbach. Philadelphia, PA: Jewish Publication Society, 2004.

*Midrash Rabbah*. Translated by Dr. H. Freedman et al. 10 vols. London: The Soncino Press, 1992.

Milgrom, Jacob. *The JPS Torah Commentary: Numbers*. Philadelphia, PA: Jewish Publication Society, 1990.

*Mishnayoth*. Translated by Philip Blackman. 7 vols. Gateshead: Judaica Press, 1983.

Monson, James M. *Regions on the Run: Introductory Map Studies on the Land of the Bible*. Rockford, IL: Biblical Backgrounds, Inc, 1998.

Nanos, Mark. *The Galatians Debate*. Peabody, MA: Hendrickson, 2002.

Nanos, Mark. *The Irony of Galatians: Paul's Letter in First Century Context*. Minneapolis: Fortress Press, 2002.

Nanos, Mark. *The Mystery of Romans: The Jewish Context of Paul's Letters*. Minneapolis, MN: Fortress Press, 1996.

Needham, David. C. *Birthright*. Portland, OR: Multnomah Press, 1979.

Neusner, Jacob, ed. *The Talmud of the Land of Israel: A Preliminary Translation and Commentary*. 35 vols. Chicago, IL: The University of Chicago Press, 1994.

Notley, R. Steven, Marc Turnage, and Brian Becker, ed. *Jesus' Last Week*. Boston, MA: Brill, 2006.

O'Brien, Peter T., *Word Biblical Commentary: Colossians, Philemon, Volume 44*. Waco, TX: Word Books Publisher, 1982.

Orr, James, ed. *International Standard Bible Encyclopedia*. 5 vols. Peabody, MA: Hendrickson, 1996.

Oswalt, John. *The New International Commentary on the Old Testament: The Book of Isaiah Chapters 40–66*. Grand Rapids, MI: Eerdmans Publishing Company, 1998.

*Philo*. Translated by F.H. Colson et al. 12 vols. Loeb Classical Library. Cambridge, MA: Harvard University Press, 1991.

Robertson, O. Palmer. *The Christ of the Covenants*. Phillipsburg, NJ: Presbyterian and Reformed Publishing, 1980.

Safrai, Shmuel and Menachem Stern, eds. *The Jewish People in the First Century*. 2 vols. Philadelphia, PA: Fortress Press, 1976.

Sanders, E. P. *Paul and Palestinian Judaism*. Minneapolis, MN: Fortress Press, 1977.

Santala, Risto. *Paul: The Man and the Teacher in Light of Jewish Sources*. Translated by Michael G. Cox. Jerusalem, Israel: Keren Ahvah Meshihit, 1995.

Sarna, Nahum M. *The JPS Torah Commentary: Exodus*. Philadelphia, PA: Jewish Publication Society, 1991.

Sarna, Nahum M. *The JPS Torah Commentary: Genesis*. Philadelphia, PA: Jewish Publication Society, 1989.

Scherman, Nosson, ed. *The Rabbinical Council of America Edition of the ArtScroll Siddur: A New Translation and Anthologized Commentary*. Brooklyn, NY: Mesorah Publications, 2000.

Schoneveld, Jacobus. "The Torah in the Flesh: A New Reading of the Prologue of the Gospel of John as a Contribution to a Christology without Anti-Judaism." *Immanuel* 24/25 (1990): 77–94.

Shulam, Joseph and Hilary Le Cournu. *A Commentary on the Jewish Roots of Acts*. 2 vols. Jerusalem, Israel: Academon, 2003.

Shulam, Joseph and Hilary Le Cournu. *A Commentary on the Jewish Roots of Galatians*. Jerusalem, Israel: Academon, 2005.

Shulam, Joseph and Hilary Le Cournu. *A Commentary on the Jewish Roots of Romans*. Clarksville, MD: Messianic Jewish Resources International, 1998.

Skarsaune, Oskar. *In the Shadow of the Temple: Jewish Influences on Early Christianity*. Downers Grove, IL: InterVarsity Press, 2002.

Skarsaune, Oskar and Reidar Hvalvik, eds. *The Early Centuries: Jewish Believers in Jesus*. Peabody, MA: Hendrickson Publishers, 2007.

Spangler, Ann and Lois Tverberg. *Sitting at the Feet of Rabbi Jesus*. Grand Rapids, MI: Zondervan Publishing, 2009.

Stern, David H. *Jewish New Testament Commentary*. Jerusalem, Israel: Jewish New Testament Publications, 1999.

Stern, David H. *Messianic Jewish Manifesto*. Jerusalem, Israel: Jewish New Testament Publications, 1988.

Strassfeld, Michael. *The Jewish Holidays: A Guide and Commentary*. New York, NY: Harper and Row Publishers, 1985.

Strickland, Wayne G. *Five Views on Law and Gospel*. Grand Rapids, MI: Zondervan, 1996.

Thayer, Joseph H. *Thayer's Greek-English Lexicon of the New Testament*. Peabody, MA: Hendrickson Publishers, 2000.

Thompson, J. A. *Deuteronomy: Tyndale Old Testament Commentaries*. Downers Grove, IL. Inter-Varsity Press, 1974.

Tigay, Jeffrey H. *The JPS Torah Commentary: Deuteronomy*. Philadelphia, PA: Jewish Publication Society, 1996.

Tomson, Peter. *Paul and the Jewish Law*. Minneapolis, MN: Fortress Press, 1990.

Vermes, Geza. *Jesus the Jew*. Minneapolis, MN: Fortress, 1981.

Vermes, Geza. *Jesus the Jewish Theologian*. Minneapolis, MN: Fortress, 2003.

Vermes, Geza. *The Religion of Jesus the Jew*. Minneapolis, MN: Fortress, 1993.

Wagshul, Rabbi Yitzchok Dovid. *Beyond Reason*. Texas: Dwelling Place Publications, 2006.

Waskow, Arthur I. *Seasons of Our Joy*. New York, NY: Summit Books, 1982.

Wilson, Marvin R. *Our Father Abraham*. Grand Rapids, MI: Eerdmans, 1989.

*The Works of Josephus*. Translated by William Whiston. Peabody, MA: Hendrickson Publishers, 1996.

Young, Brad H. *Jesus the Jewish Theologian*. Peabody, MA: Hendrickson, 1996.

Young, Brad H. *Meet the Rabbis: Rabbinic Thought and the Teaching of Jesus*. Peabody, MA: Hendrickson, 2007.

Young, Brad H. *Paul the Jewish Theologian*. Peabody, MA: Hendrickson Publishers, 1997.

Young, Brad H. *The Parables: Jewish Tradition and Christian Interpretation*. Peabody, MA: Hendrickson, 1998.

Zetterholm, Magnus. *The Formation of Christianity in Antioch: A Social-Scientific Approach to the Separation Between Judaism and Christianity*. New York, NY: Routledge, 2005.

# Appendix C
# FOUNDATIONS OF OUR FAITH

As you study the Bible with us, it is important for you to know right where we stand. But please note—we believe that real, biblical faith is marked by one's actions (James 2:17) more than by doctrinal statements. A life touched by grace and faith results in the fruit of the Spirit (Galatians 5:22–23), a transformed mind (Romans 12:2), and obedience to God's Word (John 14:15; 1 John 2:3–6).

❖ We believe in one God, as He has revealed Himself in the Scriptures. "Hear, O Israel, the LORD our God, the LORD is One." (Deuteronomy 6:4)

❖ We believe that Yeshua is the Son of God, the Messiah, the Eternal One in Whom all the fullness of deity dwells in bodily form, and who is the Word who became flesh and dwelt among us, and whose glory we beheld, the glory of the uniquely begotten Son of God, full of grace and truth. (John 1:1–14; Colossians 2:9)

❖ We believe that the Spirit of God comforts, teaches, leads, indwells, and empowers all whom God regenerates. (Acts 9:31; 1 John 2:27; John 16:13; 1 Corinthians 3:16; 2 Timothy 1:7)

❖ We believe that the Bible, both the *TaNaK* (Old Testament) and the Apostolic Scriptures (New Testament), are the only inspired, infallible, and authoritative Word of God. (2 Timothy 3:16–17)

❖ We believe that all have sinned and have fallen short of the glory of God. (Romans 3:23)

❖ We believe Yeshua's death and resurrection accomplished the atonement for all who place their faith in Him. Whoever trusts in God, in His work alone, is made a new creation in Yeshua, indwelt by the Spirit of God, and is transferred from the kingdom of darkness into the kingdom of His own Son. (Ephesians 2:8–9; Romans 5 and 6)

❖ We believe salvation is by faith through the grace of God alone, and not by human efforts. One may not earn, merit, or keep this eternal salvation. (Ephesians 2:8–10; Romans 8:29–39)

❖ We believe in the spiritual unity and equality of all believers in Yeshua the Messiah. (Ephesians 2:11–22)

❖ We believe in the continuity of God's covenants with the Jewish people, the physical people of Israel (Jeremiah 31:35–36 and parallel passages). Part of the fulfillment of these covenants is the physical return of the Jewish people to their Promised Land. (Deuteronomy 30)

❖ We believe that all Gentiles who trust in Yeshua are grafted into Israel. While this does not make them Jewish, they are full and equal participants in the covenants of promise. (Ephesians 2:12; Romans 11:11–24; Jeremiah 31:33)

❖ We believe that the Torah is a revelation of the righteousness of God and a description (along with the rest of Scripture) of the lifestyle of the redeemed community. (Matthew 5:17–19; 2 Timothy 3:16–17)

❖ We believe in the literal, physical return of Messiah to rule and reign upon the throne of David in Jerusalem. We hold to a pre-millennial view of His return. (Zechariah 14; Revelation 19–20)

# Appendix D
# CONTINUING YOUR STUDIES

Congratulations on completing HaYesod! Your adventure is just beginning. We invite you to continue learning about your connection to the Land, the People, and the Scriptures of Israel with First Fruits of Zion study resources.

## Torah Club

Torah Club can be studied by individuals or in a group setting.

The Torah Club is a subscription-based, messianic Torah-study program created by the ministry of First Fruits of Zion. Torah Club is presented in five separate, year-long volumes, keyed to the weekly Bible portions read in synagogues all over the world each Sabbath. The Torah Club is an in-depth study of the whole Bible.

As a Torah Club member, you will receive a packet of study materials every month containing written commentaries on the weekly Bible-readings and audio CDs containing additional teachings, Torah discussions, children's stories, and more. You will also receive First Fruits of Zion's award-winning quarterly publication *Messiah Journal*, and other member benefits as well. Torah Club comes with quality binders for written and audio materials and a weekly Bible reading schedule to keep you in sync.

Torah Club Bible-reading assignments are accompanied by copious written commentaries, condensing vast libraries of learning into easily digestible, weekly studies. Notes and citations invite students to delve deeper into the original sources. Discover insights from ancient Jewish sages, Messianic and non-Messianic rabbis and Evangelical scholars. For more information visit www.torahclub.org.

❖ **Torah Club Volume One: Unrolling the Scroll**

*Volume One* is Torah 101 for everyone. It is an introduction to the Jewish Roots of Christianity through a weekly study of the annual synagogue reading cycle—Genesis through Deuteronomy.

❖ **Torah Club Volume Two: Shadows of the Messiah**

*Volume Two* reveals the person of Messiah within the Torah. Like walking the Emmaus Road with Jesus: "Beginning with Moses and with all the prophets, He explained to them the things concerning Himself in all the Scriptures" (Luke 24:27).

❖ **Torah Club Volume Three: Voice of the Prophets**

*Volume Three* takes students through the weekly synagogue *haftarah* reading—the section from the Prophets that accompanies the weekly Torah portion. Messianic and ancient rabbinic insights on biblical prophecy, the end times, and the days of kings and prophets.

❖ **Torah Club Volume Four: The Good News of Messiah**

*Volume Four* guides students on a passage-by-passage study through the Gospels, and the book of Acts. See Yeshua and His world through Jewish eyes.

❖ **Torah Club Volume Five: The Rejoicing of the Torah**

*Volume Five* examines each of the 613 commandments and the institutions of Torah such as the priesthood, tabernacle, and sacrifices through the eyes of the sages, the Messiah, the prophets, the Gospels and Paul's writings.

## Books, Seminars, and Study Guides

First Fruits of Zion produces books, DVDs, audio-teachings, and study guides educating the Church about the Jewish roots of Christianity. Visit our web store at ffoz.org to browse through dozens of titles.

We also publish *Messiah Journal*, a quarterly journal dedicated to Messianic Judaism, Jewish roots, and growth in Messiah. Subscribe online at ffoz.org.

## Partner With Us

First Fruits of Zion is a non-profit ministry. We depend upon the consistent and generous support of our brothers and sisters to continue our mission of "Proclaiming the Torah and its way of life, fully centered on Messiah to today's People of God."

Learn about how you can become a sustaining supporter of First Fruits of Zion through the *FFOZ Friends* program online at www.ffoz.org/friends.